Anglo-American Economic Collaboration in War and Peace 1942-1949

ANGLO-AMERICAN ECONOMIC COLLABORATION IN WAR AND PEACE 1942 – 1949

BY

SIR RICHARD CLARKE

EDITED BY

SIR ALEC CAIRNCROSS

CLARENDON PRESS · OXFORD

1982

Oxford University Press, Walton Street, Oxford OX2 6DP

London Glasgow New York Toronto
Delhi Bombay Calcutta Madras Karachi
Kuala Lumpur Singapore Hong Kong Tokyo
Nairobi Dar es Salaam Cape Town
Melbourne Auckland
and associates in
Beirut Berlin Ibadan Mexico City Nicosia

Published in the United States
by Oxford University Press, New York

British Library Cataloguing in Publication Data

Clarke, Sir Richard
Anglo-American economic collaboration in war and
peace 1942-1949.
1. Great Britain—Foreign economic relations—
United States   2. United States—Foreign economic
relations—Great Britain
I. Title   II. Cairncross, Sir Alec
382.1'0941   HF1534.5.G/
ISBN 0-19-828439-X

Setting by Hope Services, Abingdon,
and printed in Great Britain
at the University Press, Oxford
by Eric Buckley
Printer to the University

CONTENTS

FOREWORD

For most of his working life Sir Richard ('Otto') Clarke was a civil servant. After six years as a journalist on the staff of the *Financial News* in the nineteen thirties, he served in a number of government departments before joining the Overseas Finance Division of the Treasury in 1944. Later, in 1953, he moved to the public expenditure side of the Treasury and rose to become Second Secretary in 1962. He left the Treasury in 1966 on appointment as Permanent Secretary of the Ministry of Aviation and shortly afterwards succeeded Sir Maurice Dean as Permanent Secretary of the Ministry of Technology. In retirement he led a busy life, combining numerous business interests and public duties and yet finding time to lecture and write on various aspects of public policy.

In the last year of his life, knowing that death was imminent, Sir Richard set himself to write two books on episodes in his official career. The first of these, reflecting on the development of PESC (the Public Expenditure Survey Committee), has already been published under the title *Public Expenditure, Management and Control* (Macmillan, London, 1978). The second, which he proposed to call *Adventures in International Policy*, had not got beyond half-way.

It was clearly his intention to cover his experience of Anglo-American wartime collaboration in the first two chapters, move on in the next two to the dilemmas in financial policy facing the United Kingdom at the end of the war and then turn to an extended treatment of the Marshall Plan in what would have been the second half of the book. This unwritten half would have been of special interest in view of his key role in the Marshall Plan from 1947 onwards, both as Chairman of the London Committee and as the draughtsman of important sections of various OEEC reports. Presumably he also meant to include his reflections on external economic policy in the early fifties up to the point when he ceased to be directly involved, after his promotion to an Under-Secretaryship in the Social Services Division of the Treasury in 1953. He succeeded in completing a draft of the first four chapters, carrying the story down to about the middle of 1947, and had barely started on the fifth when he died.

When, therefore, Lady Clarke asked my advice on what should be done with the manuscript I did not find it easy to make up my mind. The text was extremely readable, written from a very definite, challenging point of view, and provided a first-hand account of developments during and after the war as seen by a skilled financial journalist with access to many of the key figures in economic and financial policy. Nearly every one consulted recommended publication, especially since remarkably little has appeared for many years on the issues of policy which Sir Richard discusses. On the other hand, it would be impossible for anyone to complete the book in Sir Richard's style and from his highly individual point of view. Either the four chapters would have to appear by themselves as the first acts of a play lacking a dénouement, or they might be issued separately in article form, or they could be supplemented by further material from the Treasury files giving a more rounded picture of the background to the Marshall Plan and of the author's involvement in policy-making in the post-war years.

The last of these possibilities seemed to me to be by far the most attractive and was urged on me by others, including Sir Austin Robinson, James Meade and Professor L. S. Pressnell. In pursuing it, I had the good fortune to be given ready access by the Treasury to the Sir Richard Clarke papers for the period up to 1949 — a collection of his minutes and other relevant documents, including his exchanges with Keynes in 1945-6. This provided a rich store of material from which it was not easy to select: the choice I made has doubled the length of the book.

Not all of the papers added are by Sir Richard himself. There is, for example, a letter from Jean Monnet in mid-1941 apropos of the Consolidated Balance Sheet discussed in Chapter I (Document 1); an excerpt on sterling balances from the material submitted in the Stage II negotiations in Washington at the end of 1944 (Document 2); and Keynes's reactions to notes by Sir Richard in 1945 and 1946 (Documents 4, 8, 11, 13, and 15). Some of the papers added do not relate to the period covered by the text: it seemed desirable to give at least a glimpse of the beginnings of the Marshall Plan (Documents 24 and 25) and the debate on European integration (Documents 26 and 27) since these were matters which would have been dealt with extensively had the book been completed.

In editing the actual text I have limited myself to explanatory notes and a few minor changes. I have not sought in these notes to assess the force of Sir Richard's argument or the objections that might be brought against it. But there are some points at which the reader may need a word of caution or amplification before accepting the views expressed, and I have therefore added a short commentary of my own, much of it derived from critical notes by Professor Pressnell, to whose assistance I am particularly indebted.

The preparation of this volume has been greatly assisted by successive Treasury Department Records Officers, Mr Ford and

Mr Nooney, who gave me access to Sir Richard's papers in the comfort of the Treasury; and by Mrs Anne Robinson, who prepared the documents selected for photographic reproduction. I should like also, on behalf of Lady Clarke and the Clarendon Press, to thank the Controller of Her Majesty's Stationery Office for permission to reproduce the material in the Appendix, all of which is Crown Copyright, and for agreeing to waive fees and forgo a royalty on this material.

COMMENTARY

Chapter I begins from the Anglo-American Consolidated Statement of 1941 which it identifies (para. 8) with the 'Purvis Balance-Sheet' and the 'Stimson Balance-Sheet' and describes as 'one of the seminal concepts of the war' (paras. 9 and 16a). The discussion seems to telescope two separate sets of events, one preceding and one succeeding the Lend-Lease Act of March 1941. There was both a 'Purvis Balance-Sheet' and a 'Stimson Balance-Sheet', not just a single consolidated statement.

The first, which 'bears the marks of Monnet's thought and methods' (H. Duncan Hall, *North American Supply* p. 264 n. (HMSO, 1955)), took shape in November–December 1940 when the United Kingdom was rapidly running out of dollars. In mid-November, Arthur Purvis — at that time the head of the British Purchasing Commission in Washington, working closely with the US Secretary of the Treasury Henry Morgenthau — was casting about for a way of bringing home the need for fuller mobilization of America's productive potential on a war footing. He asked British Supply Departments to let him have data showing (*a*) the armaments needed by Britain to defeat the enemy; (*b*) the expected output of British arms in 1941–2; and (*c*) the deficiency to be made good by the United States if the war was to be won. He submitted to the President at the end of December a rough estimate of $15 billion for the deficiency and followed this up with more detailed estimates at the invitation of Morgenthau. These figures were used as a basis for the appropriation under the Lend-Lease Bill, then before Congress.

The 'Stimson Balance-Sheet' or Anglo-American Consolidated Statement of Production came later, over the summer months of 1941. Stimson took the initiative to produce a combined balance sheet of American and British arms production, partly to drive home the need for higher American production and partly to make possible a rational allocation between American and British requirements (Hall, op. cit., pp. 322–8).

Both balance sheets were conceived as methods of achieving certain changes within the United States. British production, being already within sight of capacity limits, was not an important variable. This emerges very clearly from a minute of a meeting in London on 11 August 1941 at which Purvis, three days before his death in an aircraft accident, argued that 'what was now required was a directive from the highest quarters that [US] production for civilian needs should be cut to the extent necessary to raise war production to the level required to beat the Germans . . . The consolidated statement should provide a lever to get such a directive.' The same thought underlies the letter of 1 July 1941 from Jean Monnet to T. H. Brand reproduced as Document 1.

From the Consolidated Statement Sir Richard turns to the Combined Boards (i.e. the joint Anglo-American bodies for planning and allocation of war supplies) that were brought into existence after Pearl Harbor. He concentrates on the Combined Production and Resources Board with which he spent two tours of duty in Washington, the first from just before its creation in June 1942 — some months after the other Combined Boards — and the second from February to September 1943. The CPRB was not, to put it mildly, a conspicuous success, largely because it was from the start a kind of appendix to the American War Production Board under Donald Nelson, and carried on a running battle with the service departments in Washington.

Envisaged on the American side as 'the capstone of the combined board structure' (Hall op. cit., p. 379) and by Churchill as 'a single controlling body over the Combined Boards', it was in its charter set less exalted tasks but found even those beyond its powers. Nobody, says Sherwood, ever succeeded fully in straightening out 'the enormously confused affairs of the CPRB' (*The White House Papers* Vol. II p. 658 (Eyre and Spottiswoode, London, 1948)). There was no room for it in co-ordinating aircraft supplies since the Joint Aircraft Committee already acted as a combined production board for aircraft and neither the British nor the Americans wanted to see it displaced. At the same time it could not hope to bridge the purely American gulf between the US Joint Chiefs of Staff and the War Production Board, least of all with the appointment of Nelson, head of the latter, as the American member of the CPRB. In the absence of any effective machinery, such as existed in London in the War Cabinet and the Defence Committee, for the review of requirements and programmes and the harmonization of conflicting views in a common policy, the hostility of the American Service Departments to civilian control was never really overcome.

Sir Richard describes the fruitless attempt by the CPRB to proceed from a Combined Order of Battle to a schedule of munitions requirements and hence, by comparison with production plans, to a statement of surpluses and shortages. It would seem that the most the Board could have hoped to accomplish was a series, of marginal adjustments in production programmes, and that it was futile to contemplate the preparation of a 'single integrated programme' covering the whole range of munitions of war in all their diversity. The most convincing summing-up is that of the official American account in *Industrial Mobilization for War*:

CPRB did not engage in comprehensive production planning or in the long-term strategic planning of economic resources ... CPRB's isolation from the sources of decision regarding production objectives, its failure to develop an effective organisation, its deference to other agencies and its tardiness in assessing its jurisdiction, the inadequacy of programme planning by the agencies upon which CPRB relied for forecasts of requirements, the delay of the Combined Chiefs of Staff in promulgating strategic objectives for 1943 — all these contributed to a result that saw adjustments in the American and British production programme for 1943 made by the appropriate national authorities in each case, rather than through combined machinery. (Quoted by R. Sherwood, op. cit., Vol. II p. 583.)

Sir Richard's main reflections on the activities of CPRB are twofold. He regrets that it did not begin by concentrating attention on critical shortages in crucial items like escort vessels and landing craft; and he suggests that the right course in 1942 was to cut US civilian consumption to make way for faster industrial mobilization rather than set about cutting US munitions programmes in the interests of realism. Looking at the evolution of CPRB through 1943, and in the last years of the war, he takes a more favourable view of its later activities, arguing that for the handling of the emerging problems of those years 'if CPRB had not existed, it would have had to be invented' (para. 53).

The nub of the second chapter is the contention in para. 70 that the opportunity was missed in 1942 of setting up a Combined Finance and National Economy Board which would have reviewed and compared the underlying balance of the economy in the United Kingdom and the United States and helped to bring about a true pooling of resources. This would have brought home to the Americans the dangers of putting too great a strain on Britain and the injury to their own long-term interests if this left Britain too weak to play a full part after the war in the rebuilding of the world economy. Had such a Board existed, he argues, there would have been less risk of 'a failure of communications' (para. 63) between responsible people on both sides of the Atlantic. Instead there would have developed a combined understanding and strategy on economic and financial issues. 'A steady process of adjustment . . . would in the end have left Britain stronger and more able to play a constructive role in the five critical post-war years (a great American interest) and the United States readier and better equipped to handle [her] world-wide responsibilities' (para. 70).

It is not altogether easy to share Sir Richard's optimism that such a Board could have been brought into existence and fulfilled his hopes for it. No doubt there was a failure to reconsider how the financial burdens falling on Britain in all parts of the world should be redistributed when the United States became a full partner in the war effort. A Combined Finance and National Economy Board might have encouraged such a reconsideration. But the Americans had no enthusiasm for such ideas and the British had their own reservations. For most of the war they were reluctant to expose the weaknesses of their position too nakedly to the United States and so undermine Britain's claim to be still a great power. To do this could have invited pressure 'to go on our knees' (as Keynes put it) and beg like Roosevelt's dog Fala (as Churchill expressed the same thought). Keynes in the end gave a full exposition to the Americans of the state of the British economy in the autumn of 1944, basing himself on the memoranda of the Economic Section of the War Cabinet Office, and copies of his statement were widely circulated (para. 63). But this did not prevent the sudden withdrawal of Lend-Lease a year later. There is not much evidence that what was said in the Stage II negotiations aroused American opinion over the ensuing year to the implications for post-war reconstruction of a severely crippled British economy. Would American pressure to restrict British exports or American indifference to the accumulation of sterling liabilities have given way merely through the creation of a Combined Board?

Since exports crop up at various points in the narrative it may be helpful to put the treatment of this issue in perspective. The attempt to limit British exports is dismissed as 'an obvious absurdity' (para. 62). This can hardly apply to the original White Paper on Exports issued in September 1941 since this antedated American entry into the war and was intended to prevent the use in exports competing with American goods of materials supplied under Lend-Lease. The continuation of this condition into a period when British exports fell to 30 per cent of their pre-war level was not contested by the United Kingdom until the end of the war was in sight, largely because the manpower that exports would have absorbed was needed in the all-out mobilization for war which Lend-Lease and sterling credits permitted (see para. 63 n.). As Attlee put it after the war was over and Lend-Lease had been cut off:

It has been made possible for us . . . to mobilise our domestic man-power for war with an intensity unsurpassed elsewhere . . . without having to produce exports to pay for our imports of food and raw materials or to provide the cash we were spending abroad. The very fact that this was the right division of effort between ourselves and our allies leaves us, however, far worse off, when the sources of assistance dry up, than it leaves those who have been affording us the assistance. (Quoted by Hall, op. cit., p. 472.)

The reflection with which Attlee concluded was relevant to the post-war settlement more than to the restrictions maintained in wartime. In the Stage II negotiations in Washington in November 1944 (i.e. negotiations relating to the situation that would arise once Germany, but not Japan, was out of the war) Keynes expounded the need for an early switch of resources into British exports; and although the Americans were not moved to restore complete export freedom from 1 January 1945 (perhaps from some lingering suspicion that Britain would steal a march on American exporters while the war was still in progress) they did somewhat grudgingly concede what Keynes translated as 'the certainty of complete export freedom after V-E day and, by administrative action, the substance of it from 1 January 1945'.

Early in 1945 Sir Richard moved to work full time at the Treasury where his first job was to review the export–import balance. The move is reflected in the change in focus in the next two chapters which are mainly concerned with the problem of restoring external balance after the war. In 'Towards a Balance of Payments' (below, Document 3) he circulated in June 1945 his first reflections on the means by which we could pay our way in an impoverished and un-certain world. At that time it was natural to take a cautious view of the future, and with hindsight we can see that Sir Richard's estimates of the probable volume of international trade after the war were a little too low. He thought it likely that by 1950 trade would expand to the pre-war level and might exceed it by up to 15 per cent; the maximum possible growth in the decade to 1955 was to 50 per cent above the level in 1937. In fact, however, world trade in manufactures (a more relevant measure than total world trade) was 25 per cent higher by 1950 and over 70 per cent higher by 1955 than in 1937.

Sir Richard's estimates were, however, sufficiently near the mark to bear out his conclusion that it should be possible for the United Kingdom to get back into balance within five years. If he was too pessimistic it was chiefly because he shared the contemporary pre-occupation with the danger of an American recession and envisaged a fall in US GNP after the war from $200 billion to a level fluctuating between $100 and $150 billion. He was very much alive to the critical importance of full employment in the industrial countries – as compared, for example, with a reduction in trade barriers – in producing an expanding world market. For this reason he foresaw the need to develop 'a network of much more intimate relationships' between the leading countries. Co-operation in the development of middle- and low-income countries would also depend on the inter-change of information and ideas and a close understanding of each country's 'total economic position'.

If world trade expanded and British exports were fully competitive, Sir Richard concluded that it would be possible to balance accounts within three or four years at the 1938 volume of imports. But he wanted to ensure that the rate of exchange was not unfavourable, since it conditioned competitive power, and suggested rather hesitantly an early but modest devaluation to $3.50 to £1. Keynes, however, saw no need to devalue and there was an interesting exchange of minutes that left Sir Richard not entirely convinced (Documents 4-6). Keynes was relying on a comparison of inflation rates which in his view would indicate some over-valuation of the dollar at the end of the war and hence leave sterling exporters with some residual cost advantage. He might also have contended that if the trade imbalance was so great that some eventual change in the exchange rate would prove necessary to its removal, it was preferable to defer an adjustment and rely on exchange and other controls, rather than accept an immediate burden in less favourable terms of trade and more rapid inflation.

Sir Richard was impressed by Keynes's magisterial exposition in the spring of 1945 of 'Overseas Financial Policy in Stage III' (*Collected Writings of John Maynard Keynes*, Vol. XXIV, pp. 256-95 (Macmillan, for the Royal Economic Society, 1979)). But as he explains (below, paras. 160-1), he felt that Keynes was too optimistic and in too much of a hurry. He hankered after a fall-back position which he developed in a long memorandum (Document 7, 'Financial Policy in Stage III') but which Keynes would have none of. His idea amounted to an enlargement of the sterling area to include most of Western Europe, with a pooling and rationing of dollars, freedom of trade within the enlarged area, and strong discrimination against the United States. Keynes's rejection of this idea (Document 8) contained the judgement that he did not see 'any serious risk of an overall shortage of gold and dollars in the first three [post-war] years'. Sir Richard, who feared just such a shortage, maintains that it would have been wiser to have moved more slowly after the war ended, and postponed the loan negotiations (below, para. 166). It was a mistake, he thinks, to go for early convertibility of sterling in return for a large dollar loan. We should have waited to see how things developed, borrowing more limited amounts on commercial terms and retaining our freedom of action. In the end, as he points out, the first two or three years after the war did turn out very differently from the non-discriminatory visions of 1945. We ended up with an American (Marshall) plan that stood the loan negotiations upside-down and almost made discrimination against the United States the condition for enormous grants.

There is no doubt that Sir Richard's assessment of the prospect of a dollar shortage was nearer the mark than Keynes's. It is also clear that Keynes had more faith in American generosity and less faith that there was any real alternative to relying on it. But there was more to be said in his favour than Sir Richard allows.

Keynes started out from the position that it would either be necessary to maintain exchange controls indefinitely because of the accumulation of sterling balances in wartime, or to find some alternative, given the difficulty of preserving these controls for any length of time once peace returned. His advocacy of early convertibility *may* have rested on his optimism over the post-war dollar problem. But it was prompted also by the expectation that the Americans would insist on it as the price for a substantial loan, the need for which was overriding. Just how substantial the loan had to be to sustain convertibility was a question that might have merited further consideration, and there were those who returned from Washington convinced that the loan was not big enough.

As for the idea of a grouping of Western European countries with the sterling area, Keynes's criticism was essentially that virtually all the members of the group would be short of dollars and that the arrangement would merely shift their burdens onto Britain. To form a discriminating bloc with the active support of the Americans in 1947 was a very different matter from doing it in flat defiance of America in 1945-6.

It is also possible to take a different view of Keynes's role in the negotiations. Sir Richard is critical of the selection of Keynes to lead the delegation, and similar criticisms were made at the time. The question is whether anyone else would have done better. Britain was in a weak position and the American negotiators were scared of Congress so that there was not much room for manœuvre. There is no basis for the implication (para. 186) that the sending out of Sir Edward Bridges made any real difference except probably to stiffen the Americans. These and other matters relating to the negotiation of the Anglo-American Loan Agreement in 1945 are more fully discussed in Lord Robbins's *Autobiography of an Economist*, (Macmillan, London, 1971). The best detailed account is still Richard Gardner's *Sterling–Dollar Diplomacy* (Clarendon Press, Oxford, 1956).

Whatever the outcome of the Washington negotiations, the British government was faced in 1945 with some agonizing choices. These are perhaps most vividly brought out in some of the minutes reproduced here on what could be done if no loan were voted by Congress (Documents 10-16). It must be remembered that imports were far below pre-war levels all through the post-war years (it took ten years to get back to the pre-war level), that in 1945 exports paid for only 30 per cent of total imports, and that there were heavy military and other government expenditures all over the world that were difficult to contain. It would have been impossible to get through 1946 without quite heavy borrowing. But by the end of 1946 recovery was well on the way. Then in the very severe winter of 1946-7 the fuel crisis set it back by perhaps 6-9 months so that the need for foreign credits acquired renewed urgency. Thus at the time when the Loan was finally voted in mid-1946 the outlook was much better than a year previously, and better also than a year later when the Loan was running out fast.

The anxieties of the years before the Marshall Plan are developed in Chapter IV. The US and Canadian loans provided only temporary relief, running out unexpectedly quickly in 1947. As late as May the

Treasury expected to see them last well into 1948 (Document 19). By the autumn a debate was raging over the brief dash into convertibility on 15 July and out again on 20 August (Documents 22 and 23). Many regarded this as the main cause of the early exhaustion of the loans. Others pointed to the sharp deterioration in the balance of payments after the fuel crisis and argued that convertibility had played only a limited role.

The problem of hard and soft currencies aggravated the continuing dollar deficit through the use of resources in 'unrequited exports'. For a time the problem was tackled by discriminatory devices, administrative pressure, switching of sources of supply, and so on. But it became increasingly obvious that as the United Kingdom came back into balance the right course was to alter the sterling–dollar rate and bring market forces into play to support the substitution of sterling for dollar expenditures throughout the world. Although Sir Richard does not introduce the idea into his subsequent exposition of the problem of unrequited exports and the difficulty of setting a surplus in soft currencies against a deficit in gold and dollars, his conviction of the desirability of a devaluation of sterling remained unshaken.

The most interesting part of this chapter is his account of the origins of the *Economic Survey*. An *Economic Survey for 1946* was prepared in the Economic Section of the Cabinet Office under James Meade, towards the end of 1945, and analysed the problems of the economy in financial terms, exactly as would be done nowadays. But this framework was not congenial to those whose thinking had been conditioned in wartime to balances in terms of men and materials and who were used to reallocating resources by administrative measures. This *Economic Survey* was therefore suppressed and the next draft by the Economic Section, which also treated the budget as the relevant instrument for planning a peacetime economy, was also set aside. Instead the Economic Steering Committee, made up of Permanent Secretaries under the chairmanship of Sir Edward Bridges, called on Sir Richard Clarke, who happened to be present, to draft a White Paper over the next fortnight. This was to be in terms of the physical balances to which the minds of senior officials and Ministers, like good Russian planners, were attuned.

At that stage the Minister responsible, Herbert Morrison, was ill, and in any event could make neither head nor tail of the Economic Section's approach in terms of an inflationary gap (although this was the very approach that Ministers had hailed as a great innovation in 1941). Ministers had promised to produce a plan; and this could hardly be left entirely to an Assistant Secretary. So in the end Sir Stafford Cripps, then President of the Board of Trade and aspiring to higher office, wrote the first part, entitled 'The objectives of democratic planning', of what turned out to be a three-part document.

Sir Richard, from whose manuscript notes I take this account, points out that 'there was no "planning" in the document, for no "planning" had in fact been done; but it did show the problems, hopes and expectations of each department . . . and the inter-relationship of these was tolerably expounded.' It was approved by a meeting of seventeen senior Ministers, appeared the day after the fuel crisis had led to the virtual closure of British industry (and showed what value could be attached to government plans), but was none the less a best-seller.

In the debates of those years, planning tended to be identified with the use of wartime 'physical controls': systems of rationing and allocation of 'scarce' materials and finished goods, qualitative restrictions on imports and import licensing; government bulk-buying of imports; exchange control; building controls; and so on. But while many people liked the idea of planning they were less well disposed towards controls — at any rate in peacetime. It was rare to find on the lips of those who waxed eloquent on the virtues of planning a reconciliation of the two ideas. The nearest approach by a Cabinet Minister to an exposition of the objectives, *modus operandi*, or limitations of planning is to be found in Cripps's introduction to the *Economic Survey for 1947*. It was a very muddled and unconvincing exposition and nothing similar ever appeared in later *Economic Surveys*. The interested reader will find a pungent critique of the treatment of planning in the 1947 and later *Economic Surveys* in Ely Devons's, 'Planning by Economic Survey' reprinted in his *Planning and Economic Management* (Manchester University Press, 1970).

Yet if it had been left to Sir Richard he would have had no difficulty in producing a rationale of the controls operated by the Labour government. As one of the first to preach a dollar shortage, he had no faith in the efforts to make sterling convertible at an early date or in exclusive reliance on what came to be called demand management. He would no doubt have argued that the controls were largely directed towards limiting and redirecting demand with a view to economizing dollar expenditure. Their justification rested on the difficulty (or impossibility) of relaxing the balance of payments constraint (or, later 'the dollar shortage') by other means. It had to be shown that a tighter budget would have done little to check the demand for imports, that there were logistic limits to the rate at which exports could grow, that devaluation would have weakened the terms of trade without bringing exports and imports into balance, and so on. A subsidiary justification lay in the individual out-of-balance situations in particular commodity markets and the damage likely to result from the large changes in price relationships that would have accompanied a premature decontrol. To allow such damage would have been inconsistent with the emphasis that continued to be laid on fairness in distributive shares, even after the removal of wartime incentives to high output pointed to the need to give higher priority to purely financial inducements. If the price mechanism were allowed to take over too soon, the process of adjustment would be complicated and might be delayed by large swings in price that aroused social resentments and inflationary pressure.

The *Economic Survey for 1947* was badly timed. As the fuel crisis faded, an exchange crisis loomed up, the Loan ran out fast, and Ministers had to contemplate severe cuts in dollar imports. But just as the situation was at its gloomiest came General Marshall's speech of 5 June at Harvard.

It is at this point that the text breaks off. The note on the world dollar crisis reprinted as Document 20 was intended to form part of Chapter V, an introduction to the Marshall Plan. But it, too, takes us no further than mid-1947. However, Sir Richard's papers include some that convey the gist of his thinking both about the Marshall Plan and about the economic integration of Western Europe. A few of these have been included in this volume (Documents 24–7), in token of the prominent part he played in the official thinking behind Britain's participation in the Marshall Plan.

All four documents bring out how thinking about these matters was dominated in the early post-war years by the prospect of a continuing dollar shortage. In the first it is argued that 'the central problem of Europe is the restoration of dollar viability' (Document 24, para. 14), and this is repeated, almost in the same words in the second (Document 25, para. 3). In 1948 it was expected that exports to the Western Hemisphere from the countries participating in the OEEC, even in 1951–2, would be less than two-thirds of the imports they required. The same thought recurs in Sir Richard's memorandum on 'Western and other Unions': the United Kingdom might 'regain viability pretty fast ... but France and Germany??' (Document 26, para. 15 (iv)). In 1949 officials took much the same view: 'there is no attraction for us in long-term economic co-operation with Europe. At best it will be a drain on our resources' (Document 27, para. 5).

The issue of political federation is posed in the memorandum on 'Western and other Unions'. In this, Sir Richard argues that there would be a strong case for federation if it could be completed and in full working order within five years, but little point in it otherwise. It would be worth sacrificing independence in order to prevent war for 'we are not militarily viable and never shall be again'. War apart, however, it would have 'no attractions whatever' for the United Kingdom and it would be far better to enter into a 'wholly possible' union with the United States and the British Commonwealth.

Although these were the conclusions to which he had come by September 1948 he confesses to an earlier vision:

'An Open Conspiracy of bureaucrats and business men would link the affairs of the Western European countries closer and closer together, and we should advance by almost imperceptible stages to a point at which so many questions were in fact being settled internationally that one had the substance of Western European Government without its form' (Document 26, para. 6).

The pity is that he did not live to give us his own narrative of the events of those years and his considered view, in the light of subsequent developments, of the decisions that were taken.

Oxford
February 1981

Alec Cairncross

Anglo-American Economic Collaboration in War and Peace 1942-1949

*

SIR RICHARD CLARKE

CHAPTER I

War Production: London and Washington

1. The second half of 1941 was another great climacteric period for the British, less obvious than that opened a year before by the fall of France, and calling for much greater adaptability first in leadership, planning and management, and gradually throughout the community. In May/June, it was still 'our war': we had the support of the Dominions, and increasing assistance from the United States, but the key decisions were being taken by the War Cabinet, where the responsibility for 'our side of the war' lay. Six months later, everything had been transformed. The United States was in the war; German troops were deep in Russia; Japan, having struck formidable blows at American and British sea power, was engulfing South-East Asia. 'Our war' had become the world war, in which we were a tremendously important unit, but no longer in control of the decisions.

2. Mr Churchill had of course been working towards this situation since the disasters of 1940, and President Roosevelt had been gradually working his way to persuade American public opinion to help us in 'our war'. The Lend-Lease Act had been passed in March 1941: American forces were increasingly collaborating in the Atlantic: as early as February/March 1941, staff talks had taken place leading to the fundamental strategic decision that if the United States entered the war, the strategy would be to concentrate first on defeating Germany. So it had proceeded, to the meeting in August 1941, and the signing of the Atlantic Charter. When the actual situation arrived at Pearl Harbor, a great many people in the top échelons on both sides of the Atlantic were ready for it.

3. Nevertheless, there was a wide difference between fighting 'our war', seeking the maximum assistance from the United States, and becoming a partner in a 'combined' war (with a third enigmatic 'partner' in the Soviet Union). It was certain, moreover, that as America's military and production power grew, we would become the junior partner, comparatively weaker at end-1942 than at end-1941, at end-1943 than at end-1942, and so on. We therefore had to adjust our thinking fast, and press ahead with building up combined[1] organizations to provide machinery for taking the combined decisions which would continue throughout the war.

4. My own work, in the Ministries of Supply and then Production in London, with two tours of duty with the Combined Production and Resources Board in Washington, was predominantly concerned with this series of problems; and this narrative deals only with those in which I was personally involved; and which, over thirty years later, seem to me to contain important pointers to what has happened since, and indeed to the future. I do not purport to show a complete picture.[2]

Ministry of Supply Programmes

5. I had joined Sir Walter Layton's Directorate of Programmes in the Ministry of Supply (then under Lord Beaverbrook) in April 1941. I had gone from the *Financial News* (as it then was) to the Ministry of Information in September 1939, and for the following eighteen months was shuffled between it and the Ministry of Economic Warfare, lacking perhaps the experience of the civil service in times of chaos, which is (when higher authority are all too busy and distraught to think for you) to choose some subject which seems to you to be insufficiently covered, and become indispensable in it.[3] So I was very pleased to get nearer to the cutting edge of the war effort, and accepted Layton's invitation with alacrity.[4]

6. Layton was Director-General of Programmes (DGP). He had been Lloyd George's director of statistics at the Ministry of Munitions, but like the other 'bright young men' of World War I (Salter, Keynes, Beveridge) he had not been called upon by Neville Chamberlain. The organisation's function was to act as a central link between the department and the customer — the War Office Director-General of Army Requirements (then Sir Robert Sinclair) — to keep the production programmes as far as possible in line with the requirements. Layton developed a key role in international supply, covering all war production: and his mission to USA in autumn 1940 was the first reconnaissance of their possibilities and capabilities as a source of supply.

7. Hugh Weeks, director of statistics, with a skilfully-chosen team from a variety of professions and occupations, was the anchorman of the whole organisation; Geoffrey Crowther was attached in a rather special capacity; I had a high-sounding but in fact meaningless title, but Layton's intention was always, I believe, to have me there to help with the great expansion in the international work that he envisaged for all war production. The first job that I remember doing was drafting all night the telegram containing our first Lend-Lease appropriation list of Army equipment requirements, and the summary briefs on the items.

The Anglo-American Consolidated Statement

8. In my early weeks at the Ministry, I began to see an esoteric series of telegrams from Washington, some called 'Stimson Balance-Sheet', some 'Purvis Balance-Sheet', and some 'Consolidated Statement'. These referred to a most secret and private project, the immediate substance of which was to set out a 'balance-sheet' of US and UK stocks and production programmes as then planned up to the end of 1942.

9. In my opinion, which would I believe be supported by Hancock and Gowing,[5] this was one of the seminal concepts of the war — one of the steps which literally altered the course of events favourably.

10. The original idea probably came from the fertile mind of Jean Monnet (see Document 1) and was rapidly driven forward by Arthur Purvis, the Canadian head of the British Supply Council in Washington. The decisive point was when the United States Secretary for War, Stimson, became convinced that it was exactly what he wanted to get the decisions that he needed to press forward the mobilization of American industry. He took the driving-seat and pushed with great force and urgency, setting up a special secret committee in the War Department to prepare the first draft of the balance sheet. This was immensely advantageous for two reasons: the request came to the British Government as an American initiative from a source which could not possibly be turned down although it involved disclosing to a non-belligerent some of the most secret information of the war — the stocks and eighteen months' production schedules of all the main items of equipment; and also that it brought the War Department in on the ground floor.

11. These were in my opinion the three main protagonists, but the project could not have succeeded at the London end without Layton (who carried Beaverbrook with him and thence the Prime Minister); Tommy Brand, head of the North American Secretariat of the War Cabinet Offices; and at the Washington end, Stacy May, later director of statistics of the War Production Board, specially seconded by Stimson to the War Department for this operation to reassure us that the information was being held in tight top secret military hands.

12. On 3 July, Stimson's formal request to the British authorities (wisely passed through Purvis instead of directed to a Minister — imagine such a thing happening in 1975!)[6] emphasized the importance of the balance sheet, both in planning and developing increased production in the United States, and in providing guides for allocation of US output between the US and UK forces. Purvis emphasized

speed, for the next year's War Department appropriations were just being drawn up; and 'we have reason to believe' that the results of this investigation will be a means of bringing about a considerable increase in the programme of armament production. Later he explained that the critical point had been reached at which the facilities of the professional armament producers were full, and they were now having to try to convert or expand the facilities of civil industry, which called for forceful political leadership. It must not be forgotten that US opinion, though generally sympathetic to the British, was still overwhelmingly opposed to US entry into the war, and early in August the House of Representatives had only barely by one vote agreed to sustain Selective Service. So Roosevelt had to handle the situation with immense care.

13. The operation went ahead fast. On a boiling Sunday afternoon, 10 August, I remember, Layton and I were waiting agog at his house in Sussex for the messenger with the first provisional draft prepared by the War Department Committee, and the additional material being brought simultaneously by Stacy May. It had been arranged that the final agreed 'combined' version would be prepared in London. It is easy to recall the excitement of the occasion, to see for the first time this panorama of 'combined' war production, containing our hopes and fears for the future. As soon as it arrived, we at once sat down to work on it, and had the first conclusions ready for distribution to the War Cabinet next day.

Table 1. Output and Stocks of War Equipment. *United States, United Kingdom, and Canada.*

	Stocks	Output		
	30 June 1941	1st Quarter July–Sept. 1941	6th Quarter Oct.–Dec. 1942	Total in 18 months
Aircraft				
Total combat aircraft (incl. Flying Boats)				
USA	4,250	2,750	6,720	31,760
United Kingdom and Canada	14,780	4,020	4,330	25,140
Heavy bombers				
USA	120	55	770	1,990
United Kingdom and Canada	150	200	1,020	3,490
Medium bombers				
USA	610	200	1,410	4,670
United Kingdom and Canada	2,320	720	330	3,680
Light bombers				
USA	1,800	980	1,530	9,840
United Kingdom and Canada	4,430	755	545	3,460

	Stocks	Output		
	30 June 1941	1st Quarter July–Sept. 1941	6th Quarter Oct.–Dec. 1942	Total in 18 months
Fighters				
USA	1,365	1,390	2,700	14,110
United Kingdom and Canada	7,480	2,300	2,260	13,800
Merchant shipping (incl. Tankers) (Th. Gross Tons)				
USA	6,840	230	1,210	4,840
United Kingdom and Canada	18,160*	320	440	2,300
Tanks				
Heavy and medium tanks				
USA	80	450	3,000	10,790
United Kingdom and Canada	2,210	1,250	3,030	14,040
Light tanks				
USA	350	910	1,035	6,250
United Kingdom and Canada	1,360	40	Nil	55
Artillery				
Field, medium and heavy guns				
USA	2,260	1,170	1,520	8,740
United Kingdom and Canada	5,620	1,410	790	6,380
Tank and anti-tank				
USA	1,650	2,990	5,870	31,065
United Kingdom and Canada	4,100	2,470	8,700	36,550
AA Land and naval (exc. Oerlikons)				
USA	4,600	675	3,960	14,740
United Kingdom and Canada	14,570	1,785	4,170	19,480
Gun ammunition (Thousands of rounds)				
Army artillery (including tank and anti-tank)				
USA	6,130	630	9,460	37,410
United Kingdom and Canada	10,030	6,380	18,425	85,580
AA Land and naval (over 20 mm.)				
USA	5,200	2,910	11,570	50,830
United Kingdom and Canada	18,850	6,210	9,660	51,900
20 mm Guns (Aircraft Cannon and Oerlikon)				
USA	8	510	20,400	67,570
United Kingdom and Canada	5,195	3,080	7,070	34,160

Table 1 (*cont.*):

	Stocks	Output		
	30 June 1941	1st Quarter July–Sept. 1941	6th Quarter Oct.–Dec. 1942	Total in 18 months
Small arms				
Machine guns, army and aircraft				
USA	54,720	39,020	90,860	428,480
United Kingdom and Canada	329,650	50,930	90,930	446,530
Rifles (Thousands)				
USA	1,930	106	236	1,194
United Kingdom and Canada	3,170	11	223	794
Small arms ammunition (Ball A.P. and Tracer) (million rounds)				
USA	690	670	2,480	9,310
United Kingdom and Canada	1,770	510	1,230	5,420

*British Register and Allied and Neutral on time charter to United Kingdom.

14. The Statement is a historic document; and in Table 1 are set out the figures in the final version, which was dated 3 September. It was a feat of simplicity, typical of Layton's powers of presentation and exposition. The conclusions were painfully clear:

(*a*) For Army equipment, UK and Canada were currently producing at double the rate of USA, who would not catch up until the last quarter of 1942 (it was not yet possible to do a weighted average of the lot).

(*b*) UK and Canadian output currently exceeded USA output in two-thirds of the items: this would be reversed by the end of 1942. But UK and Canadian stocks were much the larger, so they would still lead in total quantities available by end-1942 (stocks plus production) even with no supplies from USA.

(*c*) But UK and Canadian supplies would not be large enough to meet minimum requirements for aggressive warfare or to help others (e.g. Russia). The requisitions filed by Britain and others for Lend-Lease were already between one-third and one-half of the entire programme that had been planned in USA.

(*d*) To perform effectively the dual task of equipping its own forces and supplying its allies' needs, USA must marshal for armament production an amount of its production resources proportionate to that which was devoted to this purpose in Britain and Canada.

15. There is a remarkable meeting of minds between (*d*) and a leading principle laid down by the US Chiefs of Staff, General Marshall and Admiral Stark, in a report to the President dated 11 September 1941 on the military situation and the basis for the production programme.

... Past experience of the United States and other Powers should condition estimates of the capability of the United States to support a war effort, with due regard to differences in overall industrial capacity; differences in availability of materials; and an appropriate balance between the manpower to be employed in the armed forces, and the manpower to be employed in industry and essential services. Because of the present high degree of mechanisation, a greater proportion of manpower must be allocated to industry for the manufacture of equipment and munitions than was the case in former wars ...

The full report, printed in *The White House Papers*[7] of Harry L. Hopkins is a strategic document of first importance. Sherwood refers to 'the year of exchanges of information and opinion by the British and American staffs working together in secret and unofficial but highly effective co-operation'. Of course the US Chiefs of Staff could not have seen the final version of the Consolidated Statement in time, but the initial US version had been available for some weeks, and Stimson and his colleagues had clearly decided and convinced the Chiefs of Staff that even before entering the war, USA could not carry out its task of equipping its own forces and meeting its allies' and associates' needs without full industrial mobilization.

16. The Statement was immediately used to help the judgement on how much equipment the Beaverbrook–Harriman Mission to USSR could undertake to supply.[8]

16a. There were by-products of the war on the Consolidated Statement — building a group of people in war production, Services and civilian, on both sides of the Atlantic, with the mutual confidence and respect which is the root of 'combined' effort; and the sense of dimension of what a country could do which provided a rational basis for President Roosevelt's huge and challenging programmes for aircraft, tanks, and ships, pressed on him by Beaverbrook and Hopkins and announced on 6 January 1942.[9] I rely upon all this series of events in describing the Consolidated Statement, conceived as early as spring 1941, as 'one of the seminal concepts of the war'.

Combined Boards

17. The preparatory work throughout 1941 had been so good that the Churchill–Roosevelt ARCADIA conference[10] in December was rapidly able to set up four 'combined' organisations — Chiefs of

Staff, Munitions Assignment, Shipping Adjustment, Raw Materials. Food (equally important) had to wait six months. Production and Resources, to some people the key to the whole thing, was postponed, overtly because the War Production Board was only just started and its chairman Donald Nelson just in the saddle, and because Britain had not yet a Minister in charge of the whole war production field; but more fundamentally because the War and Navy Departments regarded themselves as the production authorities and would not accept War Production Board (i.e. civilian) control over their programmes. Beaverbrook had pressed Roosevelt to join assignment, production, and resources under one Board, with Hopkins (the only man acceptable to everybody) in charge; but Roosevelt turned this down, because Hopkins was known to the American public only as a prodigious spender on relief in the New Deal days, and would not be tolerated as a war production chief.[11]

18. The postponement of setting up the Combined Production and Resources Board (CPRB) was sensible in all the circumstances, but it was in my opinion a great mistake in effect to put it under the chairman of the War Production Board; for the crucial problem of the control of war production was unlikely ever to be solved (and it never was), so that whenever the CPRB might be set up, placing the War Production Board in the lead made it certain that it would never be able even to begin to perform the functions that were to be laid down in its charter:

The Board shall:
(a) Combine the production programmes of the United States, the United Kingdom, and Canada, into a single integrated programme adjusted to the strategic requirements of the war, as indicated to the Board by the Combined Chiefs of Staff, and to all relevant production factors. In this connection, the Board shall take account of the need for maximum utilization of the productive resources available to the United States, the British Commonwealth of Nations, and the United Nations, the need to reduce demands on shipping to a minimum, and the essential needs of the civilian populations.
(b) In close collaboration with the Combined Chiefs of Staff, assure the continuous adjustment of the combined production programme to meet changing military requirements.

19. It is difficult to believe that a satisfactory arrangement could not have been made, e.g. Stimson as member with a War Production Board deputy, or indeed an outside figure such as Averill Harriman, which would have enabled the CPRB to play a role consistent with its charter. But the Americans had a lot to think about at the time; and the British in the period after ARCADIA were heavily involved in their own affairs — and indeed the position could have been retrieved only with great embarrassment to Nelson.

Ministry of Production

20. When Churchill got back to England, he was at once faced with creating a Ministry of Production. It was necessary to have a Minister in charge of all war production in order to sit with Nelson on the CPRB and to handle the international work. More important, industrial mobilization was so advanced that there was no spare room for the Supply departments[12] to put new projects, and there were continuous problems of priority for capacity and labour: these had formerly been settled by a Cabinet committee, to nobody's satisfaction. Finally, the course of the war was at its worst, with the Prime Minister under great pressure to take new action.

21. The Prime Minister announced the setting-up of a Ministry of Production on 4 February 1942, and appointed Beaverbrook. This appointment was anathema both to Ernie Bevin, Minister of Labour, and to the Service and Supply Ministers. Bevin feared that he would try to take over the control of labour; the Supply Ministers thought that the new structure would destroy their responsibility and that a monolithic machine would be created with incessant and arbitrary forays by the Beaver (whose intention was to take over the Ministry of War Transport too). In the preparation of the White Paper defining the Minister's work, Churchill tells how 'every point of detail in dividing the various responsibilities had to be fought for as in a battle' and of 'the long and harassing discussions which took place in my presence between him and other principal Ministers'.[13]

22. When published on 10 February, the White Paper had met the essential points of the Beaver's opponents, who fully appreciated the need for a Ministry of Production, provided that it limited its tasks to those that obviously required central decision or central initiative (of which there were plenty); but Bevin was not prepared to concede any responsibility for labour and manpower control, nor the others any derogation from their responsibilities to Parliament for running their departments. Beaverbrook initially accepted this, but in a few days, racked with asthma and nervous exhaustion, he resigned. This was fortunate, for his great qualities were really the opposite of those required for this task.

23. The new Minister, Oliver Lyttelton, was a conciliatory appointment. Sir Henry Self had already been appointed Permanent Secretary; and Layton had gone to the new Ministry with Crowther and me. With Layton's departure, Weeks became Director-General of Statistics and Programmes at the Ministry of Supply,[14] and then began to share his time with the Ministry of Production, finally moving there

altogether. Slowly the Ministry built up; a difficult process at the best of times, with the lower posts much more difficult to fill than the higher.

24. Layton's objective at this stage was to create a Joint War Production Staff (JWPS). He brought together in one committee the users and producers of war equipment, and intended to make them the body to decide equipment strategy, and to serve them by a joint staff drawn from the Ministry and the Supply departments. We produced valuable papers; of particular value, for example, in discussing and bringing into focus the Minister's objectives, stretching right across war production, for his visits to Washington (two in 1942). An inevitable awkwardness was that the Service departments would normally be represented by their officers in charge of supply, who were already closely in touch with the Supply departments. Moreover, at this stage of the war there was rapidly diminishing room for manœuvre in the UK production programmes, and this was not a sensible forum for dealing with individual and highly specific priority points. My own opinion was (and indeed is) that to be really effective it should have been started much earlier, as soon as the departments' programmes had begun to take shape; and I was not at all surprised that meetings became rarer in 1943, when Layton retired.

CPRB Set Up

25. By the end of May, the Americans and ourselves decided that CPRB could now be set up; and Lyttelton took a very strong Service and Supply Mission to Washington. We flew at night by Boeing Clipper from Foynes (Shannon) to Gander (Newfoundland) to Baltimore. When I awoke, I saw below not the icy desolation of Newfoundland, but the emerald-green fields of Ireland: in mid-Atlantic, the pilot had had bad weather reports and decided to return.[15] The next night all was well. We arrived in Washington in the evening, very hot, and I found it much changed from my first visit in January 1939.

26. Wartime Washington was always confused, though the administrative achievement nearly always turned out to be much better than it ever seemed likely to be. Naturally enough, there had been no change in the CPRB situation. Nelson was friendly, able, obviously under great pressure, and had obviously not thought at all or been briefed about CPRB. Our enquiries and those of our Washington team showed no progress either; although much valuable work was done on the specific matters of business to be carried out with the Americans, and, as always, in discussions between the London and Washington British.

27. However, we had the first meeting of the Board, with Nelson and Lyttelton (deputy Sinclair), to whom later the Canadian Minister of Munitions and Supply, Mr C. D. Howe, was added. Brand and the very bright American lawyer, Milton Katz (and later Sid Pierce for Canada), were the secretaries. Monnet was of course there. It was decided to have an 'international' staff to start with under Colonel H. S. Aurand, a very competent professional soldier in the US War Department who moved on after a few months to other duties. Roy Allen, the British Supply Council statistician and myself (totally unexpectedly, for I had not even brought a change of clothes) were to be the 'British' members, and there were some bright young War Production Board people: we were to have a separate suite of offices, specially security-protected, in the Social Security Building, now WPB's headquarters.

28. The British team was reasonably strong. Sinclair was chairman of the British Supply Council as well as deputy member of CPRB; and his record and remarkable gifts took him at once into the heart both of military and war-production Washington. Monnet had his unique contacts. On specific questions, e.g. the need for more escort vessels, the whole British network could and did exercise great pressure. But the real reason for the existence of CPRB was to contribute to the very large problems, particularly the relation of requirements to resources, and this proved intractable.

Requirements and Resources

29. We found that Stacy May, after his great part in promoting expansion in 1941, had now decided that the President's targets of January 1942 were much too high; and that if the Services (US and Allied) were planning operations on this supply basis, they could be in great difficulty. He believed that if these targets were reduced, this would increase, not decrease, production. This had become firm War Production Board doctrine.

30. Much time was spent in trying to determine what were the Army 'requirements' corresponding to the agreed strategy of the Combined Chiefs of Staff. The British system was to decide upon an 'Order of Battle' for a date, say, two years ahead. They would then calculate the unit equipment, reserves, etc., that these forces would require, and the estimated wastage in the mean time; subtract the initial stock; and there the 'requirements' were, independent of the expected supplies. The Americans were asked to do the same, but it ran counter to their thinking. Their 'Army Supply Program' (ASP) was essentially a production requirement (adding in Allies' needs where

known); and it was never possible to relate this back to the needs of
a strategy; their system was almost certainly simpler than the British,
and in any case had to give figures consistent with the President's
production targets for 1942 and 1943. When the CPRB formally
asked the Combined Chiefs of Staff for the US Army requirements,
the ASP landed on our desks next day with a resounding thud; and
that was the end of it.

31. I now wonder whether the War Production Board and thence
CPRB were tactically wise in pressing the Army requirements problem
so hard. Much the biggest combined production problem in summer
1942 for at least eighteen months was ocean transport — merchant
shipbuilding and escort vessels — and landing craft. The cumulative
production of ships did not exceed the cumulative sinkings until
autumn 1943. The escort vessel programme did not begin to yield
significant output before 1943: at Casablanca (January 1943), the
Combined Chiefs of Staff specified escort vessels (for ocean convoy)
as: 'the one item of insufficiency on the gigantic list of equipment
which seriously affected all the strategic requirements of the time'.[16]
At TRIDENT in May 1943 the Combined Chiefs of Staff reported:
'that sufficient personnel and material were available for all proposed
operations: no serious deficiencies were apparent, with the exception
of steel for landing craft construction'.[16] General Marshall wrote that
at Teheran in December 1943: 'of all the problems of implementation
of strategy, the greatest by far was the critical shortage of landing
craft'.[16] If CPRB could have begun its existence in June 1942 with a
powerful memorandum to the Combined Chiefs of Staff identifying
this as the crucial area of combined production problems for 1942
and 1943, this might not have been successful, but it would certainly
have won respect.[17]

32. However this may be, the fact was that the CPRB lost its first
major engagement; and moreover on what was known on the American
side to be a negative issue, seeking to reduce requirements and
programmes.[18] It never recovered.

Faster Mobilization

33. The alternative way to handle the problem of lack of balance
propounded by Stacy May was to press for faster mobilization of
labour and consumer goods industry, so that in fact the larger
programmes for 1943 could be carried out, and room found without
undue pain for the new critical ocean transport and marine requirements. This was never considered as far as I know. It would have
involved looking the other way, towards James Byrnes,[19] taken from

the Supreme Court on 1 October 1942 to become what was in effect Assistant President on the Home Front. This would have been difficult. The 1941 Consolidated Statement and the US Chiefs of Staff's report in September 1941 had shown that as the war developed (and Japan was not then in the war) something approaching a total war effort would be needed to meet world-wide requirements. But there was no understanding of this at all in the Government generally or the public, who had a universal confidence that United States industry could do whatever was required. Moreover, war production was going ahead well in 1942 (nearly 4 times 1941); and the War Production Board might be being unduly pessimistic about the ability to meet the President's programmes for 1943.

34. A highly expert statistical report commissioned by CPRB in 1944, and published in 1945,[20] described what actually happened:

(a) At June 1944, USA had 18 per cent of its labour force in the armed forces and 22 per cent in war production – about 40 per cent in all.

(b) UK had 22 per cent in the armed forces and 33 per cent in war production – about 55 per cent in all. [It could properly be argued that these figures were made possible by North American supplies of munitions, materials, food – but there were services for US and Canadian forces in UK on the other side; and nearly five years instead of 2½].

(c) US civil consumption per head in 1944 was about 4 per cent above 1941: UK's was about 16 per cent below 1938, virtually the same from 1941 to 1944.

35. These comparisons of total mobilization are well known. In munitions production, USA overtook UK early in 1942; had a fine expansion in 1942, and produced about 2½ times UK; but the rate of momentum fell in 1943, and with UK still expanding to its peak, US production in that year was less than 4 times UK, and little more in the following year. So the US war production at its peak was little over 4 times UK's, notwithstanding bombing, the smaller proportion of US forces, the immensely greater US manufacturing productivity, and 2.8 times the population.

36. If the Americans could have achieved 45 per cent mobilisation instead of 40 per cent this would have increased their munitions labour force and production by about 25 per cent (to 5 times UK), and would have given the Combined Chiefs of Staff an extra capability equivalent to the whole UK war production. Admittedly, the verdict in the end was that they had 'enough', except for such critical shortages as landing craft – but that was enough to do the operations

currently planned. With a fillip to production, particularly of the critical items, and clearly on the way by mid-1943, or perhaps a mix of more soldiers and more munitions, there could conceivably have been faster timetables. And if the war had gone badly — collapse of the Soviet armies on any major front, loss of decisive mid-Pacific naval battles, Japanese breakthrough into India, Ceylon, Australia — there would have been great reserves of munitions and ocean transport to call upon.

37. So there was much to be played for in mid-1942:

(*a*) the only practicable way to retain the President's objective
(*b*) the possibility of a shorter war
(*c*) some supply insurance in the event of new disasters
(*d*) sacrifices for the US civil population which would have been significant compared with what happened, but nowhere near 'total war'.

38. At this distance of time, nobody can say what would have happened to a CPRB initiative, or who would have supported it. 'Might-have-beens' are unprofitable, but there are four lessons to draw, relating to all affairs, and not just to war:

(*a*) everyone accepted the conventional WPB policy without thinking of the alternative — to release more resources. When there is unanimity without solid thought behind it, one should always be suspicious;
(*b*) 'balance-sheets' between requirements and resources can sometimes be resolved by increasing the latter, not by reducing the former;
(*c*) the system by which the war was being fought, both in USA and UK, was separating the conduct of 'the war' from the conduct of 'the civilian economy'. I shall return to this later; it extends far beyond this particular situation;
(*d*) maybe the statistical apparatus would not have been able, by mid-1942, to pick out the crucial points. So the first thing to do, in all new adventures, is to look after the statistical apparatus.

Raw Materials

39. From the start, the Americans had seen raw materials, rather than industrial capacity or labour, as the most troublesome limitation on their war production potential: in this their troubles were the opposite of the British, who at the outset found it most difficult to get enough industrial capacity and were then continuously and critically short of labour, but except for steel were rarely very short

of raw materials. The difference was natural, for the Americans were increasing their total production, whilst the British were converting theirs, and were also able to draw supplies from USA. In the event, at the level US mobilisation achieved, the difficulties were overcome — some by the marvellous achievements of US technology, e.g. the creation of a synthetic rubber industry virtually from scratch to be able to produce 600,000 tons a year by early 1944 (so that the problem became the shortage of capacity to produce tyres and tubes!), and some by a systematic development of supplies and economy in requirements.

40. This rapidly became an important function of CPRB, in combination with the Combined Raw Materials Board (CRMB), whose US executive secretary was Lincoln Gordon. Normally a combined committee of the two boards was set up, to try to get at a realistic balance sheet. One of the first was for copper, where ammunition requirements called for half the total supply; and the attempts to substitute steel for cartridge cases and the recovery of battle scrap were proving unproductive. Examination showed, however, that the production facilities fell short of the ammunition requirements at the critical times, so that the shortage could be of facilities, not copper. Again, at the crucial time, expenditure was low, so the requirements could fall.

41. A similar committee was set up for aluminium and magnesium; which showed that the huge expansions of production in progress in the United States would match the expansion in the aircraft programmes.

42. For steel, a tremendous apparent shortage appeared, but this proved to be a consequence of the inadequate US allocation system: in November 1942 they invited Arnold Plant, who managed the British Steel allocation system, to advise them; and adopted something very like the British system; and with the aid of vigorous expansions of capacity, the realistic requirements and supplies began to fit.

43. The breadth of these studies was widely extended in 1943, notably into the supplies which were becoming increasingly for the civilian economies and world-wide: this was certainly one of the constructive contributions of CPRB, particularly because the joint examinations with CRMB of the requirement/supply balance sheets tended to overcome fears of shortage which would have resulted in panic action, either in cutting back military requirements or in excessive diversion of resources to increasing material supply.

The Lyttelton Mission: November 1942

44. Lyttelton's visit to USA with a strong Mission in November was much more important than that of June, for we were getting to the end of our resources of manpower, and our dependence on US supplies had reached a scale, itself a tribute to the relations developed in 1941 and 1942, that we needed to know what we could rely on. There were three fundamental topics:

(a) integration of British and American aircraft programmes, with special aim of improving quality (not just numbers);
(b) increase of the US shipbuilding and shipping programmes;
(c) guarantee of minimum supplies of major importance that we needed, notably escort vessels, auxiliary aircraft-carriers, tanks, heavy trucks, locomotives, 20mm weapons, rubber.

45. The Mission was successful; and the President wrote a letter to the Prime Minister, backed by departmental agreements on merchant ship tonnage, aircraft, and ground Army equipment which went a long way to meet our requirements. Lyttelton attributed this success largely to the victory at El Alamein; and partly to a decision taken just before the visit to put a ceiling on the expansion of the Army and Air Force: on the other side, he noted the bitter controversy and struggle between the War Production Board and the Services, and the Navy's fight against the aircraft and merchant shipbuilding programmes.[21]

46. There was of course the usual meeting of CPRB, but the significant point was that none of the substantial topics were discussed in CPRB, and that Lyttelton's instructions for his Mission and his subsequent report on it did not mention CPRB at all. These were all topics of the kinds that were envisaged for CPRB at the time of its conception; and this occasion marked the end of any intention that anyone might have had of using the CPRB as a means of integrating the combined production programmes.[22]

A Reorganized Ministry

47. In the early months of 1943, there was a major reconstruction of the Ministry of Production. Layton, who had borne a tremendous load since Dunkirk and had been one of the creators of combined Anglo-American war production, retired ill. I have never known a man with a sharper eye for the key point, a clearer and more lucid writer of reports, a wider international comprehension of war; and he was one of the few men whom Beaverbrook could not bully. Yet he was in many things indecisive; and one always sought in vain for the sharp cutting edge in his attitude to the organizations which he

believed in, such as the Liberal Party and the European Movement. He was one of the most lovable of men, and I both enjoyed and learnt much from my years with him.

48. Sinclair was brought back from Washington to become chief executive of the Ministry: Sir Henry Self, then Permanent Secretary, succeeded Sinclair at CPRB: John Henry Woods, the personification of common sense, succeeded Self. This form of organization was a wartime one, distinguishing between the 'executive and policy' work, mostly done by the industrialists, academics and others brought into the service by the war, and the 'secretariat' work, done by professional civil servants. In this case it worked effectively; but Sinclair and Woods could have run anything. A powerful and talented organization[23] developed – programmes and planning, raw materials, regional, production, non-munition supplies, with all sorts of offshoots such as the Radio Board (under Sir Stafford Cripps), a strong battery of scientific advisers, etc.

49. The arrangements which had been made with the Americans were worked into the final deployment of resources, and from then on the war production side of the Ministry was concentrated on getting the last gram of production of the most essential supplies.

CPRB – Mark II

50. I returned to Washington in February 1943.[24] As I had expected, I found the scene changing. Monnet had gone to North Africa, to begin yet another chapter in his extraordinary career: in his correspondence he was expressing his concern at the scale of the British effort, and the fear that we should exhaust and do ourselves permanent damage, which we did.

51. There was not much war production activity left in CPRB. There was a regular reissue of an increasingly refined Consolidated Statement, without commentary, valuable as an authoritative statistical return for both assignment and production purposes. A first-class half-yearly report was produced giving factual comments and graphs on the main war production programmes, on the manpower situations in the three countries, and the raw material and other supplies with which CPRB was concerned. Towards the end of 1942 a CPRB Truck Committee had been set up, for the heavy trucks (made only in USA) were a critical limit. Another area was locomotives. But most war production problems were being solved by the Supply departments and their missions in Washington with their American opposite numbers, reinforced where necessary by high-level personal visits.

52. There was the continuing work of the Combined Committees on copper, aluminium, steel, already described: the situation was continuously changing, but it rarely deteriorated to a difficult extent. But other materials were now coming into the picture, with mixed military and civil uses, and new committees were set up for hides, leather, footwear and for paper and pulp. CPRB was now having to cover a much wider range, not only for the needs of US, UK and Canada, but for liberated territories and the successive stages of relief and rehabilitation, and in some cases the needs of countries which had been starved of supplies for many years.

53. The list of committees as recorded in autumn 1943, each with its own characteristics, is formidable — cotton piece-goods and then other textiles, medical supplies, coal (for Europe), tyres and tubes, agricultural and food machinery, public utility equipment (for liberated areas), machine tools, internal combustion engines, conservation of materials, etc. As the war drew into its final years, the medley of such problems became hardly manageable — certainly if CPRB had not existed, it would have had to be invented.

54. I returned to London in September 1943, before this latest phase was effectively under way, and it was never my task to follow the progress closely. There is no doubt in my mind that drawing up balance sheets for each of this variety of goods, and examining them in a reasonably objective way, must have made more sense at the end, and perhaps even more if the war against Japan had lasted much longer. But if all those who had thought about CPRB before ARCADIA had foreseen the kind of thing CPRB would have been doing in less than two years' time, they would have had to recollect very firmly that war is full of surprises.

Notes

1. 'Combined' always referred to US/UK (and sometimes Canada).
2. The subject has had much less attention that it deserves. Apart from the brilliant *British War Economy*, by Hancock and Gowing, (HMSO, 1949), and the official histories of particular aspects and departments, inevitably of varying quality, which appeared over the next decade, there was a very valuable chapter by Sir Hugh Weeks, in *Lessons of the British War Economy* (National Institute of Economic and Social Research, CUP 1951); but very little else.
3. However, I can legitimately mention one interesting work which I did for the two departments — a substantial pamphlet on 'Britain's Blockade' (Oxford Pamphlets on World Affairs No. 38) of which large numbers were sold or distributed in six languages, the first edition in October 1940 and an up-to-date one in October 1941. At the airport at Djakarta in 1950, I found a copy of the Dutch language version for sale on the bookstall!

4. He took me to the canteen at No. 10 Downing Street for dinner, which also had its significance to a man of 31!

5. op. cit., pp. 384 ff.

6. [This hardly does justice to Purvis's position in Washington where he was virtually an Economic Ambassador (as Lord Salter described him) exercising a more powerful influence in some directions than Lord Lothian the British Ambassador to the USA. Ed.]

7. Edited by Robert E. Sherwood, Vol. I pp. 413-23 (Eyre and Spottiswoode, London, 1948).

8. [At the end of September 1941 a mission to Moscow led by Lord Beaverbrook and Averill Harriman negotiated and signed the first agreement to regulate the flow of British and American supplies to the USSR. The mission was preceded in mid-September by a conference in London on long-term requirements between representatives of the Service and Supply Ministers and Chiefs of Staff of the United Kingdom and United States. Ed.]

9. [The President's departmental advisers had aimed at lower targets and in discussions with the President, Hopkins, and the Service and Supply Staffs, Beaverbrook used to good effect 'the comparative statement of British and American production prepared by Monnet for the Supply Council'. H. Duncan Hall, *North-American Supply* pp. 341-2 (HMSO, 1955). Ed.]

10. [The ARCADIA Conference was organised immediately after Pearl Harbor and stretched from 22 December 1941, when Churchill, Beaverbrook, and their advisers arrived in Washington, until Churchill's departure from the White House on 14 January. At the Conference important decisions were taken on grand strategy, on American production targets, and on immediate supplies of munitions from America to Britain. One of the main results of the Conference was the setting-up of combined machinery for British–American collaboration which underwent little change throughout the war. It brought into existence the Combined Chiefs of Staff and the Combined Boards, except the Combined Production and Resources Board which was not created until June 1942. Ed.]

11. Sherwood, op. cit. Vol. I p. 483.

12. Ministries of Supply and Aircraft Production, and Admiralty.

13. Churchill, *The Second World War* Vol. IV pp. 54-74 (Cassell, London, 1951).

14. His place as Director of Statistics was taken by Kenneth Usherwood, later chairman of the Prudential Insurance Co.

15. This illustrates the problems of direct East–West flight even in June at that time. Flying with us were Dr Evatt, the able but peppery Australian Minister for External Affairs, who roundly abused the pilot for his 'cowardice' in turning back, and his colleague on his tour, Mr W. S. Robinson, the great Australian non-ferrous-metal industrialist. In his memoirs, *If I Remember Rightly* (edited by Geoffrey Blainey and published by F. W. Cheshire, Melbourne, 1967), Mr Robinson recalls this unusual flight. He and Dr Evatt were in the bridal suite of the Clipper: 'this, however, was right over the stern and it took an experienced acrobat to keep in his bunk with the continuous swaying and rolling of the craft . . .' Mr Churchill, who arranged their accommodation, had experienced similar troubles in the bridal suite in his flight from Bermuda to Plymouth after ARCADIA.

16. Sherwood, op. cit., pp. 682, 728 and 558 respectively. There was always some doubt about the Navy Department's handling of landing craft supply, for it was an Army requirement: in March 1942 tenth on the Navy's priority list; in October second; in November (with the North African campaign launched) back to twelfth. Production reflected these decisions as zero in first half 1942 rising to 106,000 tons in February 1943, falling to 51,000

in July, and then reaching an average of 120,000 a month (supported by total priority) in the first half of 1944.

[The Conference at Casablanca in January 1943 between Roosevelt, Churchill, and the Combined Chiefs of Staff followed the battle of El Alamein and the American landings in North Africa in November 1942. In May there was a similar conference in Washington which was given the name TRIDENT, and in August there was a further conference in Quebec referred to as QUADRANT. In December Roosevelt and Churchill met Stalin for the first time, at a Conference in Teheran. All four conferences were concerned with high strategy: including, for example, the planning for the invasion of Sicily at Casablanca, and of Normandy at TRIDENT. Ed.]

17. From the time of his arrival in Washington, Sinclair used every opportunity to press the substantial point, then escort vessels. In relation to the Army requirements, Admiral King (Chief of Navy Staff) and Admiral Leahy (chairman of the US Joint Chiefs of Staff) were telling the President on 25 November 1942 (Sherwood p. 655) that it was the aircraft programme (not the Army programme) that was causing delays in the naval programme.

18. It is hardly surprising that not long afterwards both the War Department and the Navy Department were pressing the President (unsuccessfully as it happened) to replace Nelson (Sherwood p. 696).

19. James F. Byrnes 1879-1972, American lawyer. Associate Justice, US Supreme Court 1941-2; Director of Economic Stabilisation 1942-3; Director, Office of War Mobilisation 1943-5; US Secretary of State 1945-7. His first remark to Hopkins was 'There's one suggestion I want to make to you, Harry, and that is to keep the hell out of my business.' (Sherwood p. 632).

20. 'The Impact of the War on Civilian Consumption in UK, USA, Canada' (HMSO, 1945). The UK statisticians were Harry (later Sir Harry) Campion and Roy (later Sir Roy) Allen.

21. See footnote 17 above. But Lyttelton's papers on his Mission suggest that looking into 1943 there were considerable problems of shortage, which suggests that a more effective mobilization of the economy from mid-1942 might even as early as this have been making the 1943 situation look more promising.

22. After the Mission, I was allowed to return to London (having been there without prior preparation since June), and was succeeded by Crowther. As all other ordinary people did, I flew from Montreal to Prestwick in the bomb-bay of a Liberator: my clearest recollection is one of Angelo's attributes, described by Lucio in *Measure for Measure*, III. ii. 119 ('When he makes water his urine is congealed ice.').

23. Apart from the Minister, who became Lord Chandos, four of the HQ staff in 1943 ultimately were promoted to the House of Lords, seven became knights, and one a dame, Elizabeth Ackroyd.

24. In winter, the journey by Clipper took a week, and often longer. The route was Foynes–Lisbon (where we stayed at Estoril, with Germans at one end of the dining-room and British at the other — it was not unknown for people to have to wait for weeks there) — Bolama (Portuguese Guinea) — Fisherman's Lake (Liberia) — Natal (Brazil) with its wonderful dawn chorus — all day across the Brazilian jungle to the 100-mile-wide Amazon estuary and the port of Belem — Trinidad — Puerto Rico — Bermuda (delightful three days, for all the US Clipper ports were frozen) — Baltimore; and then Washington in deep snow. The journey was also made memorable for me by long and agreeable conversations with the Zionist Moshe Sharett, who became Israel's Foreign Minister in the first half of the 1950s.

CHAPTER II

'Combined War' and 'Debtor's War'

55. When I returned to the Ministry in about October 1943, I was plunged into the problem of 'Stage II', the period in which the war was against Japan alone, the Germans having been defeated in 'Stage I', and 'Stage III' when Japan had been defeated too. The Combined Chiefs of Staff had originally thought that Stage II would last three years: this was reduced to two years in April 1944, and then eighteen months. It was thought that the war with Germany would end at end-1944, so we could see the war stretching ahead into its seventh year. The scale of war effort to be applied during Stage II, and the ability of the British economy and people to withstand this sustained further strain posed formidable problems, which for those of us who had been concerned solely with war production were new and forbidding.

56. To the reader of the 1980s, who recalls that the war with Germany actually ended on 8 May 1945 and the war with Japan on 14 August, so that Stage II lasted only three months, there must appear some incongruity here. The war with Japan was in fact ended by the atom bomb, which could not be foreseen even by the Combined Chiefs of Staff (for it was not known whether the first one or two would work). It was argued at the time that after the destruction of the Japanese Navy and the tremendous bombing, the Emperor was already on the verge of surrender, provided that his face could in some way be saved (as indeed it ultimately was); and an ultimatum had been sent at the end of July. Nevertheless, the invasion of the Japanese mainland had been regarded as one of formidable difficulty, given the expected fanatical resistance; and as late as June 1945 plans were being made for the main invasion operation in 1946. It had been thought necessary to make concessions to the Soviet Union to persuade them to join in. And it is a matter of historical fact that in their decision to drop the atom bomb, Truman, Marshall, and Stimson had been governed primarily by the need to avoid risking the lives of perhaps millions of American soldiers. So the eighteen-month decision cannot be regarded as having been unrealistic.

57. Of course it was a great stroke of fortune that ended the war so quickly. But it did mean that Stage III, with its immensely greater (though entirely different) problems both for Britain and USA came

at a moment's notice; and bad decisions were taken by both, the ill-effects of which lasted for years.

'Combined' and 'Debtor's' Wars

58. The work on Stage II brought together the dual kinds of war management that had been going on since Pearl Harbor and the ARCADIA conference. Half of Washington and half of Whitehall — Roosevelt, Churchill, Hopkins, the combined organizations, Services, supply departments, food, shipping, etc. — had been fighting a 'combined' war. There were great clashes of opinion. But even at the worst of these, British and Americans were fighting the same war and accepted each other's point of view as being objectively and genuinely held. Many of the most publicized differences were personal. Nobody would believe, for example, that if Bradley had been British and Montgomery American (or both British or both American) or if Eisenhower had been British, the conflicts would have been very different, or necessarily resolved differently. It made for inter-dependence, of course, that at the time of the initial Normandy landings, the number of United States and British Commonwealth divisions in contact with the enemy world-wide was equal, and before that, through 1942 and 1943, the British exceeded the Americans by over 50 per cent, and that in 1943 and 1944 the United States were supplying over one-quarter of the British Commonwealth munitions.[1] It was beyond question a 'combined' war, and was so regarded by those engaged in it.

59. The other half of Washington, and the other half of Whitehall, were engaged in what I can only call a 'debtor's war', in which Britain was receiving 'assistance' from the United States, on whatever terms the latter reckoned that they could impose. In the period when it was 'our' war, which we were fighting with the indispensable help of the United States, this was a true state of affairs, and it was legitimate, though probably in the long run unwise, for the Americans to impose the conditions they did. But none of the protagonists in this half of the war management — the State Department, the Treasury, and the Lend-Lease Administration on the American side, and the Treasury and the Board of Trade on the British — appear to have recognised sufficiently the effect of the entry of the United States into the war, and the change from 'our' war to a 'combined' war. The United States, far from having to take such cautious steps to help us as the isolationists would tolerate, was committed irrevocably to the defeat of Germany and Japan, and could not conceivably do the former without our full help and our active forces (as shown above) 50 per cent bigger than theirs.

60. I had not encountered this 'second half' until the work on Stage II, which had to deal with Lend-Lease and the national economy as well as with Services, munitions, shipping, etc. It was anyway much too late to change it, for we did not come to grips with Americans on Stage II until autumn 1944, and by then they were dominant. But I mention this, and have tried to think constructively about it, because finance and national economy are just as important to long and total war as the subjects covered by the Combined Boards in 1942–5.

A 'Combined Finance and National Economy Board'

61. A Combined Finance and National Economy Board, led perhaps on the American side by Mr Morgenthau, could certainly have got rid of misunderstandings and nonsense and might have created a constructive approach all round. It would not have involved changes in administrative systems but it would nevertheless have been a tremendous change on both sides from the 'debtor's war' (as it had properly been) of 1940 and 1941. However, there were changes too on the military side, and I doubt whether Treasury men are less flexible than soldiers!

62. The following illustrations show some subjects in which such a combined Board could have had a real part to play from early-1942 onwards. I exclude here the obvious absurdities like the attempt to limit our exports (in 1944, 30 per cent of pre-war) and to constrain our gold and dollar reserves ($1,500 million at end-1944 and short-term indebtedness of $12,000 million and rising fast), which could not have survived if there had been any combined machinery, for their only rational purpose (if such existed) was to ensure that at the war's end the British economy would be crippled. Nor will I include the anomaly that the Soviet Union was given Lend-Lease with no conditions at all: fair enough if the conditions applied in the 'assistance' period had been removed later.

(a) Comparative state of the economy — manpower, maintenance of essential services, civil consumption, balance of payments.
(b) Guarantees of undertakings before any discussion began at all on post-war international financial and trade arrangements that Britain would be in a strong enough economic position to play her part in them as a full founder-member and not running on the escape clauses.
(c) Financial needs of third countries (e.g. Middle East).
(d) Sterling area balances and 'dollar pool'.
(e) Reciprocal aid.

63. CPRB commissioned its major report under (*a*) in late 1944, (Chapter I, n. 20), but that was never meant as a policy tool: what was needed was a paper showing 1941, published in 1942, and then yearly.[2] The relevance of this need became clear in autumn 1944: opening the Stage II negotiations, Keynes made a wonderful exposition of the state of the British economy. It had been thought that this was all well known to the American officials and their seniors on the 'debtor's' side; but it came as a great shock. Fortunately, Sinclair had insisted that copies be made for wide circulation (why worry about security?) and a huge impression was made, which helped towards a successful agreement (never to come into operation). This was not a failure of 'public relations': it was a failure of communications between the responsible people on the 'creditor' and the 'debtor' side; and it shows why Congress was always quoted as an ogre that had to be appeased — naturally, for those who gave evidence 'for us' on the Hill were unfamiliar with our true situation.[3] This was exactly the kind of failure of communications that the 'combined' system was designed to prevent, and did.

64. In (*b*), it was odd to be expending large and skilled resources in negotiating huge imaginative agreements, depending on a US–UK axis, to be recommended world-wide, when our economy depended wholly on external aid and would remain so. In (*c*), we were picking up the cheques from North Africa to Burma: we did it, but it was bad for the post-war world that we were left to do it alone. I include (*d*) because here too there were misconceptions and hostility which did us great damage, and would have been much helped if approached via (*c*). There may have been security issues involved, but nothing like those of disclosing our aircraft production forecasts and stocks in spring 1941!

65. Reciprocal aid began formally with the agreement on 23 February 1942, and provided for US to give US forces, supplies and services free, here and in overseas theatres. It became highly complex, involving the whole Commonwealth (except Canada), and a changing list of commodities (e.g. in some cases raw materials), with the changes imposed by 'debtor's' Washington in order to prevent our gold and dollar reserves from rising. Some peculiar anomalies developed: Britain of course got no reciprocal aid from any part of the Commonwealth except Canada, and thought it right to pay the Colonies' reciprocal aid to US: Australia, as a US base, gave much more reciprocal aid to US than she received from them in Lend-Lease, and New Zealand about the same — so here the Americans were receiving aid and earning dollars! The authority on this complex is Professor Sir Roy Allen,[4] whose conclusion is: 'Relative to her resources, the

UK contribution in the form of reciprocal aid to the United States may have been rather less, but certainly not much less, than the US contribution in the form of lend-lease aid to the British Empire.' The relevance of a possible Combined Board is that it could conceivably have prevented some of these anomalies from arising; and it could certainly have ensured that the full weight of Professor Allen's conclusion would be included in the 'debtor's war' negotiations.

66. The purpose here is not to suggest 'might-have-beens', but to try to develop the lessons to be drawn from the second world war, and their bearing on future problems. Every Foreign Secretary since the war, and a Prime Minister at Suez in 1956, has had to learn from bitter experience that he cannot conduct effective foreign policy without the backing of 'finance and national economy'. In a desperate war of survival, as in 'our' war of 1940 and 1941, all resources must be urgently mobilized, as ours were, whatever the cost for the nation's future. But a moment arises, as in my view it did sometime in 1942, when with powerful allies totally committed and in the field, it becomes possible and indeed necessary to begin to inject some thought about the nation's future into the planning of the war — not the housing and health and social security 'after the war', nor indeed providing more consumption during the war, but the future of the industrial, financial, trading, economic base upon which everything depends.

67. Our failure to do this, or our inability to do it because of the 'debtor' system for running the 'finance and national economy' half of the war, was an important cause of the paradox that we 'won' the war, but at the same time 'lost' it.

68. An illustration that springs to my mind, I believe in 1943, was a meeting between Lyttelton and the Central Electricity Generating Board on a proposal for new equipment. They put their case well, and finished by telling the Minister that if they could not order this equipment at once there would inevitably be a power crisis in 1947, with no possibility of any subsequent action to prevent it. The facts had been carefully examined, and were not challenged. Lyttelton simply said, 'I am very sorry. I have not the resources. I cannot do it.' In the United States or Canada, such a request could not have been refused at any time even if Government approval was needed. There were similar cases on the railways, and indeed over the whole infrastructure.

69. It is almost literally impossible to imagine the chaos that would have happened in the prosecution of the war if the 'combined'

organization and concepts and network of contacts had not been created. On the 'finance and national economy' side, there was no 'combined' apparatus and everything was done on a 'debtor' system, and the chaos followed. It did not openly appear until Stage III, for the British economy was being shored up by Lend-Lease and Canadian Mutual Aid and the growth of sterling debt all round the world. Only three days after Japan's surrender, Lend-Lease came abruptly to a stop; and the abyss opened immediately ahead. The existence of a Combined Board would not have closed that abyss of August 1945: the Combined Chiefs of Staff had no part in the decision to drop the atom bomb.

70. My contention is that a Combined Finance and National Economy Board, working steadily through 1942, 1943, 1944, 1945; and developing a combined understanding and strategy as they went along to deal with the kinds of current problems listed in paragraph 62, would have led to an entirely different situation by the end of Stage II, not by some dramatic *coup*, but by a steady process of adjustment at the crucial points which would in the end have left Britain stronger and more able to play a constructive role in the five critical post-war years (a great American interest), and the United States readier and better equipped to handle the immense world-wide responsibilities which continued to confront them in Stage III.

71. Events might not have turned out like that, just as on the military side differences between the partners could have led to a complete diversion in the conduct of the war, with the Americans devoting more resources to Japan. But with a failed Combined Finance and National Economy Board, Britain would have been no worse off than she was in the end anyway. Perhaps the 'civil' depart-ments could not in 1941, even with the support of their Washington missions, have devoted the creative effort and power of conviction to the development of one Combined Board that the 'war' departments did for the creation of six: they could certainly have enlisted strong support from Monnet, who was arguing strongly, though unsuccess-fully, for adoption of complete pooling and abolition of Lend-Lease in a 'combined' war. An attractive project could probably have been created, both for the Americans and ourselves; and if Sir John Anderson, as Lord President and in charge of the Home Front, and member-elect of the new Board, had accompanied Churchill to ARCADIA, it is difficult to believe that Roosevelt would have said 'No', except perhaps to postpone until he had got James Byrnes into place to be the US member.

72. But even if he had said 'No', or if subsequently the Americans

had tried to wreck the Board, we would at least have known where we stood and could have managed our war effort (still on a 'combined' basis) accordingly, and our attitude to post-war discussions with the Americans with this knowledge.

Interval for OVERLORD

73. The analysis and policy determination for Stage II had been completed by the spring of 1944, subject only to the decisions about the military effort, which were to be made at the next President–Prime Minister meeting at Quebec in September. It is simpler to deal together with our policy and the subsequent negotiations with the United States and then Canada in the autumn, at the expense of chronology; and deal now with two very important Stage I operations, one in the months immediately before the Normandy landings and the other in July–August.

74. The internal transport for the movement of troops and equipment to their starting points for OVERLORD [the code name for the Anglo-American invasion of Normandy in June 1944] was one of the earliest points of trouble. At the beginning of the war, the railways had stated that they could carry any load put upon them by the war. But there were great crises in 1940 and 1941;[5] and with inadequate physical capacity and control of the railways and their relations with other inland transport, here was a truly dangerous inadequacy of the infrastructure for coming events. The traffic continued to grow, and by 1943, ton-miles of freight carried were 50 per cent above pre-war, and passenger-miles up by 68 per cent; and this was believed to be about the peak that was practicable, given the possibilities of equipment, labour, etc. Neither the amount of tonnage nor the number of passengers was greatly above pre-war: in 1937, the biggest of the five pre-war years, the goods traffic was 297 million tons and passenger journeys 1,295 million, whereas in 1943 these figures were 301 million tons and 1,335 million respectively. What had happened, through diversion of imports to the western ports and the change in the pattern of the economy, was a very large increase, both for goods and passengers, in the average length of haul.

75. There had been weakening of equipment — locomotives and wagons taken abroad for the Services; locomotive plants turned over to make tanks; repair and maintenance greatly reduced. The locomotive problem was identified fairly early, and a big programme started, which gave 360 in 1942, 800 in 1943 and 1,070 in 1944 (total stock about 20,000). The same situation was developing in USA, where the tank production was also taken out of the locomotive

plants, and their production was expected to rise from 2,500 in 1942 to 5,000 in 1944. This was one of the items at the core of Lyttelton's priorities in his November 1942 visit to USA (para. 44), and standard types were adopted. It was always sensible on shipping grounds to produce most in UK, but the competition with repair, for steel plate, and for boiler makers was always intensive. There were going to be huge demands for liberated Europe, for the Persian supply route to the Soviet Union, and India had a request for 4,000. Some additional money was made available for extra work on track, but the figures were still small.

76. With the peak of British carrying capacity reached in 1943 (a peak confirmed by the actual figures for 1944) the problem of how to handle the increased load for the invasion required a special approach, and a committee of officials (Official Committee on Inland Transport, or OCIT) was set up in February, with the Ministry of Transport providing a chairman, and all the big transport-using departments, and the Ministry of Labour and the Ministry of Production (Austin Robinson and me), represented. We were told four things:

(a) 2,000,000 tons of coastal shipping were to be withdrawn for use in OVERLORD (estimated at about 1.4 million tons of goods a month);
(b) operational traffic would be about 1.2 million tons a month;
(c) London and all the southern ports were to be kept free for the invasion, so that imports, from the outset diverted to the west, had to be diverted to the north. It could reasonably be expected that this would increase the average length of haul again, and create new pressures on the railway system at new bottlenecks;
(d) everything had to be ready by 1 May.

77. The first task was to establish the dimensions of the problem. (a) and (b) together were about 10 per cent of the freight tonnage (but we knew nothing about the ton-miles or the routes): (c) could not be measured by any normal statistical process. Nor, in spite of the Ministry of Labour's hard work, could one reasonably rely on estimates of increased total traffic capacity, for equipment, weather, V-bombs and air-raids, etc. had to be taken into account. The statistical apparatus of the railways, though voluminous for some purposes, was no good for ours. So we had to do some intelligent guesswork, and Austin Robinson got down to it on the backs of envelopes. Some members of the committee thought this was arbitrary and indeed perhaps rather irresponsible, for they had never seen figures before except as measurement of established facts. But nobody could think of any better way to proceed, or had better envelopes, and so it was done.

78. The practical policy question was that we must run no risks with OVERLORD, but if we doubly insured, the reductions that would have to be made in transport of coal, steel, materials, and perhaps even food, would have reduced important and critical parts of the economy to a virtual standstill with great potential damage, incidentally, to the next phases of OVERLORD. That is why, by some means or other, we had to make a judgement, not between, say 11 and 12 per cent deficit, but between 10 and 15 per cent.[6]

79. This provided the basis for a number of alternative policies, which we evaluated as well as we could in the same kind of way (much easier than the first step). We decided against trying to create a system of priority, calling for a licensing system to authorize use of the railways — obviously impossible in the time, and hopelessly bureaucratic. We decided against trying to close particular lines to non-OVERLORD traffic: the goods would turn up somewhere else, maybe worse. So in the end we decided to leave coal and essential food alone, but cut other bulk traffic, such as steel and timber and fertilizer and industrial and constructional materials, very heavily for a three-month period beginning 1 May. This was of course 'unfair', for some firms had stocks and some had none. But major industrial dislocation was avoided. Mr Forbes-Smith, formerly of the London and North Eastern Railway (LNER), the transport officer of the Ministry of Supply, who was a tower of strength throughout, told his big railway-using manufacturing contractors throughout the critical areas that if they got a message from him they were to put nothing on the railway until he countermanded the message (on the real bottlenecks like the London–Tilbury line this was potentially important).

80. Sir Michael Barrington-Ward, of the London and North-Eastern Railway, in charge of railway operations nation-wide, gave the committee a weekly review of the situation. At the beginning in February–March, the extent of the restrictions which were having to be imposed at the exchange points seemed menacing to the amateur, with a responsibility for getting it cleared up in a period of weeks. But it did gradually improve; and at the last meeting of the committee Sir Michael was able to report 'traffic is moving freely throughout the whole system'; and we were able to go on to our next jobs.

81. I hope I may be forgiven for mentioning one lesson that I learnt from the proceedings, nothing whatever to do with the substance. I cannot remember a case at which Sir Michael Barrington-Ward, formerly a divisional general manager of the LNER, ever referred to the LNER — or indeed to the LMS (London and Midland and Scottish)

and the other systems created by the 1921 Railways Act. The exchange problem was 'between the Northern and the Eastern' or 'the Midland and the Central' or whatever it might be. It was all lucid, but when I heard the practical operator thinking in terms of the railways systems of before the first world war, I was bound to ponder. I knew that Lord Stamp and his brilliant No. 2, Sir William Wood, had devoted immense efforts to making the LMS an effectively integrated organization; and the same happened on the Southern; whilst the Great Western had been one unit, steadily absorbing others, for a hundred years; and the LNER had financially done the worst of the four. It was always clear that if a merger is not made one entity you do not get the economies of scale which are its only justification. I saw this then for the first time, but never forgot it when concerned with mergers. When I had to merge five Ministries (or parts) myself twenty-five years later, I took this as the central task, and anyone who failed to adapt himself to his part in his new Ministry, backward-looking and not forward-looking, got short shrift. As a non-executive director of a variety of businesses since, I put my weight in the same direction (on the rare occasions when this was needed). So OCIT had its by-products, for better or for worse.

Canadian War Finance — Stage I

82. I had been asked by the Treasury to visit Ottawa late in July 1944 in order to meet Keynes and Sir Wilfred Eady, who were coming from Bretton Woods to carry out a difficult war finance negotiation. Our financial relation with Canada was a 'debtor' one, in the terms of this chapter; and a generous one, with a combination of interest-free loans, gifts, and Mutual Aid on similar lines to Lend-Lease. But what worried the Treasury was that the Mutual Aid appropriation for April 1944–March 1945 was not nearly enough. Not only was the total cut, but it also had to look after the needs of the Soviet Union, China, France, UNRRA. So about half of the prospective sterling area deficit with Canada was uncovered. If nothing could be done, this would have to go 'on the cuff', to be turned into a loan or to be cancelled later.

83. Keynes insisted that we could not borrow in Stage I or Stage II; so other methods would have to be found. He had to prove that borrowing was impossible, and that our borrowing strength in North America must be reserved for Stage III.

84. The next step, getting away from the 'debtor' concept for the first time, was to begin to compare the UK and Canadian war efforts throughout the war, and to say that if the UK effort had been

substantially bigger in proportion to resources, why should the British be paying money to Canada net? With the later CPRB report (Chapter I, n. 20) this could have been proved clearly and decisively — UK 55 per cent of manpower for Services and supply; Canada, including one quarter of agriculture as war employment, about 40 per cent (the same as USA). But the arithmetic was not yet fully established; and we used different and more complex figures, but no less convincing. If the war efforts had been identical in relation to resources, however, the same principle was there: why should the different deployment of effort require one partner to pay the other money?

85. With the Canadian officials accepting these two steps (paras. 83 and 84) what was possible? The Canadian Government and Parliament would certainly not in August 1944 produce something new in principle, or increase the 1944-5 Mutual Aid appropriation. But there were many military payments issues, which the Canadians had formerly resisted hard if it meant their 'paying out money' but could do if they wanted to meet us on the points made in paras. 83 and 84. Here are four illustrations.[7]

(a) Very many Canadian airmen had joined RAF, not RCAF, squadrons. The cost of their equipment, supplies, etc. was borne by RAF. If they had been in RCAF squadrons this cost would all have been met by Canada. There was a big increase in RCAF squadrons; and it was agreed that Canada would pay for advanced air training of Canadians in UK since April 1943;

(b) higher capitation payments for Canadian forces;

(c) payment by Canada for reserves and transit stocks behind the supplies for their forces; the former system provided that Canada paid only for the equipment actually at the moment of issue, with the British paying for everything in the pipelines and storage dumps needed to have the equipment there when needed;

(d) rebate of taxes on Mutual Aid contracts.

There were others, and the total was put at about $650 million, which seemed likely to leave the position fairly manageable up to 31 March 1945. We had a huge Stage II problem with Canada, that could not without great awkwardness be handled by a 'debtor' system, so we were inevitably due back in Ottawa by the winter.

86. This had been a case in which the Treasury after repeated disappointments had been pessimistic, so it may be worth mentioning a note by Sir David Waley of 18 August: 'The telegrams seem to mean that by a surprising feat of diplomacy our negotiators have got the Canadians to accept claims which close the gap for the current year'.

87. The settlement was recorded in the War Cabinet minutes, with the names of the three protagonists in the negotiations — not a very frequent occurrence!

Stage II — The British Plan

88. I have noted that we started work in the Ministry of Production and other departments in the early autumn of 1943, and that the papers were finished, subject to the decisions of the Quebec Conference of September 1944, in the late spring. There were four questions:—

(*a*) what would be our war effort in Stage II;
(*b*) how much Lend-Lease (and Canadian Mutual Aid) would we need;
(*c*) what were our objectives for Stage II in other fields, notably freedom for export;
(*d*) by what line of argument and negotiation could we get what we wanted?

89. The first point (*a*), though very difficult to decide objectively, had much earlier been pre-empted by the Prime Minister. At Casablanca, January 1943,

he had said in categorical terms that our interest and honour were alike engaged and that the determination of the British Parliament and people to devote their whole resources to the defeat of Japan after Germany had been brought to her knees was not in doubt. The War Cabinet would be fully prepared to enter into a formal treaty or pact with the United States on this point . . .[8]

90. Churchill repeated this pledge at TRIDENT in May, and its substance was duly recorded in the report of the Combined Chiefs of Staff.[9]

91. Even if it could be assumed that the war with Germany would be over by end-1944 (quite optimistic at the time, before OVERLORD's difficult problems had been overcome), and the war with Japan would take two years after that (the official view was three), we would still be fighting up to end-1946 — a seven-year war without respite. When making the Casablanca pledge 'to devote our whole resources' to the war against Japan, one of the most important decisions of the war, which fortunately never had to be carried out, the economic, financial, industrial, social implications (and the effect on the nation's post-war ability to survive as an effective Power) clearly never entered Churchill's mind — a powerful illustration of the consequences that can flow automatically from separation of the 'war' half of the war from the 'finance and national economy' half of the war. It appears that none of the other members of the War Cabinet, Labour or Conservative, took the point either. However,

it must be noted that the Chancellor of the Exchequer was excluded from the War Cabinet from 1940 to end-September 1943, when Sir John Anderson took over at Sir Kingsley Wood's death.

92. However, at QUADRANT in August 1943, grave differences appeared between the British and US Chiefs of Staff on the share that UK was to have in the major assault against Japan:

Actually, the dispute was on the issue that Britain demanded a full and fair place in the war against Japan from the moment when Germany was beaten. She demanded a share of the airfields, a share of the bases for the Royal Navy, a proper assignment of duties to whatever divisions she could transport to the Far East after the Hitler business was finished. In the end the Americans gave way.[10]

93. The matter was not settled until the Quebec Conference of September 1944. The Chief of US Navy Staff, Admiral King, was unremittingly hostile and the Chief of Air Staff, General Arnold, was unwilling, because they already had many more planes than their bases could accommodate. Churchill made a firm offer:

. . . for the British main fleet to take part in the major operations against Japan under US Supreme Command . . . a fleet train of adequate proportions would be built up, making the warships independent of shore-based resources for consider-able periods . . . As a further contribution, the RAF would like to take part in the heavy bombing of Japan . . . a bomber force of no mean size could be made available . . . As for land forces, when Germany had been beaten we should probably be able to send six divisions from Europe to the East, and perhaps six more later on . . . in South-East Asia we had 16 divisions which might ultimately be drawn upon . . .

The United States had given us the most handsome assistance in the fight against Germany. It was only to be expected that the British Empire in return should wish to give the United States all the help in their power towards defeating Japan.[11]

94. The President overruled his Chiefs of Staff, and it was agreed that the British role would be to liberate Burma (completed in Slim's remarkable campaign in May 1945) and Malaya, and both the Navy and the RAF should participate in the assault on Japan.

95. As for (b) in para. 88 above, it was obviously impossible for the Joint War Production Staff to make final estimates during the winter of 1943-4. On the other hand, given what the Prime Minister had promised, and taking account of the substantial requirements for occupation of Germany and elsewhere (including notably the Middle East and India, where we were incurring cost of about £500 million a year), it was possible to establish limits for Service and Supply. The first estimate, in early 1944, put the figure at the end of the first year of Stage II around 75 per cent. This was clearly unacceptable, in spite of Churchill's valiant words; and the figure ultimately used after the Quebec Conference, and incorporated in the proposals for

the Washington negotiations in October, was 56 per cent of mid-1944 to be reached at the end of the first year of Stage II, with an average of over 70 per cent in that first year.

96. The corresponding requirement for Lend-Lease munitions for the first year was $3.1 billion, or 54 per cent of 1944. Non-munition requirements (food, oil, shipping, materials, etc.) were put at $2.5 billion against $3.9 billion — here a little over 60 per cent of 1944–5. Large reductions had been made in coverage in order to avoid 'Export White Paper' difficulties. So we were over all asking for about 60 per cent of what we were currently getting (when certain other items were taken into account) whilst our defence effort would be about 70 per cent on the average in the first year.

97. For (c), the recovery of the economy, the two essentials (apart from getting the Lend-Lease) were the freedom of our exports from restriction, and stopping attempts to prevent our gold reserves from rising, and taking such steps as possible to increase them.

98. Finally (d), on strategy, we had painfully evolved the doctrine of 'proportionate aid'. This was less straightforward than it looks, for Lend-Lease originally assumed that we were using all our resources for fighting the war. When we were fighting a partial war, where should the Lend-Lease line be drawn? Would the US taxpayer be prepared marginally to finance our economic recovery? So the concept developed of maintaining munitions Lend-Lease proportionally to the reduction in war effort. In this case, to avoid argument, the bid was lower — 54 per cent against an average war effort in the first year of 70 per cent.

99. There was also an underlying concept that the 'proportionate' war effort had some relevance to whether countries were 'doing their share'.

100. With all this went a total analysis of our trade and external financial position; the extent to which we should have manpower available to begin to restore consumer-goods industries, housing, infrastructure. In fact, our prospects for progress by the end of the first year were pitiful — 3.4 million needed (including exports) and an estimated 2.6 million likely to be available to get minimal progress. Finally, no loan in Stage II.

Stage II — The US Negotiation

101. The Prime Minister had a very good discussion with the President

at Quebec, who expressed agreement with the basis of our Lend-Lease programme (but expressed in numbers, not proportional) and was helpful on our export point; and a combined committee was set up to process it all (shades of a 'Combined Finance and National Economy Board'!). It might perhaps be thought paradoxical for the Prime Minister to have been pressing the President so hard for a bigger share of the war against Japan that he had to overrule his Chiefs of Staff, and then come round again for the money to pay for it; especially when what was probably the strongest UK finance-national-economy team ever to visit Washington was just about to arrive to prove that Britain was very near the end of her financial and economic tether. On the short-term aspects, indeed, the first leg of the paradox may have helped us.

102. The Mission, headed by Keynes and Sinclair, and with an enormous array of expertise to enable it to deal, together with the local delegations, with all questions on every item of our programme, assembled in September 1944; and the first meeting of the combined committee (headed by Mr Morgenthau) was held in October. I was not on the Mission, and cannot deal with it at length; but I think four points can be made.

103. First, the basic document, introduced by Keynes and then circulated widely, made a huge impact. There was still the euphoria of OVERLORD and the belief that the end of Stage I was near. Alas, in my opinion, the impact came at the wrong time. As I have said earlier, such a document produced in 1942 and repeated in 1943 and 1944 could have had a cumulative and lasting effect. But by September 1945, Roosevelt was dead and Churchill out of office; there were new faces in Washington; Stage II was finished and by the atom bomb with its awesome consequences for the future. Americans, if they wanted to look anywhere except their own backgardens, were looking at the future, not the past.

104. Second, the negotiation of the Lend-Lease programmes was a success. Some points were lost, some gained.

105. Third, there was a disappointing outcome on freedom of export. We had hoped to get it from 1 January 1945: they would not accept it before the end of Stage I.

106. Fourth, a great many devices were examined to enable them to strengthen our gold reserves at once. Some were found practicable, others not: the total was much less than we had hoped.

107. Taken as a whole, however, it must be regarded as having been probably the most successful of the 'debtor system' negotiations with USA; and it must be regarded as an unhappy stroke of fortune that frustrated its spirit in 1945.

Stage II — Canadian Negotiations

108. Keynes and Sinclair proceeded to Ottawa in November, where I joined them. This was truly a follow-up from the August negotiations; for it was still a problem of how we could deal with the 1945-6 (and Stage II) sterling area deficit with Canada, and how we could handle this through the mutual aid technique which we had been developing in the summer. The arithmetic was worse, for in Stage II we would not be getting the income from Canadian forces which we had managed to increase so substantially; and we would still need munitions, food, materials. The current deficit for 1945-6 (Stage I basis) was put at about $1,200 million, compared with the out-turn for 1944-5, which might be of the order of $560 million. It would be about the same on Stage II, for our receipts from the Canadian services would be reduced (ultimately) by about $540 million, which was equal to about 50 per cent of the expected purchases of munitions in Stage I.

109. Our preferred course was the pooling plan, which would embody the principle for the common effort against Japan:

(*a*) Canada would provide munitions freely for the pool, the level of Canadian production being fixed according to the same proportionate reduction as UK's munitions production, or otherwise.
(*b*) The United Kingdom would provide freely all supplies and services, except pay, for Canadian Forces outside Canada.
(*c*) Canada would provide freely all war services incurred in Canada on our behalf — e.g. inspection and inland freight on munitions.
(*d*) The finance of the Air Training Plan had in the past been kept separate from the general financial arrangements; the arrangements for winding it up would likewise be separate, but we hoped that these could be agreed in the same pooling spirit now proposed.
(*e*) Canada would provide food for UK and for British Forces, etc., on Mutual Aid; the scope of Mutual Aid would be limited to this and to ancillary services.
(*f*) Other transactions between Canada and the sterling area would be financed as usual on a cash basis.

The only cash transactions between the two countries would thus have been in respect of the pay of Canadian troops outside Canada and in respect of raw materials, manufactured goods, and other commercial payments. We believed that this would not lead to any substantial transfer problem between Canada and the sterling area.

110. This all looked nice and clean, and indeed convincing on the pooling doctrines, which were by now becoming familiar in Ottawa. But one could not avoid the fact that Canada, not wanting to play a significant role in the war, would have to pay much more than she had expected. The munitions and related expenditures would come from War Appropriation, which would ease the Mutual Aid Appropriation — but not very acceptable to the Defence Ministers. Otherwise, however, they would have to increase the Mutual Aid Appropriation, which they had cut in 1944-5. There were some suggestions of our borrowing some of the deficit, but this was of course rejected. There was indeed a relatively straightforward dilemma, which had to be left unresolved for the present: on the other hand, there was a strong view among some of the Ministers that 'so far we have always managed to see Britain through'.

111. In February 1945, the Canadians told us that they were intending to provide Mutual Aid in 1945-6, but they pressed hard for a concession on the commerical policy point that worried them most — UK discrimination against Canada in favour of imports from the sterling area. This was not a difficult or costly concession to make to Canada, but it would also have to be given to USA — a different dimension altogether. However, an acceptable concession was worked out.

112. On the finance side, the Canadians adopted the ingenious expedient of getting an Appropriation of $2,000 million for War and Mutual Aid together to last five months, i.e. to the end of August, with the intention of introducing a new budget after their general election was held, due at the beginning of June. By what must certainly be regarded as a remarkable coincidence, therefore, our affairs were looked after to the end of Stage II.[12]

'Debtor System' with North America

113. The following tables[13] show what happened in the two phases 'our war' to end-1941 and the 'combined war', for which the figures have been taken to end-1945:

Table 2

	Sterling area balance in US dollars ($ billion)			Sterling area balance with Canada ($ billion)		
	Sept. 1939 –Dec. 1941	1942–1945	Total	Sept. 1939 –Dec. 1941	1942–1945	Total
UK imports etc.	5.7	29.8	35.5	2.1	7.6	9.7
exports etc.	−1.5	−8.7	−10.2	−0.7	−4.1	−4.8
Rest of £ area	−0.3	0.3	—	0.1	0.7	0.8
Miscellaneous	−0.3	0.1	−0.2			
Gold and Dollar deficit	3.6	21.5	25.1	1.5	4.2	5.7
Financing: Gold and US dollar reserves	1.5	−1.8	−0.3	0.2	0.4	0.6
Sales of investments	0.6	0.2	0.8	0.5	0.6	1.1
Loans etc.	0.4	0.6*	1.0	—	0.6	0.6
Miscellaneous†				0.8	−0.8	—
Grant, Lend-Lease‡ Mutual Aid, etc.,						
UK and Colonies	1.1	20.9	22.0		3.2	3.4
Rest of £ area		1.6	1.6		0.2	

*   including Lend-Lease settlement
†   increase in UK sterling liabilities
‡   less Reciprocal Aid

114. It is of some interest to note that in the period of 'our war', we had to cover 70 per cent of our deficit with USA, and 100 per cent of our deficit with Canada in disinvestment in one form or another — payments of gold, sale of investments, loans. In the following period, the sterling area had no disinvestment at all *vis-à-vis* USA. In fact, after all the toils and tribulations, we managed very well as soon as the war was 'combined'. Taking the six years as a whole, we got 94 per cent of our deficit with USA covered free, and 60 per cent of our deficit with Canada.

Exports

115. While these negotiations had been going on, there had been a lot of talk about how the necessary export expansion was to be achieved. Exports in 1944 were about 30 per cent of 1938: nobody could see a tolerable balance of payments unless exports were 150 per cent of 1938, and some thought more. The Board of Trade asked all the trade associations; the individual items were examined one by one; and on this theoretical and statistical analysis there was universal pessimism. Moreover, there were two very fundamental difficulties.

116. First, the responsibility within the Government was obscure:

the Board of Trade was supposed to be responsible for reconversion of industry and for exports; but the Ministry of Production were responsible for releasing capacity for reconversion; and several other departments (e.g. Fuel and Power, Food) were potentially heavily concerned. So there was nobody responsible for taking a grip on the problem.

117. Second, exports were 'unpopular'. Ten years' intensive propaganda and three sterling crises later had had their educational effect: but in any discussion between Ministers, the easing of the consumers' position, of housing, and the repair of the infrastructure, necessarily took first place. Little attempt had been made to convince Ministers as the war proceeded that our whole economy was underpinned by North American aid and sterling borrowing, and with the end of Stage II, the abyss would open before us.

118. In the Ministry of Production, with support from Keynes and the Treasury we were trying to develop the idea of an 'export programme' — a target for each industry for which it would receive the support of mixed business—civil servant groups in the relevant departments, services, favourable treatment by controls, regional organization, etc. The scale and build-up of the required export programme was not dissimilar from that of the Ministry of Supply production programme from the beginning. Some quotations from a minute to Lyttelton of October 1944 may be interesting:

If there is a clearly defined export programme, it will be possible to mould reconversion to see that it is carried out: once we have our export objectives clear, military programmes can be adjusted to release firms and industries for the export programme. But if we vaguely say 'we want more exports' it will never be possible to exert the necessary pressure . . .

Can a programme of this scale be achieved without the same organisation and drive which went behind the Ministry of Supply programme? Will the programme do itself?

There are disadvantages compared with 1939-42 . . . but also advantages . . . the firms know the departments and the departments know the firms . . . But these are wasting assets. The Government's industrial machine will evaporate. Already the governmental machine is in the doldrums; at the end of Stage I it will collapse unless its constituents are made to feel that there is a real job to be done. In a year's time, when the crying need for exports is patently obvious, the Government will be powerless to do anything about it, for there will be no machine left . . . We must therefore start now. Otherwise, reconversion will be frozen against the export trade . . .

The similarity with 1939 is striking and disturbing. There is the same network of ineffective and policyless committees. There are the same arguments for inaction; 'the Treasury cannot afford it' is now 'we cannot deal with exports until there has been some civil easement'; 'we do not know the Army requirements' has become 'how can we say what foreign countries' requirements will be'; 'these civil firms cannot do the high quality work required for armaments' has become 'the firms we want for exports are all making armaments' . . . and so on.

The type of programme that we want now is different; the responsibility between Government and industry is different . . . but the need for a policy and for action to carry it out is hardly less pressing than the 1939 job was.

Should we not have a Battle for Exports Committee, with the departments required to work out a programme, develop a policy to implement it, and organise the executive drive which is needed to carry it through?

We really have to find a sensible set-up in which industry will work within a required framework laid down by the State, while the State will provide all the assistance it can to industry.

119. This kind of idea never got anywhere. The arguments in paras. 116 and 117 had their force, but I believe that by the last quarter of 1944, Ministers had had such a gruelling that they could not summon up the power and energy to drive along a campaign for national reconstruction and recovery, at any rate while Stage I was still going on. Of course this idea was contrary to the traditional doctrine of the Board of Trade, but they could not reasonably produce highly pessimistic papers without some course of remedial action. It is worth noting, moreover, that this line of industry–Government relation had great similarity to the plan that Monnet developed later (for industrial development, not exports) which turned out to be the corner-stone of French recovery; and that in the field of exports, the idea of a close common interest and co-operation between industry and Government was highly developed in the 1970s among many of our competitors. Indeed, this could have been the basis for a post-war continuation of the favourable wartime relations here, sadly lost later.

120. However, in fact the performance was better than expected, for we had underestimated the hunger for goods: from 1944's 30 (1938 = 100), the volume of exports was 46 in 1945, nearly 100 in 1946, a little over 100 in 1947; and after the 1949 devaluation (with bad terms of trade), the volume was over 160. But the fact remains that from then on we were losing our share of world trade year after year.

Move to the Treasury

121. During autumn 1944, the Treasury had asked the Ministry of Production for my transfer, where they wanted me to be Assistant Secretary in charge of a division called 'Export–Import': the Treasury (Overseas Finance: OF) was strongly organized on the territorial side, but weak on the 'general' side. It was ultimately agreed that I should serve both until the end of Stage II,[14] and then be full-time at the Treasury. This obviously committed me to remain in the civil

service for, say, the first two years of Stage III, a possibility that I had never considered; but the work was so exciting and exacting, and the intellectual and executive challenge so formidable, that I accepted with no more ado.

122. In fact, from March 1945 onwards, I devoted most of my time to the Treasury; and this all comes conveniently in the next chapter: but there were two 'Ministry of Production' activities that can best be mentioned here.

The Ferguson System

123. In about July 1944, a very remarkable Ulsterman came to see Sinclair. He was Harry Ferguson, certainly one of the world's greatest dozen inventors and engineers of this century, and a visionary too.[15] He was born in 1884, and as a young man before the first world war was the first Briton to design and fly his own aeroplane. In 1917 the Irish Board of Agriculture asked him to improve the quality of Ireland's tractors, and this set him on the tractor road. He began to develop a new kind of tractor altogether, which was not commercial until 1936. The essence of his concept was that whereas the conventional tractor pulled the plough and was really a substitute for a horse, in the Ferguson system the tractor and the plough (or any other implement) were a single machine. This had great advantages in flexibility, simplicity, safety. The production and commercial arrangements on both sides of the Atlantic, including his 'gentleman's agreement' with Henry Ford I, are too complex to be described here, but the purpose of his 1944 visit was to find a UK producer.

124. The essence of Ferguson was that besides being a marvellous engineer (75 per cent of the tractors in the world are based on his system), he was a great showman, and in addition to his system, he had the Ferguson Plan to solve the world's food problem. This was what attracted him and Henry Ford I together — first world war and second world war. So he brought with him brochures to exhibit a world market for twenty-five million Ferguson tractors, every country from China to Chile. By 1944 one had seen a lot of claims of this kind, and his brochures did not even mention the social and economic rural revolution that would happen in the underdeveloped countries. It looked like charlatanry.

125. However, if the potential market was five million, and with the Ferguson and the Fordson being made here, this was beginning to look like a great new post-war export industry. Sinclair put Ferguson in touch with Sir John Black, head of Standard Motors, who had an

aircraft engine shadow factory at Banner Lane, Coventry. But they needed a lot of steel and dollars for the machinery and engines. Ferguson laid on one of his demonstrations, at Feltham, for Sir Stafford Cripps (then President of the Board of Trade) and a distinguished group of anyone who could help. I have never seen an audience of critical men so utterly convinced in ten minutes. He had a small roped-off field. He first announced 'This is how it was done in Mesopotamia 2000 years ago'; and a horse came in pulling a plough; it could just get diagonally across the field, and was ignominiously withdrawn. He then said, 'This is how we do it now', and a Ferguson came in, driven by an eleven-year-old boy, and proceeded to plough every square inch of the field.

126. Then all that remained was to get the steel for about 70,000 tractors a year; and Cripps did that; and to get about $8 million from Eady (on no account to be disclosed publicly), and the project was launched. As usual there were rows, and at the end it became part of Massey-Ferguson; but the new industry did get established.

Potsdam Conference

127. This was my last assignment for the Ministry of Production for Stage II. There was a technical point that had to be settled. The US man was at Potsdam, and I had to follow him there. But the work did not take long, and my recollections are those of a much privileged tourist — the Soviet Asian troops lining the road from the airport; the Army organisation that had actually provided me with a bed; walking round the military avenues in the hot mid-July evening, and seeing the houses where the Big Three were living and the crowds around them; a concert by Truman's favourite Army pianist; standing by the huge buildings, talking in whispers. Next day a drive to Berlin, seeing the chaos of the Chancellery; but more memorably the hundreds of piles of rubble, with old men and old women picking at them hour after hour to seek anything to eat and sell; and over it all a dank smell of decay.[16] Back by air across the bombed-out Ruhr. A notable experience, difficult to remember when you see West Berlin, Dusseldorf, Essen, thirty years later.

End of Ministry of Production

128. The Ministry was losing ground in 1945, for it needed a new function for Stage II and Stage III. At the end of May, when the Coalition broke down, it became obvious that its day was over, for in the 'Caretaker' Government, Lyttelton was both President of the Board of Trade and Minister of Production; and it was unlikely that

if a Labour Government were returned, it would move in our direction. In my opinion, it had done a good job in 1943 and 1944.

129. Finally, one cannot record the end of the department without recalling Sinclair's huge contribution, both in Washington and in London (and in Ottawa too). From my personal point of view, apart from continuous kindnesses, he taught me much (as Layton did) which has stood me in good stead for thirty years. But looked at more widely, his remarkable quality was always his power, both intellectual and through integrity, to convince people, British or Americans, soldiers or civilians, sometimes by writing and sometimes by talk. However urgent the situation was, he never hurried; for you can never convince people faster than they are capable of being convinced, crisis or no. He was never at ease with men like Keynes, with their wild flights of paradox and fancy. He had limited objectives, sometimes very wide indeed, and nearly always succeeded in attaining them by convincing the men who needed to be convinced.

Notes

1. Hancock and Gowing, op. cit., pp. 367 and 373.
2. The British figures for 1941 were much the same as 1944.
3. On the export limit controversy, for example, they probably did not know that from 1941 to 1945 we had no manpower to develop our exports, like it or not.
4. 'Mutual Aid between the United States and the British Empire', *Journal of the Royal Statistical Society* Vol. CIX Part III (1946).
5. Hancock and Gowing op. cit., pp. 268–80, and then 480–90.
6.. I never kept the papers embodying the guesswork and thence of the 'transport balance-sheets' referred to with approval by Hancock and Gowing, op. cit., p. 490; and so cannot here without great research publish them as I would have liked. I learnt accidentally a great many years afterwards, that no doubt as the consequence of some petty bureaucratic squabble, they were never included among the official published statistics of the war effort.
7. There were extraordinary anomalies within the field of war accounting, not at all confined to our relations with Canada. In Professor Roy Allen's study of Lend-Lease and Reciprocal Aid, he made very sophisticated calculations leading to an average exchange rate of $7 to £1 for munitions and military stores (some as low as $3 and others above $10), and the official rate of $4 to £1 for everything else. This gave an average for Professor Allen's analysis of $5.3 for Lend-Lease and $4.7 for reciprocal aid. The payments between UK and Canada were real money. The Air Ministry supplied the RCAF with Mosquito bombers at the UK price of $40,000 (airframe): MAP paid the Canadian producers $56,000; and there were inevitably many cases of Canada selling weapons into the pool at the higher price (equivalent to the $7 rate above) and taking them out at the lower. The capitation charges for the Canadian Army (wherever it was) were based on the average for the UK Army (wherever it was). Exports from Canada were free of duties and charges, but Mutual Aid contracts for export were 'internal' and paid the duties — average about 10 per cent, but tanks 20 per cent and ships negligible

(we did not discover this until our 1944 visit!). This could not have been done differently without immense labour and contention: it simply illustrates the absurdity of the 'debtor' system.

8. Churchill, op. cit., Vol. IV p. 612.
9. Churchill, op. cit., Vol. IV pp. 709, 722.
10. Churchill, op. cit., Vol. V p. 81.
11. Churchill, op. cit., Vol. VI pp. 134-7.
12. [There is a good deal more to be said about the Canadian position in these negotiations. The situation in Quebec made them doubtful whether they could go on financing Britain even in wartime. Article XI of the Canadian Act giving Mutual Aid limited it, not to the end of the war, but to 'a date to be agreed upon by the two Governments'. In the post-war transition they were offering to finance the sterling area's Canadian dollar deficit in return for the adoption by Britain of a 'liberal' international trade policy as expressed in Article VII of the Mutual Aid Agreement. Ed.]
13. R. S. Sayers, *Financial Policy 1939-45* (HMSO, 1956). From Tables 12 and 13.
14. Nobody believed, in making practical arrangements, that Stage II would last to anything approaching end-1946.
15. There is a good biography by Colin Fraser, *Harry Ferguson, Inventor and Pioneer*, (John Murray, London, 1972); and Dr G. B. R. Feilden, FRS, gave a lucid lecture about him at Queen's University, Belfast, in 1970. [For a slightly different view see Sir Miles Thomas *Out on a Wing* pp. 238-9, 336-41 (Michael Joseph, London, 1964). Ed.]
16. Singularly, I experienced the same smell at an exhibition of Picasso's war paintings later in the year — the human race at its nadir.

CHAPTER III

Stage III and the US Loan

130. When I joined HM Treasury *de facto* early in 1945, there was heavy occupation with Stage III overseas financial policy. The previous autumn's negotiations with USA had settled Stage II, it was hoped, and Canadian Stage II was being gradually worked out. So although strictly speaking Stage III was still estimated to be nearly two years ahead, the strategy was being actively discussed; and Keynes was writing one of his most masterly papers, which was to provide the basis for 1945 policies.

Overseas Finance

131. Overseas Finance (OF) was one of the four sectors of the Treasury alongside Home Finance, Supply, Establishment. It was headed by Sir Wilfrid Eady, who had started in the Ministry of Labour, had set up the Unemployment Assistance Board, and came to OF via the chairmanship of Customs and Excise: in my opinion, his great strength was as a negotiator, and particularly of persuading into agreement difficult and hostile people: his lack of Treasury background and expertise stood him sometimes in ill stead, and he was never very effective (but who could have been?) as the administrative counterweight to Keynes. Below him (we would now call him a Deputy Secretary) was Sir David ('Sigi') Waley, a Treasury man since before World War I, who turns up everywhere in Europe in the histories and biographies of the 1920s, with razor-sharp intelligence, likeableness, and the cynicism and waspishness born of thirty years of British and European finance. Under him was the charming Irishman Ernest Rowe-Dutton (another European specialist); in charge of about eight territorial divisions each under an Assistant Secretary (some Treasury and some from outside).

132. On the periphery were the two great forces — the internal one, Keynes, the creative power of OF (and Home Finance too), and the external one, the Bank of England, with its huge knowledge and experience and prestige and independent status (and also the source of all balance of payments statistics), usually represented by Mr Deputy Governor, Lord Cobbold.

133. OF was a different kind of institution from anything in my previous experience. The 1-1-1 form of organization and lack of general divisions looked odd, until one saw that it was more like a club than a Government department, with its intellectual quality, its absence of hierarchy and formal organization, mutual respect for each others' views from top to bottom, and very ready acceptance, as I found personally, of new members. The effectiveness of this pattern of organization, traditional to the Treasury, depended on the nature of the problems and the extent to which they were assignable to individuals, with the general implications discussed casually at tea-time. The great 'systems' problems, which required detailed co-operative analysis, were a different matter altogether; and as they became more prominent, the structure changed.

134. Keynes fitted admirably into the old system, for he regarded the huge 'systems' problems as being within his field in much the same way as the Assistant Secretary in charge of Western Europe regarded our relation with Sweden as being within his field: but this was where Keynes's unique quality lay. The Bank of England, on the other hand, was a hierarchical institution, which worked out its own philosophy and policy; but in my opinion at that time found it difficult to convey them to the rather amorphous OF. The combination of OF, Keynes, and the Bank of England had immense potential power in developing overseas financial policy; but they were a difficult troika, with their varying forms of organization and style of working, personal relationships, and conceptual differences; and therefore in the aggregate a lack of effective Whitehall executive power.

Commonwealth Wool Conference

135. This may be the place to fit in the first negotiation on which I specifically represented the Treasury. It sounds a long way from the stratospheric work of Stage III policy, but these commodity problems, and the unscrambling of wartime arrangements, often with a lot of money involved, occupied considerable time and activity in the next two years, and the Treasury (sometimes OF and sometimes the Supply side) was always in up to the neck.

136. This Conference[1] was to decide how to wind up the situation created by the British Government's agreement with Australia and New Zealand at the beginning of the war (and South Africa later) to purchase their whole wool clip for the duration of the war plus one year. The problems of detail and of price were formidable and often tendentious; but the agreements stood; and now in April 1945 the Conference had to sort it out. There were large and powerful

delegations from the wool-growing countries, containing both officials and wool-growers (Australia, for example, had the Permanent Secretaries of both Commerce and the Treasury): for wool's future was of great importance to their economies. The UK Delegation was strong too, led by H. J. Hutchinson (Ministry of Supply and later Secretary of the Coal Board); with officials and the wool control organization.

137. The arithmetic confronting the Conference looked bad. The acccumulated stock was two years' world consumption of Dominion wool; and the estimated time taken to dispose of this and the current clips, on reasonable assumptions about expansion of consumption, would be 12–13 years. This could not happen without continuous wrangling about how fast Britain should dispose of her stock. Meanwhile, this stock would be permanently overhanging the market. The original idea was to agree a formula fixing the priorities between offers from stocks and from current clips; but discussion showed that there were too many uncertainties and too deep a conflict of interest to keep such a formula for long — and this began to open a vista of repeated and increasingly ill-tempered conferences.

138. So it began to appear that the only prospect of success was to resolve the conflict of interest by pooling the stock and operating it as a four-country common enterprise. This would involve the three Dominions in buying back half the stock, the total value of which was then £171 million (the halves were thus £53 million Australia, £17 million New Zealand, £15 million South Africa — large sums). On the other hand, it gave much the best prospect of stability and reliability of the market; and as a joint Commonwealth enterprise it was politically attractive. I found S. G. McFarlane, the Australian Secretary of the Treasury, receptive; and we worked out a kind of profit-linked instalment plan, which would make it look easier for the Dominions to pay their halves. The Australian Delegation agreed, and we were home and dry, for New Zealand and South Africa would surely then agree, and did.

139. The basic scheme having taken shape, the Conference was able to write the constitution for the new Joint Organization (JO), settle all the details, and propose that the scheme would come into effect on 31 July 1945, with detailed arrangements for a short transition until JO could physically take over. The four Governments agreed, and proceeded with the legislation.

140 In the end, thanks partly to the speed of European and worldwide wool textile recovery and partly to the skill of JO's operations

and the stability of the market, with prices much higher then expected, it was possible to liquidate JO at January 1952, less than seven years after the Conference, with a shared profit of the order of £200 million. One can say that it was 'lucky': that at every material point in consumption and price the virtually unanimous views of the UK and Dominion experts were proved very wrong within two years.

141. The conclusion which I drew is that where the future is genuinely very uncertain, no international agreement can sensibly be based upon an arbitrary assumption about the future course of markets or demand, for then one side or the other is bound to feel aggrieved in the end. Some means must be found, if this is at all possible, of making an agreement that expresses a community of interest.

Long-Term Viability

142. At the beginning of the year I had worked out a paper 'Towards a Balance of Payments' setting out policies for getting a strong economy in 1950. [This is reproduced as Document 3. The draft is dated 11 May 1945.] Without such policies, it seemed to me, the loans that we got to cover the intervening period would be wasted; and Governments are much more able to get results, if they will, over the medium-term period than over the short. The paper was much more a 'national economy' paper than an 'OF' paper; but Eady had asked me for some notes too; and the paper created much interest in OF, notably by Keynes. Some of the main points may be relevant to the subsequent discussions.

143. Volume of world trade. I reckoned that by the end of Stage III, (1949 or 1950) the volume of world trade would be in the range 0–15 per cent above 1937. By the end of the first decade after the war (1955), I put the range at 10–50 per cent above 1937.[2] The difference between the top and bottom of the ranges was caused primarily by (i) level of US national income, (ii) rate of European recovery, (iii) rate of growth of medium and lower income countries, (iv) extent of restrictions (which I put lowest; definitely much less important than employment in the high-income countries and development — notably agriculture and infrastructure — in the medium and low). Indeed, international agreements in these fields appeared on analysis much more important for world trade than the traditional preoccupation with tariffs and import restrictions.

144. Inflation and deflation up to 1950. This was much less discussed in OF than I expected. My own paper thought of it largely in terms of USA employment and impact on world trade. Yet we had the

experience of the sharp world inflation of 1919 and 1920, slump of 1921, and then gradual expansion; and I cannot remember anyone predicting this again: confidence that the US and UK controls would check it; but the main fear was that USA would be unable to re-employ the returning soldiers and munitions workers. This illustrates the combined traumatic effects of the depression of the 1930s and the great productive power of the 1940s. Nevertheless, even speaking after the event, it must have been known that the physical damage and destruction of commodity supply in Europe and Asia vastly exceeded that of the first war: in the Treasury by the middle of 1945 we were being warned by the Ministries of Food and Supply of big increases of prices, which could be catastrophic for the real purchasing power of a US loan.[3] But I would not claim to have been smarter than anyone else in drawing the conclusion.

145. Exports. An attractive presentation was to say that by 1950, one quarter of Britain's manufactures would need to be exported. There were two profound difficulties, not yet overcome:

(a) Very important industries (notably coal, steel, cotton) needed major reconstruction; the modern part of industry and the public utilities were based on the economy of the 1930s, with 15 per cent unemployed. On top of this was wartime dislocation and under-maintenance. So great expansion was needed. We should be willing to import all the machinery required in 1946-8; but machinery supply was not necessarily the limiting factor.

(b) How could industry be persuaded to concentrate on exports?

146. Imports. The difficulty here in food would be in getting back to the cheap European and Southern Dominions sources of supply, instead of North America; our food was costing us 25 per cent more per unit (at constant prices) than pre-war.

147. Balance of Payments 1950. Taking all this together, with import-saving such as oil refining, my conclusion was that the prospect was just about manageable given a high level of world trade; and provided that there had been effective action in industry. The former turned on effective international machinery with USA (and probably with others) of a 'Combined Board' kind, to co-ordinate on full employment and overseas development, and multilateral machinery which would not interfere with these objectives.

148. Finally, I raised the question of the $4.03 exchange rate, established in 1939.[4] I was afraid that our whole position would be endangered (e.g. incentive to export) if sterling became over-valued; and although the 'purchasing power parity' was not out of line in

1945, I thought it odd that the same £/$ rate should prevail when Britain was the biggest debtor as when Britain was the biggest creditor. The point having been raised, there was great interest, and Keynes commissioned further calculations which showed that the case was not strong enough.[5] However, by 1947, it was widely reckoned that sterling was over-valued and of course in 1949 it went on to the rocks altogether. Jobbing backwards, I still think that a modest devaluation (say, by 10 per cent) in 1945, as part of our deal with the Americans, would have given us a smoother run through the rest of the 1940s, and might well have avoided the massive devaluation of 1949.

Policy for the US Loan – March to September 1945

149. When Keynes produced in mid-March his great paper 'Overseas Financial Policy in Stage III',[6] neither he nor anyone else could have imagined that in six months' time there would be a Labour Government, the war would be over, Lend-Lease would have stopped, and he would be negotiating in Washington. His paper inevitably became the policy for the Loan negotiations.

150. First, he emphasized what we had done. We had retained our financial independence from the United States and developed the sterling area and extended sterling agreements with Sweden and others to a point at which we could present a credible alternative to unacceptable American proposals. We had succeeded in avoiding substantial debt in overseas currencies or gold; and our gold and dollar reserves were moving up towards the £500 million that would give room for manœuvre.[7] We had sterling liabilities of about £3,000 million, subject to the continuation of the Japanese war, and our war expenditure in the Middle East and India.[8] All this had been done while retaining good temper and good feeling with our creditors. Lastly among the successes, he listed the stabilization policy on prices and wages; he reckoned, indeed, that we had retained most of the advantage of the 1939 devaluation *vis-à-vis* USA, and that sterling would be under-valued rather than over-valued elsewhere (which, when he saw my paper, led to the arguments described in para. 148).

151. Keynes drew favourable conclusions, with reservations, about our industrial competitive power:

Even the celebrated inefficiency of British manufacturers can scarcely (one hopes) be capable of offsetting over wide ranges of industry the whole of this initial cost-difference in their favour . . . It is when it comes to making a shirt or a steel billet that we have to admit ourselves beaten both by the dear labour of America and by the cheap labour of Asia and Europe . . .

If by some sad geographical slip, the American Air Force (it seems too late now to hope for much from the enemy) were to destroy every factory on the North-East Coast and in Lancashire (at an hour or day when the directors were sitting there and no one else) we should have nothing to fear.

[What has happened to German and Japanese industry since 1945 makes this look, perhaps, a little less amusing a paradox than it appeared at the time.]

152. Second, Keynes went on to the failures, and to their critical nature for the future. Unless we could master them, the prospective load would by beyond our unaided powers:

(*a*) overseas expenditure of the Service Departments in Africa, the Middle East, India, and the Southern Dominions. This local expenditure was outside Treasury control and even outside Treasury (and probably the Service departments') knowledge. This totalled £574 million in 1944, nearly as much as our total net disinvestment world-wide of £640 million — i.e. here was the cause of virtually all our wartime external financial problems. Would this stop, or even be reduced significantly, after the Japanese war? Could the expenditure be brought under control?
(*b*) preparation for exports (see above, para. 118);
(*c*) burden of relief and reconstruction overseas: (i) UNRRA (United Nations Relief and Rehabilitation Administration), (ii) areas not yet within UNRRA, (iii) occupation of Germany, (iv) our own liberated territories in the Far East. Treasury was preparing to limit our expenditures under (i), (ii), (iii); (iv) should be a charge on the whole Commonwealth.

153. So Keynes concluded: 'What is the upshot? Unless there is a great change in our handling of our matters in the next year, those factors will probably put a quantitative burden on the financial machine in the first three years after the war far greater than it can carry without further financial aid from the United States.'

154. Keynes put three basic choices — 'Austerity', 'Temptation', 'Justice'. 'Austerity' was complete financial independence of the United States. This required at the very best, and assuming success in dealing with the three factors in para. 152 above:

(*a*) the continuance of war rationing and war controls more stringent than in 1945 for say three to five years after the war;
(*b*) the national planning and direction of foreign trade, both imports and exports, somewhat on the Russian model;
(*c*) a serious retardation of Colonial development and Far Eastern re-habilitation and a strict limitation of all overseas activities, whether military or diplomatic or by way of developing our trade, wealth, and influence, which involved any considerable expenditure.

155. Keynes did not want to rule this out as impossible for he had to keep an alternative alive. A year later, when I had the task of preparing a contingency plan in case the US Congress rejected the Loan,[9] I was able to paint a less apocalyptic picture, partly because by then there had been several months' peace and economic recovery, and partly because world political-economic opinion (including powerful forces in the United States itself) would reckon that the Americans had behaved outrageously, and would draw conclusions for themselves. But in attacking this as a 'choice' of our own volition, Keynes was obviously right. I would myself go further, and say that no Ministers would have been willing to reject any American proposal for a Loan Agreement (unless it raised some issue clearly unacceptable to the electorate as a whole — and it is difficult to imagine what such an issue might be) if the only alternative was 'Austerity' as expounded by Keynes.[10]

156. 'Temptation' was a possible US course for providing us with very large amounts of credit on condition that we accepted all the US doctrines (as they were at the time), e.g. free convertibility of sterling balances; major reduction in imperial preference; convertibility and non-discrimination. Keynes thought that some of our US friends might offer this: he opposed it because it would concentrate our world indebtedness on USA, would involve large loan service, would be directing our economic policy under financial duress, and would end up by our paying exactly the same figure to the Americans as the Russians were claiming in reparations from Germany. However, our friends in Washington were not very powerful in autumn 1945.

157. The third was 'Justice', which was an approach to a general reconsideration of the proper division of the costs of the war:

> For a hundred good reasons we have had to accept during the war a post-war financial burden entirely disproportionate to what is fair . . . We did it in the interests of getting on with the war without waste of time or loss of war-like efficiency. As a result, we, and we only, end up owing vast sums, not to neutrals and bystanders, but to our own Allies, Dominions and Associates . . . This does not apply particularly to USA; indeed to them (and Canada) proportionally least of all. It applies all round. Nevertheless it is only through appropriate action by USA and Canada that there is a prospect of a general resettlement . . . [if the North Americans can do this] we shall be made able to be their partners and co-adjudicators in setting up a post-war international economy of the character on which they have set their hearts.

158. The following were the proposals:

(a) US to refund to us as a sort of retrospective Lend-Lease the $3 billion (£750 million) which we spent on purchases in USA in 1939–41 before Lend-Lease.

(b) We would accept *de facto* convertibility in the Bretton Woods sense within a year after the end of the war without waiving other transitional regulations. (Conditional on (a) and (e)).

(c) We undertake funding arrangements proposed for sterling balances which would leave not less than $3 billion (£750 million) liquid and fully convertible.

(d) We would then approach sterling area countries, not necessarily uniformly but perhaps normally: (i) each would contribute 25 per cent of either its total balance or war-increment; (ii) 25 per cent would be fully liquid and convertible, (iii) 50 per cent would be funded; (iv) any country refusing would have all its balances blocked; (v) figures to include post-war demobilization and terminal liabilities.

(e) In addition to (a), US would give us a call on dollars exercisable over, say, ten years up to a large amount (say $5 billion, or £1,250 million) at a token rate of interest and easy repayment terms.

159. Canada was also expected to contribute, say an additional $500 million to the total in (e), and to clear up various outstanding liabilities from early in the war. South Africa should make a gift of £50 million of gold to pay for retrospective costs of the war. Australia and New Zealand did not present great problems. The sterling balances of non-sterling countries likewise. So the roster ran round the world.

160. The immense breadth of concept and mastery of detail made a great impression on those who read it, especially when one realizes that it was all done in Stage I, with the expectation of another eighteen months' war. Keynes wanted to get ahead with the negotiation as soon as Stage I was over and the Stage II appropriations approved. From the beginning he showed a total optimism that 'Justice' would be accepted, and feared that delay would be fatal. It was by no means obvious that this timing was right, especially after Roosevelt's death in April, and the evidence of a more hostile temper in Congress, and later of course by the replacement of Mr Churchill — all the old Anglo-American landmarks disappearing. And it was odd to expect the British or the Americans to determine their long-term policies and embody them in a long-term financial agreement while the war was still going on or immediately afterwards.

161. The explanation, in my opinion, both of the optimism and of the urgency, is that Keynes regarded this agreement with the United States as the capstone of the great constructive effort on which he embarked in 1941 to create a world-wide multilateral financial system.

To see sterling convertible at an early date was a major objective —
perhaps, apart from getting the money, his most important objective.
He could not tolerate that after he had overcome for three years all
these obstacles which were intrinsic in the task, the edifice would
collapse — and because the British had not played their part. So of
course he had to believe that the Americans would help him to
complete this masterpiece of his public service. He may well have
felt that his health would not stand a negotiation in 1946 or 1947;
and he had more mistrust than he probably should have had of the
ability and willingness of Ministers, Treasury, and Bank to carry the
project along. Nevertheless, both the optimism and the urgency
turned out, in my opinion, to be counter-productive.

162. The plan described above was Keynes's first approach, and it
changed before the delegations sat down in Washington on 11
September. But there were two problems, there from the first draft,
which were never resolved.[11]

163. The treatment of sterling area balances — cancellation, freeing,
funding. There was certainly great indignation about the growth of
this indebtedness. Yet, even the moral argument did not all run one
way. There was the banker's morality: if a customer deposits his
money, you don't take it away. More difficult, these countries were
all 'underdevelopeds'. Australia and New Zealand did make contributions of £20 million and £10 million ('about right') and South
Africa would never have paid a penny. Did we really intend to be
negotiating independence with India and Ceylon with one hand
and holding out the begging bowl with the other? Sir Archibald
Rowlands, formerly Finance Member for India, said that if we
mentioned 'Justice' we should never get another word in edgeways.
It was remarkable that the Americans were pressing us, for if we had
proposed such things ourselves we would have been submerged with
cries of 'British Imperialism'.

164. However, the £750 million to be contributed from sterling
balances (the same as the proposed retrospective Lend-Lease) remained
as a problem; and without this operation our future international
balance sheet was in ruins. First, should it apply to everybody?
Keynes was leaving out Burma, Malaya, Hong-Kong (presumably to
be brought in when liberated). Some wanted to omit the Crown
Colonies (and some even Eire as an integral part of the British
monetary system). Some wanted to limit the operation to India,
Egypt, Iraq. The proportion of private and banking holders varied
very widely, and only in two or three of the countries was the
public holding large enough to make the Keynes cancellation-

funding–freeing practicable; and the 'sanction' of total blocking seemed increasingly impracticable. Jobbing backwards, if the Treasury had taken continuous score, country by country, settlements could have been reached every few months while we were there fighting and had great purchase thereby. But once it was 'post-war debt' we were done. Keynes's preference was to require countries to exchange sterling from their currency reserves and substitute local currency. But this too encountered difficulties; and in the end the only tenable course was an *ad hoc* agreement with each country, according to the tactical situation in each case. So we put Keynes's formula in the US–UK loan agreement without having decided how to carry it out. If Keynes had lived, this might have been his main preoccupation in 1946.

165. The other great problem, particularly for Eady and me, was to find a practical alternative to 'Justice', or rather 75 per cent 'Justice', 50 per cent 'Justice' or worse. Like Keynes, we did not think 'Austerity' would be acceptable to any Ministers in sight. So we sought others, not necessarily to be mentioned to the Americans, but to give Ministers more room for manœuvre.

166. The simplest plan, which had much to commend it in any case after the collapse of the war, but for which nobody could have persuaded Keynes, was to abandon the concept of a 'Grand Design' negotiation in autumn 1945, for several years' money, sterling balances, convertibility, non-discrimination. We could easily have said 'We are willing to sign the Bretton Woods Agreement and participate in the International Commercial Policy conference; but we are not willing to accept any prior commitments at all until we see how the new world develops: we would be willing to negotiate in 1947.' We would have borrowed, say $1,000 millions (some from Export–Import Bank and some, no doubt, also from Canada), and would have undertaken to accept a loan for the residue of Lend-Lease at the rate of any ultimate major loan. After the abrupt end of the war and the cessation of Lend-Lease, the Americans could not have refused or tried to impose strings. In fact events by 1947 showed that the multilateral theologians' concepts of the course of events had been utterly wrong, and that the doctrines of the 1945 negotiations had fallen into the background of US policy except as a far-ahead (and useful) ideal, and that the combination of the Communist threat to Europe together with the world dollar shortage had persuaded the Americans to grant billions of dollars in pursuit of European discrimination against USA! So the idea of postponing the 'Grand Design' negotiation, and borrowing relatively small amounts if necessary expensively, would have been well justified by events.

167. But this was no backstop for Ministers on a failure to get adequate terms under 'Justice', no alternative to 'Austerity'. Eady and I worked out in June an idea called 'Plan 2',[12] the essence of which was to create as big a multilateral group as we could (sterling area, French, Belgian, and Dutch areas, Scandinavians, etc.) to trade freely between themselves — about 75 per cent of pre-war world trade — and to pool and allocate their dollars. The group could have associates: Canada might be prepared to be paid 50 per cent in sterling and 50 per cent in dollars if they could see a multilateral group taking shape, and with no alternative markets anyway: it could borrow from USA. Later history showed that technically this could be done: not unlike the trade and payments organizations set up by OEEC in 1948.

168. But would these other countries have agreed to join in 1946; and would they have been a source of strength; and would the Americans have applied pressure against them? One can say with certainty (in the light of after-knowledge) that none of the Europeans would have turned down such an offer of British leadership and participation unless it was impossible for them to do so: this was what they were continuously seeking in the late 1940s. They would also have known that the Americans had refused their chief wartime ally a loan on acceptable terms; not necessarily a good prospect for US co-operation. Could USA have made credible offers to France, Belgium, Holland, all to be approved by Congress? The answers must be 'don't know'. But although the material problems of 'Austerity' would still have been there, we would have been engaged simultaneously in a great creative endeavour.

169. Eady put this to Keynes as a possible fall-back position very moderately and tactfully, but Keynes would have nothing of it. He was never a man to conceal his disagreement, and few could write a ruder rejoinder. Eady sensibly dropped the point, for at that stage a battle with Keynes could not have yielded anything. But nevertheless I must quote the last sentence of Keynes's rejoinder, leaving the reader to judge whether this should be taken as an illustration of his ruthless debating style or (my own opinion) as his fundamental view on 9 July 1945: 'I do not think there is any serious risk of an overall shortage of gold and dollars in the first three years.'

170. The last step before the war ended, and with it Lend-Lease, was a visit by Clayton (US Assistant-Secretary of State) here for an UNRRA meeting, to tell us politely that to any loan would be attached strings about sterling balances, convertibility and non-discrimination.[13] Sir Stafford-Cripps called a meeting on August

Bank Holiday, 6 August, at which what one might call a preliminary inquisition took place. We got quite a good mark for convertibility, we gathered, but less so on non-discrimination; and this all came back in the early rounds of the negotiation when it actually began. It took both the Americans and ourselves a long time to get away from the concepts of the 'debtor's' war; having missed the opportunity to set up a Combined Finance and National Economy Board in 1941. I suspect, indeed, that this did not happen until March 1947, when we unilaterally announced our decision that no more British funds would be available for Greece as from 31 March 1947.

Import Programme Machinery

171. There had of course been control of (predominantly) dollar imports through the war, operated through a Treasury Committee called the Exchange Requirements Committee, with a Board of Trade sub committee called the Import Licensing Committee. By spring 1945, however, the senior Treasury people were coming to the opinion that this was not going to be adequate in Stage II and Stage III, and that it would be necessary to have a committee dealing with both sides of the balance sheet; and also dealing with imports as a whole (dollar and non-dollar) — for in the traditional Treasury way, food imports were handled by the division responsible for food, material imports by those responsible for materials, and so on, so there was great scope for duplication.

172. The cancellation of Lend-Lease brought this to a head, and it was decided at the operating level to concentrate the whole operation on my new division OF(EI), where the work was done with great brilliance by one of the Principals, J. F. Cahan, a Canadian who ultimately became Deputy Secretary-General of OEEC, and was tragically killed in a car accident.

173. There was a top-level committee, the Balance of Payments Working Party (BPWP), under Eady's chairmanship, which began each operation by expounding the situation fully to the top people in the relevant departments. Cahan would then send out instructions for import schedules to the operating (not the financial) people in each department: they would return them and would be examined; and so the total would be built up. This would then be compared with the rest of the balance of payments prospect; and from there would develop the picture to be put to BPWP, and the alternative proposals to be made to Ministers.

174. This basic system lasted under different names until the effective

end of import control in the 1950s: it became immensely complex from 1947, when the failure of convertibility forced us into a bilateral system; and the secretariat of the committee was extended and became responsible for long-term as well as short-term balance of payments analysis. It did not solve the balance of payments: but it did provide the apparatus.

Import Policy in 1945

175. There was a continuous flow of decisions, for which principles had to be sought:

(a) Should we insist on customers buying at home instead of importing? For machinery, we decided that there would probably be advantage in allowing the imports, and letting the home manufacturer develop his exports. Of course there were exceptions, if the import could reasonably be deferred, or if home supplies were readily available. But the doctrine was pro-import, with particular emphasis on strengthening the economy by 1950.

(b) How far should we subsidize UK production in order to save imports? This was always regarded as being reasonable for agriculture. But it could be argued that the case was just as strong for coal (prices 25 per cent too high) and thence transport and electric power. Nothing came of this, probably rightly, though another interesting comment on the exchange rate. Similar to these was the question whether it was right to 'save foreign exchange' by importing bauxite and manufacturing it into aluminium here at a cost far above that of imported Canadian aluminium.

(c) The question of direct discrimination against US and Canadian goods. The doctrine at that time was to discriminate strongly against buying their goods, but not to discriminate much if we were importing the goods at all. But we were being careful, both under Lend-Lease and then for fear of prejudicing the Loan.

(d) How long would import control last? At the first meeting of the Import Licensing Committee that I attended, I said 'at least five years'. General consternation; for the Board of Trade had expected to start relaxing immediately after the war.

(e) Should the Ministry of Food be pressed to buy more imports in order to allocate them to the manufacturers of processed food for export? Not unnaturally, the Ministry was so preoccupied with home consumption, that it did not pay much attention to the (very large) export potential. But food was an integral part of the 150 per cent export target, and we reckoned that if the conversion rate was 2:1 or better, export would be well worth while.

176. However, here were the policy points beginning to arise that would involve immense complication in the following years; and they are mentioned here, so to speak, as introduction.

The Loan Agreement

177. The negotiation began on 11 September, less than a month after the cessation of Lend-Lease, and little more after the accession of the Labour Government. 'Urgency', indeed, and Keynes at the height of optimism:

Keynes, in his talks with Ministers just before leaving for Washington, was almost starry-eyed. He was very confident that in the coming negotiations he could obtain American aid that would be ample in amount, and on most satisfactory conditions. He told us that he thought he could get £1,500 million ($6 billion) as a free gift or 'grant in aid'. There would be no question of a loan to be repaid, or of a rate of interest on the loan. Nor did he, at this stage, say much to us about 'strings', conditions to be attached by the Americans to any aid from them . . . This undue optimism, as it soon proved to be, naturally predisposed us against concessions, which Keynes proposed later . . .[14]

178. Keynes and our Ambassador, Lord Halifax, were leading for us: Vinson,[15] US Secretary to the Treasury, and Clayton for the Americans. At the British end, the Ministerial team was Dalton, Bevin, Cripps.

179. Keynes appears to have opened with a *tour de force* of Britain's war effort and post-war plight — the basis of 'Justice' — as he had done the year before in the Stage II negotiations. But he speedily learned that the Americans now were interested in the future, not the past, and that the old soldier, showing his medals, would not be a persuasive advocate.

180. By early October[16] Keynes reported that Vinson had made clear that neither a grant nor an interest-free loan was practical politics; Vinson had emphasized that he was not worried about the money ('only peanuts to me') and was solely moved by the judgement of what was politically possible in the present mood of Congress and the public. Clayton proposed a $5 billion loan, repaid and serviced over fifty years, starting in five years' time, at $150 million a year (actuarially a little over 1 per cent interest); and was willing to consider escape clauses in conditions of particular difficulty provided these were postponements of instalments, not cancellations.

181. As soon as some card had been played by the Americans, there was immense activity in Washington and London. London was still unwilling to let Keynes explore the possibility of interest; and found

$150 million (£35 million) too much anyway. On the other hand, although London greatly disliked waivers and escape clauses ('legitimised defaults that would create conflict sooner or later') they were not taboo.

182. The 'strings' were perhaps more specific than expected, but not outrageously so. An attempt to include the abolition of Imperial Preference in the package was warded off. We had always agreed to participate in the International Commercial Policy Conference, which ultimately led to GATT; and we agreed (a genuine 'string') not to discriminate against USA goods after end-1946. They insisted that we take action on the sterling balances, but as pointed out above, neither we nor they knew how to do it: and the only point at issue was whether we undertook to approach these countries or whether the Americans would come too: the actual text was much the same as in Keynes's great paper of mid-March. They insisted that we accept the Bretton Woods Agreement virtually immediately (again something we intended to do, but not under duress): they insisted (the biggest 'string' of all, though again an integral part of Keynes's mid-March paper) that we made sterling convertible one year after the Loan's enactment.[17] This brought the negotiation to the verge of breakdown.

183. On the principal side, the figure was $3¾ billion (£938 million), interest at 2 per cent repayable in fifty years beginning December 1951 (annuity $112 million). A waiver of interest was allowed if we failed to earn on current account as much as would have been required to pay for our pre-war imports at constant prices. Besides this Loan, there was a further loan of $650 million (£160 million) on the same terms, representing a very generous settlement of all outstanding claims for the war — a total of $4,400 million (nearly £1,100 million).

184. So in the last analysis, having no alternative to 'Austerity', Ministers decided to accept the strings and take the $4,400 million loan. Looking only eighteen months ahead, it cannot be denied that the Loan was a terrible fiasco. Some have tried to attribute the fiasco to the Government, the Treasury, and the Bank. Others would put more weight on what Keynes said wouldn't be serious in the first three years — the US current surpluses of $6 billion in 1946 and $12 billion in 1947. Dalton emphasized the very rapid increase in US and world prices, particularly after the breakdown of controls in 1946. These are not easy matters to judge.

185. However, there is one weakness for which I would criticise Keynes himself, OF, and the Bank. The most difficult part of the

problem was to put a money equivalent on the 'strings', realizing that we were concerned with real life and not with 'stable prices' and 'steady progress'. What was the difference in the 'strings' acceptable for $6, 5, 4 billion? Again, what difference to these did the payment of small amounts of interest, waivers, etc. make? Might it perhaps have been better to start with the 'strings', make a maximum and minimum evaluation of each — and *then* see the range of resources required? If this will be too much for Congress, take one away, and so on.

186. Lastly, the negotiation itself. It was certainly not successful, for the outcome was much worse than Ministers had been led to hope; and it lasted three months and generated ill temper. Dalton says that at one stage Bevin suggested that Keynes should be replaced by Eady: Dalton refused, probably rightly, in midstream, though it did prove necessary to send Sir Edward Bridges at the end. The truth was that in the Roosevelt regime, Keynes had an excellent relationship with Morgenthau; but he had nothing in common with Vinson. Sir Frank Lee told a story of one of the interminable discussions of waivers in a roomful of Americans:

VINSON. I'm not clear what happens to the waiver if something entirely unexpected happens to you . . . suppose you found a billion dollars in a cave?

KEYNES [like lightning]. Mr Secretary, I am willing right now to include a clause providing that the waiver clause is immediately cancelled if we find a billion dollars in a cave.

187. Compare this with Eady's handling of Snyder, the next Secretary of the Treasury, in August 1947, when he had to go and tell him that we had to suspend convertibility but wanted the rest of the Loan too: 'As I was going along to the Treasury, I remembered that Snyder had started as a small-town banker in the Middle West. So as soon as I was shown in, I walked straight across to him and said quietly, "Mr Secretary, I must tell you that there is a run on the bank".'

188. Again, the terrible conflicts with London: 'The thought that anyone in London could suppose that this [a telegram he had received approved by Ministers] was a starter suggests that dangerous and indeed demented advice is abroad.'

189. With the whole prepared 'Justice' concept manifestly unacceptable; with Vinson unquestionably the key American in the negotiation; and a new Government, largely inexperienced in this field; it is by no means obvious to me that Keynes was the right leader for the delegation.

Notes

1. The history is excellently described in Edwin McCarthy's *Wool Disposals 1945-1952: The Joint Organisation* (privately printed, 1967).
2. The actual figures for 1949 and 1950 were 9 per cent and 22 per cent respectively above 1937; the actual figure for 1955 was 55 per cent above 1937 – the top of the range in both periods, reflecting the high US activity.
3. By 1948, US primary food and raw materials prices were about 50 per cent above 1945; and both US and UK wholesale prices were about double pre-war.
4. 'It will be very difficult to get multilateral order and to get the exchange rates of the liberated and enemy countries on to a sound long-term basis if the £/$ rate is fluctuating at the same time. We shall be bound in practice to a stable £/$ rate as soon as we allow convertibility ... The danger that we shall find ourselves saddled with over-valued sterling becomes even more real when we consider that concessions on commercial policy will inevitably accompany convertibility; as a founder-member of the Commercial Club I doubt whether we could at the outset invoke the escape clause by which we are allowed to impose import restrictions when our balance of payments is adverse ... I feel very hesitant to suggest what we should do in these circumstances. But we should be a good deal better placed to take these risks if the rate was $3.50 than we are with the rate of $4. At least we should surely not leave the Americans under any illusions that the $4 is something fixed and immutable.' (Document 3, paras. 31-3).
5. [For the exchange of minutes see Documents 4-6. Ed.]
6. [The paper is reproduced in *The Collected Writings of John Maynard Keynes* Vol. XXIV pp. 256-95 (Macmillan, for the Royal Economic Society, 1979). Ed.]
7. £610 million at end-1945. [The figure in the text is based on the less comprehensive data then available. Ed.]
8. £3,688 million at end-1945: £2,454 million within sterling area and £1,234 million in non-sterling countries.
9. [Reproduced as Document 10. Ed.]
10. Keynes said in a private letter to Dr Dalton on 28 October, 'The fact that the Americans are becoming aware that there is no way out remotely compatible with the present domestic policy of the Government except on the basis of substantial US aid is one of the hidden unmentioned snags in our path'. Dalton, *High Tide and After* p. 77 (Muller, London, 1962).
11. During the late spring, Keynes invited some of us and the leading Canadian officials (for whom he had a great respect) to a week-end at King's College, Cambridge. It was an idyllic occasion, and with the work too, and I was always pleased to have seen Keynes simultaneously at the height of his power as host and teacher combined. His purpose, as I recall it, was to convince the Canadians of our multilateral intentions.
12. [See below Document 7: 'Financial Policy in Stage III'. Ed.]
13. Clayton's UNRRA engagements were virtually a cover for a series of meetings on post-war commercial policy in London. The talks in August 1945 followed earlier talks in December 1944/January 1945 and in April–June 1945. See *Foreign Relations of the U.S., 1945* Vol. VI (Washington, 1969).
14. Dalton, op. cit., p. 73.
15. Keynes told Dalton (op. cit., p. 75) that his 'most conspicuous gift was the accuracy with which he could spit into a distant spittoon'.
16. [A month earlier, even before he reached Washington, Keynes was writing from Ottawa that a grant was unlikely. In the first few weeks in Washington

little progress was made because the Americans insisted on talking trade policy before discussing cash and Keynes had persuaded the Cabinet before leaving that there was no need to take the trade experts. The line taken by Clayton was that Britain could have 'collective credits', i.e. credits that Britain could service if she would bind herself to adopt free, non-discriminating trade. Ed.]

17. [This does not make clear that the real bone of contention was *non-resident* sterling, i.e. sterling held outside the sterling area. Keynes had already offered to make sterling held by the sterling area countries convertible after a year. Ed.]

CHAPTER IV

From US Loan to Marshall Plan

190. The year 1946 was a lull before the storm, or perhaps more accurately, a lull between two storms. Admittedly, we did not know until mid-July whether we would get the US loan, but as the weeks and months passed of more or less acrimonious debate in Congress, with rumours and counter-rumours about the outcome, it became increasingly clear that if the answer was 'No' we could find a course that would enable the United Kingdom economy to survive, and that the Americans' foreign economic policy would be in parlous plight, and bound to seek some line of new development from which we might readily benefit. Meanwhile, our demobilization and reconversion of industry were proceeding well. The external financial position was more encouraging than might have been expected a year after the end of the war: early in March, after a tough negotiation by Eady and Cobbold, we got a reasonable agreement with Canada, with a loan analogous to the US loan and also clearing up the past; and there was no evidence anywhere of unwillingness to continue to hold sterling.

191. The import control system operated by OF(EI) for the Balance of Payments Working Party was working satisfactorily. The two very large programmes — food and raw materials — were managed by people in the departments who had done exactly the same operation in the war for their departments' shipping programmes, and had no difficulty in adopting the financial limitations instead. The smaller departments, lacking this experience, found the idea of programme-making more difficult, but the policy criteria were clear (generally free for machinery — 70 per cent of applications accepted) and tight for consumer goods. The problems arose bilaterally; 'token' imports designed to give very small quotas to USA, Canada, Switzerland to 'encourage them for a better future'; and imports from 'war-shattered' countries (France, Holland, etc.) to help their recovery and to help pay for their imports from us. These points, small in substance, created great philosophical arguments, and a sharp stimulus to bilateralism in Europe, and were not cleared up until the new European organizations were built in 1948 and 1949.

192. For Ministers, the only contentious issue on the import programmes was that of extra imports of 'variety' foods from North

America, such as citrus, canned goods, milk powder, dried eggs (beyond a certain level). The Minister of Food would argue that if we could not get food to increase the ration, we should buy these. But to buy these once meant continuing to buy year by year, and when the extra rationed foods became available we could not cut back. The amounts of money became significant — for example £10 million for fruit as a special addition when the US loan was approved. Looking back thirty years, nothing impresses me more than the tenacity with which these battles were fought. The Chancellor saw the dollars draining away; and knew that every concession would be followed by more demands: and Mr Strachey saw the situation in the shops, and did not really believe that the Government should impose any limit on his overseas expenditure.

Balance of Payments for 1946

193. In the first half of 1946, we had two BPWP reports: one at the beginning of February to fix a firm programme for the first half of 1946 and a provisional one for the second half; and one in April (later revised in the light of the Loan) to fix the second half and a provisional programme for the first half of 1947, and the next in October etc. It may be interesting to compare the series of programmes for 1946:

Table 3. UK Current Account 1946 (£m)[1]

Estimate made in:	February	April	October	Actual
Imports (f. o. b.)	1075	1120	1160	1082
Exports and re-exports (f. o. b.)	−550	−770	−910	−920
Government (net)	400	380	320	323
Invisibles	−155	−40	−95	−190
Deficit (+) or Surplus (−)	+770	+690	+475	+295

194. The progress is shown in this way for three reasons. First, it explains any inconsistency between the 1946 outcome and the estimate used in the Washington negotiation (£750 million for 1946). Second, it shows that the actual imports for the year, despite price movements, shortages of supply, etc., were virtually equal to the amount decided in February: they total 65 per cent of 1938 at constant value of money. Third, the fact that the forecasts were steadily improving had encouraged the concept of a 'lull'. I must add, however, that in the course of June (before we knew whether the Loan was coming) I had formed the opinion (greatly helped by the Bank's statisticians) that it was a lull before a storm — one could not yet say how big a storm — and had warned the Chancellor, who had thoroughly taken it on board. I shall of course come back to this later.

Bulk Purchase

195. Early in January 1946, an operation began which to some civil servants looked very odd from a constitutional point of view. The Government had to decide whether to reopen the Liverpool cotton market or to nationalize it. The novelty was that it set up a committee of officials to advise it. This question of terminal markets had been a political one for years. The 'capitalist' view was that the market was the most efficient system of distribution, that it gave the British consuming industry a marginal advantage, that it earned foreign exchange. The 'socialist' view was that it created speculation. There was no possibility of an 'objective' argument to decide what was best in the public interest, the kind of assessment that civil servants are qualified to make; and some thought it essentially the responsibility of Ministers to make up their own minds, and not require officials to disclose their own political views either to their colleagues, as was inevitable in any discussion, or to Ministers.

196. There was no new 'objective' evidence: State trading had been successful in the war, as part of the apparatus of shipping and industrial control, but that was irrelevant in the long run. The Commonwealth Wool Conference, after a lengthy discussion between all the interests concerned, decided that the Bradford wool tops market provided the best system. Keynes, who knew immensely more about the commodity markets than anyone else, expressed himself as being very hostile to all methods of procuring imports, regarding Government purchase as atrocious and private importing as shockingly inefficient. But he was strongly in favour of bulk purchase of cotton, following his experience with Sir Frank Platt in the creation of the Lancashire Cotton Corporation, and thought it essential for any reorganization of the Lancashire manufacturing industry. But he saw no case for bulk purchase of non-ferrous metals.

197. The Treasury therefore supported closure of the Liverpool cotton market, but was in favour of opening the London Metal Exchange when practicable. However, we did not carry the official committee on cotton, which (us dissenting) recommended the opening of the Liverpool market. When the report reached Ministers, its conclusion was rejected on the classical grounds that the market 'created speculation', and legislation followed accordingly.

198. However, Dalton should have the last word:

I must confess that this particular experiment in State trading worked badly in peace-time. It lost money, and failed to bring the steady prices we had promised. If Platt [who had been Cotton Controller] had still been in charge, and in his prime, it would, I am pretty sure, have been a very different story. But as things were, the Tories scrapped it later, and I could hardly blame them.[2]

What Happens If?

199. The ink was barely dry on the Loan Agreement when I was commissioned to report on what we could do if Congress rejected, and this task lasted until 13 July. It was obvious that we would have resources, both financial and moral, available to us that we would not have had if the situation had resulted from breakdown of the negotiation; and also the longer the delay before the rejection the better, to give more time for our and the rest of the world's recovery. But the task would be formidable. One could not make detailed calculations; and indeed the strategy was more relevant than the figures. The strategy was most clearly set out in a paper written at the end of February (which had the approval of Keynes and was generally supported by Keynes, who could be excused for not liking the subject much!); and a simplified version was then submitted to Ministers. The following was the original document:[3]

1. Our economic aim would be:-
    (i) to reinforce and extend the sterling area system, linking trade arrangements with it.
    (ii) to borrow what smaller sums we can from USA (e.g. Export–Import Bank, pledging investments, etc.).

2. If we could do *both*, we reckon that we could wriggle through to end 1948 at the following cost:-

    (i) *Food.* Retarded recovery of consumption. We could hope to avoid *new* food austerities (except for certain items like dried eggs and canned milk). But easements would be very slow coming, because US is the marginal supplier. In particular, easements would be very slow in sugar (worst), dairy produce, and possibly fats.

    (ii) *Manufactured goods.* We could hope to avoid hampering reconversion by cutting raw materials and machinery supplies. But consumers' recovery would be slower because we should have to export more.

    (iii) *Tobacco, films, private motoring.* The severity of cuts (assuming we gave priority to food, materials and machinery) would depend largely upon the extent to which we could borrow from USA. But we could hope to avoid desperate slashes. [Cut US tobacco by 20%, films by one-half, retain basic petrol rationing].

    (iv) *Military and political expenditure.* Maintenance of Forces in Middle East and India would be possible only if we could induce the locals to lend us the money to finance them. We could not afford to continue to supply Germany on the present basis. We could not afford to finance European relief and reconstruction except to the extent that we could afford to allocate UK exports to these purposes.

    (v) *Empire countries* would have to go short of US goods. This would be possible for Australia and New Zealand, and also for Eire, but not at all easy for the Colonies. South Africa (and probably India) would almost certainly decline to play on sharp import restriction. Canada would be in great difficulty, but would have to lend us money in order to sell her goods, and would have to limit her imports from USA.

3. By the end of 1948, we should have to balance sterling area payments with USA. This implies direction of our exports. It means development of Middle East oil (but see 2(iv) above), Rhodesian tobacco, UK films, Malayan tin and rubber, gold production throughout the Empire, pressure to increase UK sugar, livestock, dairy produce, long-term supply from Dominions and Argentina of meat and dairy produce; more UK steel production, develop African supply of US type cotton, strong attempt to get timber from Russia etc.

4. The difficulty would be to reconcile our energetic sterling area policy with the need to get *some* money somehow from USA. The levers for the latter, in order of importance, would be ocular demonstration of:-

(a) the political effect of drastic reduction of our overseas commitments.
(b) loss of US markets in the sterling area.
(c) loss of US markets in UK.

But the levers would probably not work unless we left the door ajar for economic co-operation between USA and the sterling area. We *must* avoid economic warfare with USA.

5. In strict economic terms, rejection would hurt us much more than it hurt USA, but we could scramble through somehow. The crucial fact would be that it would force us willy-nilly to cut our overseas commitments, which would radically affect the world political balance. This means big risks. But it would also carry with it a reasonable likelihood that we should get some financial assistance from USA nevertheless and indeed perhaps a more realistic economic relationship with USA. At the same time, appreciation of these facts suggests that rejection is rather unlikely.

200. The point that was really important here was that the UK import programme could not play a big role, partly because we should use gold reserves rather than critically weaken our economy, and because the big dimensions were outside — overseas military and political expenditure, sterling area dollar spending, oil, etc. The big issues had to be decided in any case, US Loan or not; and it may be that in real difficulties, free of the US 'strings' and with no moral obligation to help them with their military obligations, it might have been easier. Thirty years later, when one sees the relative success of Germany, Japan, France, which were forced to make great social and economic changes, one cannot be absolutely sure that our right long-term course was to display remarkable ingenuity to retain the status quo.

201. Nobody thought of this then, for the defeated countries appeared as a terrible problem and expense. Nevertheless, some had two thoughts, and on sending the papers to the archives on 15 July, I added a covering note:

The House of Representatives approved the Loan on July 13th by 219 votes to 155. This particular exercise can therefore be said to have been completed and can be relegated to the archives. However, it descends there with mixed feelings on the part of at least one of the protagonists in the various discussions contained in it, and it seems rather likely that in some years to come Anglo-American financial relations will have got into such a tangle as a result of the Loan that this file will be sought for proof by the one party that we had to have the Loan and by the other that we could have done without it.

RWBC

Keynes's Death

202. One cannot leave this period without mentioning the death of Keynes, both the great man himself and his immense impact on the Treasury. I cannot usefully add to the hundreds of thousands of words written about him, the flow continuing thirty years later. But I will give the note I made in my diary on that day, 22 April 1946:

Appalling news of death of Keynes. Felt bereft, as on the death of Roosevelt. He is the man whose abilities I would soonest have been able to match. The extraordinary thing about him was his intellectual attraction and zing — always fresh and interesting and original and provocative.

The pity of it all is that he negotiated the US Loan; this is what killed him, and he did it with great brilliance, but badly, over-complicating and finessing against London and against himself. We have not yet seen the beginning of the complexities and difficulties which this settlement has thrust upon us. I feel that he got some wrong ideas into his mind and became committed to them and felt bound to defend them ultimately against his better judgement. [I was very shocked at the time by his belief that there would be no dollar shortage in 1946–8, and that convertibility could move quickly and smoothly; and I never liked running a sterling balance plan internationally without knowing exactly how we were going to do it; nor could I share his unreal optimism about US intentions.]

His death leaves the Treasury in a terrible hole. Keynes has been the Treasury over the last few years; he has determined policy, spurred on the officials by criticism and help, conducted the major negotiations. This dependence upon Keynes has been good for the Treasury in some respects; it has been bad in others, for it has prevented the officials from developing an individual technique of thought. He has been the brains and the conscience. Now, at the beginning of a period of far-reaching negotiations, the controller of the basic strategy (and of 75% of the tactics) has gone. A frightful gap is left in Bretton Woods; another in the sterling balances. I expect Cobbold will increase his influence; and I wonder whether the Treasury will find a means of providing stimulus.

But what a wonderful career! Aged 31 in 1914; finished the war as Treasury representative at the Peace Conference; then the 'Economic Consequences' (one of the greatest and most influential books of our time); then 15 years in academic life culminating in 'The General Theory'; back to the Treasury with the masterly war-time Budgets, the conception of Bretton Woods; and the gradual domination of overseas financial policy.

The Signs of Storm

203. I mentioned that as early as June, some troublesome signs were beginning to appear. The first was shown in an analysis of the trade returns for the first four months of 1946, about the earliest moment

that could be expected to give meaningful results. Simply, we found that 38.4 per cent of our imports came from the US and Canadian dollar area, compared with 23 per cent in 1938: only 8.5 per cent of our exports went there, compared with 10.9 per cent in 1938. For South America, the movement was the same: in Western Europe, the clear opposite. Anyone looking from outside would think that we were deliberately unbalancing our payments with each group as far as we could; a bilateral policy in reverse: 'We use our exporting power to pay off debt to the sterling area countries and to permit Western European countries to incur debt to us or cancel their holdings of UK securities — while we pay out gold and dollars to the Americans in unprecedented quantities.' Nothing new in this, but menacing to see it already happening with such force.

204. Two weeks later came the Bank's estimates of the sterling area's payments for the first and second halves of 1946:

Table 4

	1st half 1946 (£m)	2nd half 1946 (£m)	Total (£m)
US dollar area	−85	−171	−256
Canada	−96	−96	−192
Latin America	−31	−26	−57
Sweden, Switzerland, Portugal	−16	−18	−34
Belgian area	−16	−5	−21
French area	48	38	86

This was exactly the same story; but with one modification. The rest of the sterling area, as well as ourselves, were in deficit with every one of the difficult countries. The figures looked like a sterling area deficit with the dollar area of £450 million:

Traditionally we have financed deficits with the American Continent with surpluses in the rest of the world, but on present indications this may become chronic early in 1947. We run grave risks of achieving overall balance in our international accounts consistently with an outflow of gold and dollars; which means in effect that the burden of the world's transfer problem with North America becomes concentrated upon our reserves.

205. So by the end of June 1946 (i.e. within six months of the Loan Agreement which was based on a different philosophy) we had identified and diagnosed the problem; and had advised the Chancellor, who had asked the Balance of Payments Working Party for a report. It was clear that we could not change the pattern of our (and other countries') trade without a fair amount of State action and conflict with our convertibility and non-discrimination commitments. Not until we got the 1947 programme, however, could we begin to judge the dimensions.

The 1947 Programme

206. When the programme was submitted in October, it revealed a difficult and unsatisfactory position. It caused no conflict between Ministers, for the Chancellor and the Minister of Food had settled the 'variety' food programme outside. But there had been a big increase in prices (with more probably to come with the abandonment of US price controls). The total volume of imports was 82 per cent of 1938 compared with 65 per cent in 1946. There was no sign of any ability to switch to non-dollar food and raw materials. It could not be said at all that we were over-importing; and it would have been impossible for Ministers, with the Loan three months behind, to slash consumption.

Table 5. UK Current Account, 1946–1947 (£m)

	Actual 1946	Estimate for 1947 at Oct. 1946	Actual 1947
Imports (f. o. b.)	1082	1463	1560
Exports and re-exports (f. o. b.)	− 920	−1300	−1146
Government (net)	323	175	149
Invisibles	− 190	− 85	− 190
Deficit (+) or Surplus (−)	+ 295	+ 253	− 442

As had been feared, the estimate of imports did turn out too low: that of exports was too high, aiming at 150 per cent of 1938 by the second half of 1947 (already reached 100 per cent by end-1946) but this target was a casualty of the winter industrial crisis. Moreover the 'Government' figure was artificially low, allowing for substantial sales of surplus military stores.

207. It was estimated, probably conservatively in all the circumstances, that the drain on the reserves in 1947 would be of the order of £500 million (£250 million more than the estimated general current deficit): this would exhaust the Canadian Loan by end-1947 and the US Loan at latest early in 1949. Obviously by that time there was no possibility of multilateral convertibility being established. So the big problem of sources of supply and receipts was fully confirmed.

Remedial Measures

208. The Treasury proposed the following line of attack:

(*a*) Special steps to develop our exports to the 'desirable' areas if necessary at the expense of exports elsewhere.

(*b*) Development of long-term sources of supply in the sterling area and Europe, e.g. Western European steel, dairy produce, bacon, Rhodesian tobacco, etc.

(c) Examination of UK food production in order to reduce dollar expenditure on food to a minimum.

(d) Examination of oil policy; oil is a very heavy user of dollars, not only for purchases of petroleum products from US countries, but also the dollar expenditure of the British countries.

(e) Consideration of the extent to which buyers of our exports can be obliged to pay for them in goods or convertible currencies.

(f) Crucial importance of the recovery of Western Europe to the solution of these problems. We cannot afford to finance European reconstruction ourselves: which adds more weight to *our* urgent need that they should receive substantial help from USA and the international institutions.

209. This was all agreed early in November, and the Treasury was told to arrange for studies with the departments. These problems were going to be with us for several years, and they recurred again and again. I doubt whether we got as much progress year by year by leaving it to the departments as we would have done if the Treasury had had the steam and resources to drive at full speed: it might indeed have been a good case for bringing in a business man with civil service experience, of whom there were still many in 1946. We may have underestimated the immense difficulty of making any progress, particularly under (a) or (b), except what might happen in the ordinary commercial way; and did not organize enough.

210. In each case, the essence was time. For example, in exports, the Government had expounded a firm policy to industry that 'all exports were good exports, provided they were paid for'. This had been successful in getting our exports back to pre-war by the end of 1946. This instruction could not be reversed off-hand. So indirect methods had to be applied, such as quiet words to big firms, and more selective development of the Government's own export services, and setting up a Dollar Exports Board. Exports to USA recovered fast; in ten years' time, USA had overtaken Australia as our biggest market; and ten years after that, USA took nearly as much as the whole EEC. Government policy had played a valuable role in this extraordinary development of the US market, but it was really the richness and openness of the market, and the great opportunities which it presented for £1,000 million a year of British goods. But nothing could have been done at end-1946 that could have helped our dollar exports much by, say, 1950. In 1947 and 1948, the 'hard currency' rule was made specific, but the more positive guidance was more important.

211. For the important foods, switching of sources of supply depended mainly on the world situation — the meat and dairy produce depending on the feeding-stuffs, etc., each again with its own time-cycle. Great effort had been put into long-term contracts (e.g. Commonwealth sugar) and this could switch supplies at a cost, both in money and in politics. But here was obviously an important area. The idea of great new tropical developments, like the ground-nut scheme, was very long-term indeed, with huge risks. As the food trade returned to private hands, with the trade flowing freely, a great deal of non-dollar trade developed. It was naturally important to press for substitution of US by Rhodesian tobacco, but everyone in the trade knew that we had a non-discrimination commitment, which was a discouraging background for expenditure on changing customers' taste and new development in Rhodesia. Raw materials raised different problems to food; if there was enough coal (and we were also willing to buy azaleas!) we could get Belgian steel. Throughout this field of switching sources of supply, the problem was to find those points where positive action could yield something, apart altogether from such commodities in which supply conditions could reasonably·be expected to improve anyway. But such positive action was bound to take a period of years, as an Import Diversion Committee showed. However, the performance of the Americans in scouring the world for scarce raw materials for the Korea war in 1950 suggests that their mix of Government and private enterprise is in a different class to ours in this kind of situation.

212. Agriculture was always regarded as a 'dollar-saver', though it was never clear which production pattern was best, and whether the structure of the industry could be shifted that way, except by a tremendous effort.

213. The relevance of oil was not dissimilar from what it was in the early 1970s. There was heavy expenditure on American companies' oil, both here and in the sterling area: we became very insistent in persuading them to develop a petroleum equipment industry in the UK to meet their capital needs. Shell and BP were pushing ahead with their developments world-wide, which were also very costly in dollars. Then there were expensive tanker costs. Huge refinery programmes were being built, both by Americans and British. On the other hand, the development of Shell and BP was manifestly favour-able to the balance of payments, for only about 40 per cent of their cost was incurred in dollars. So in fact this was a huge investment of dollars in order to get very large dollar savings. One note of the time reckons that the oil bill, taking the whole thing together, would absorb about one-third of the US credit. Nor could we find criteria

to pick out priorities effectively, for the oil industry is interwoven. So we limited UK consumption by retaining petrol rationing, but broadly speaking went ahead with the rest. The outcome was that by the 1960s and early 1970s we were getting our whole UK oil requirements at no cost in foreign exchange. But here again, time was the essential factor.

214. Then there was the fifth question, why should we tolerate a dollar deficit of £500 million and a rest of world surplus (i.e. giving them loans or paying off our debt) of £250 million? In the short run, if you could reduce the £250 million surplus that would not reduce the £500 million dollar deficit, but it would then save resources. In practical terms, the Government had learnt by the end of 1946 not to give loans; but investment to develop European production of dollar goods for our market was well worth while; and the biggest 'unrequited' exports were to the rest of the sterling area. The right way to handle this, as developed later, was to have regular meetings of a 'Sterling Area Statistical Party', which led to suggestions, some stronger than others, about the individual countries' limits *vis-à-vis* the various currency areas.

215. To sum up; there was unquestionably progress to be made on all these fronts, but for anything other than changes in market conditions, where positive action needs to be taken by Government, the time-scale was at least five years.

ITO

216. Meanwhile, the work of creating the International Trade Organization. We had a Commonwealth meeting in the autumn, an interesting one because Australia for the first time began to show a possibility of joining; and whilst Mr Fraser, the New Zealand Prime Minister, had been expressing violent hostility in his visits earlier in the year, they were unlikely to stand out if Australia came in. The most important point, for them and us alike, was to ensure a high level of employment, particularly in the United States; for in the last analysis, international trade depends on employment. We went so far as to draft a convention to be agreed simultaneously with the instrument setting up the Organization, but this was overtaken by the Americans' own Full Employment Act.

217. We continued with the full Conference at Church House, where we began to get the provisions that countries needed and were likely to continue to need — the rules governing how countries could impose quantitative restrictions (q.r.) on imports when in balance of

payments difficulty, and the rules governing how far these could be discriminatory.

218. In the end, ITO never came into being, for the US Government of the time thought it would be rejected by Congress. In my opinion, the other Governments should have abandoned it forthwith, for it was outrageous for successive US Governments to take the initiative in creating a scheme, and in imposing prospective participation in it on other Governments as a condition for financial assistance, and then for this not to be endorsed by the US legislative body. However, it was possible for the US Government to adhere to it by calling it the General Agreement on Tariffs and Trade: and this has turned out to be a useful regulator of conditions for world trade.

Economic Surveys: 1946 and 1947

219. In August 1945, Sir Stafford Cripps had been pressing for a 'five-year plan', and Sir Edward Bridges put the question to James Meade, the Head of the Economic Section, and set up a Steering Committee, under his own chairmanship, of Permanent Secretaries. Meade thought it best on the other hand to concentrate on the short-term — the immediate problems of general scarcity. The *Economic Survey for 1946* (submitted in December) was therefore an analysis of national expenditure and income, directed to the problem of 'closing the gap' between resources and demands, seeking a variety of means of reducing Government expenditure and private investment.

220. This system was not universally accepted. I wanted to put the emphasis on the manpower budget:

I am not at all sure that you are comparing like with like. There is an implicit assumption that all types of resources are thoroughly mobile, both industrially and locationally and market-wise. The new method is extremely difficult for Ministers and senior officials to understand. If we had balanced the manpower budget and showed an inflationary gap nevertheless, would we then create unemployment in order to close it?

As I see it, the purpose of overall planning is to ensure a global consistency of Government programmes and policies, and to do that one has to relate it very closely indeed to the individual programmes, recognising a wide range of error in all these global statistics and not attempting to allocate too precisely. The questions that Ministers really want answered are, 'Are the Government's plans nonsense? What are the expectations which we can reasonably hold out to consumers? What should be our main objectives of policy?' It seems to me that two things stand out a mile:

(a) the need to balance our payments, apart from military expenditure, by the middle of 1947, and
(b) the need for the most rapid possible contraction of the Armed Forces.

221. These arguments continued. I was never heavily involved, for my preoccupation was in getting our balance of payments needs properly incorporated in whatever kind of plan was made. But there was a clear distinction between those who thought in terms of national income and expenditure and inflationary and deflationary gaps, and those who thought in terms of the best co-ordinated deployment of physical resources.

222. Towards the end of 1946, the Economic Section produced its 1947 *Economic Survey*, which put much less emphasis on the critical questions for Ministers than the Economic Steering Committee thought necessary. They therefore submitted a very tough programme:

(*a*) postponement of raising of school leaving age
(*b*) conscription of young women for national service (e.g. textiles, etc.)
(*c*) cut in the housing programme
(*d*) big reduction in Services and supply.

This was agreed by the Ministerial Planning Committee, but it was all turned down by the Cabinet (only one member of the Planning Committee could be there).

223. Here was a dilemma, for the Government was irrevocably committed to publish its 'Plan' for 1947. Sir Edward Bridges and the Steering Committee put the task of writing this document on me; and it turned out to be rather a heavy one (a thirty-six-page document in all) which had to go through nine drafts and two Ministerial meetings.[5] We had only just started when the appalling weather and transport interruptions stopped the distribution of coal to the power stations; and on 7 February Mr Shinwell had to announce a complete surprise – the virtual cessation of power supply to most of industry and only intermittent supply to the domestic consumer. This crisis lasted for three weeks. It cost £200 million in exports; it was clearly damaging for the Government's credibility; and it was manifestly true that if stronger measures had been needed to deal with the manpower and the balance of payments situations, stronger measures still would now be needed.[6]

224. *Economic Survey for 1947* was issued early in March, as the power crisis was drawing to an end. It was eagerly awaited, and 300,000 copies were sold or distributed. Unexpectedly to those of us who had been working on it for six weeks and knew its deficiencies, the reception was quite good. There was an introduction by the Prime Minister, and a long Part I on economic planning, written personally by Sir Stafford Cripps, setting out his concept of planning

in a democratic society. This itself is of some historic interest, for he was the only Cabinet Minister in the 1945 Government who thought in terms of economic planning, rather than in terms of nationalization (Morrison) and fiscal policy (Dalton).

225. Sir Stafford Cripps's system emphasized throughout the difference between 'totalitarian' and 'democratic' planning, the need to sustain the flexibility of our economic life, the fundamental importance of certain basic industries and services — coal, power, steel, agriculture, transport, building — to our entire productive activity, and the need for a long-term plan for each. Then he called attention to the need for economic 'budgets' (manpower and national income and expenditure, supplemented by foreign exchange, investment, and scarce fuel and materials) to compare the future resources of the economy with the future claims upon it; and finally to the development of methods for balancing these 'budgets' — basically the use of controls and fiscal means in a concerted way in accordance with the Plan. He emphasized, however, that Government could not do 'fine tuning':

The execution of the Plan must be much more a matter for co-operation between Government, industry and the people than of rigid application by the State of controls and compulsions. The Government must lay down the economic tasks for the nation; it must say which things are the most important and what the objectives of policy should be, and should give as much information as possible to guide the nation's economic activity; it must use its powers of economic control to influence the course of development in the desired direction. When the working pattern has thus been set, it is only by the combined effort of the whole people that the nation can move towards its objective of carrying out the first things first, and so make the best use of its economic resources.

226. Thirty years later, it is difficult to see how a system of this kind could have worked. It had always been necessary to have long-term plans for the basic nationalized industries, related in some way to the prospective growth of the economy: we can also envisage 'plans' of a less committed character resulting from discussion between the Government and large private sector industries. But I do not see how this could be done for more than a small and selected number of industries; nor how the Government could decide which were 'essential' and which 'non-essential', especially in view of the overriding requirement for 'flexibility'. However, under the Marshall Plan, the concept of a long-term plan came up in a different form.

227. Before leaving the 'Cripps' unattributed note on economic planning it is amusing to recall that in the debate in the House of Commons (*Hansard* 12 March, Col. 1351), Mr Churchill spoke very favourably of paragraph 9:[7] 'which carried us back to the old days of

Adam Smith and John Stuart Mill . . . and might have been conceived by Mr Gladstone or Mr Bright. I wonder who was the civil servant who wrote this for his Socialist masters. Out of the 2,000,000 we have at present, he should be the last one to be sacked.' But this was drafted by Cripps himself.

228. Part III was a full review of July 1945 to December 1946, describing the success of demobilization and reconversion, the growth of industry and agriculture, the performance of imports, exports, and the balance of payments. By the end of 1946, the rate of national output was not significantly below pre-war — an increase imposing a heavy strain particularly on coal (18 per cent below 1938) and power. The volume of exports at the end of the year was 11 per cent above 1938, and the balance of payments better than expected. Building was not far short of pre-war. This progress looked good, but it was rarely remembered that there was 15 per cent unemployment in 1938, so that national output would have to be about 10 per cent above 1938, with infrastructure to match, to provide a reasonable economy.

229. Part IV set out the situation in 1947:

We have hardly enough resources to do all that we *must* do. Whether we reckon in manpower, coal, electricity, steel or national production as a whole, the conclusion is unavoidable. To get all we *want* production would have to be increased by nearly 25% . . . The Government has examined the national needs for 1947, and has decided that first importance must be attached to payment for imports and to basic industries and services, particularly coal and power.

The situations in each of these critical sectors, and the Government's comments and targets on each, were set out frankly and at length. At the crucial stage in each of them, it was clear that the Government was not in control. The recommendations were hortatory. The coal programme depended 'above all' on increased output per worker, and then on the achievement of fuel economies (with no indication of how this was to be done, by price or by new controls). Allowance was made for increased building labour, with timber supply increasingly critical. Most cases depended on more labour, but the Government had no means of getting labour into the required places.

230. No attempt was made to conceal the fact that 'the Emperor had no clothes'; and no-one could reasonably criticize the Government for failing to develop at a moment's notice such a mix of specific and general policies and the political authority and administrative power to carry them out. But if they had started both with the politics and with building the administrative machine in 1945, the resistance to the 1947 crisis might have been more effective.

Import Programme July 1947 to June 1948

231. In April, Ministers had to get to grips with imports and the balance of payments for the period between mid-1947 and mid 1948. Apart from the rate at which the Loans were being exhausted, our convertibility operation stood for mid-July, and the scale of the loss could not be forecast. The BPWP (Balance of Payments Working Party) arithmetic was as follows:

Table 6. UK Current Account 1946–1948 (£m)

	Actual 1946	Actual 1947	Programme mid-1947–mid-1948
Imports (f. o. b.)	1082	1560	1770
Exports and re-exports (f. o. b.)	− 920	−1146	−1270
Government (net)	323	149	150
Invisibles	− 190	− 121	− 100
Deficit (+) or Surplus (−)	+ 295	+ 442	+ 550

The following are the relevant points:

(a) increase in food and raw material prices (10–15 per cent);
(b) fuel crisis had cost about £200 million; and winter weather had heavy cost in agricultural output;
(c) the dollar deficit was put at about £650 million, which would in effect absorb by mid-1948 the whole of the rest of the United States and Canadian credits.

232. The effect of (c) would have left us in such an impossible position in 1949, dependent solely on our reserves, that the Treasury felt bound to recommend really drastic cuts in the hard currency import programme − £200m, of which £150m would be food. It recommended also that the export target of 140 per cent of 1938 volume, to be reached by end-1947, should be altered to 140 per cent by the second quarter of 1948 (in spite of the winter delays). The Treasury's essential point was that unless these proposals were accepted, we would not be able to sustain a tolerable level of imports after mid-1948.[8]

233. At the first round of Ministerial discussion the £150m food cut was reduced to £100 million. Then followed controversial discussion by Permanent Secretaries, in which the majority favoured the £100m cut, though some thought it would damage industrial morale and productivity.[9] It was decided to recommend that the Americans should be told at once that the intention was to cut food imports on this general scale; to ask for relief on non-discrimination; but not to ask for assistance. In the end, by the end of June, the

£150m hard currency food cut had come down to £50 million; so that the total import-saving was £100 million, and a general deficit for 1947 of about £450 million was to be expected; and from the middle of 1948 there would be very little left except our gold and dollar reserves to cover our hard-currency imports.

Second Half of 1947

234. For those in Treasury Chambers, the first half of 1947 (apart from getting more sterling balances under control) had been very unsatisfactory, with this long argument about the balance of payments, leaving us completely at risk in 1948, and with the total failure, marked by the Economic Survey for 1947, to get the manpower and productivity situations manageable.

235. In order to begin to make some headway, and to lead towards some progress in 1948 — or more strictly to avoid new critical dilemmas in 1948 — a series of operations for the second half of 1947 was essential:

(*a*) maximum help for and pressure upon the Americans, French, etc., to get the possible Marshall Plan created, and in a form suitable for UK and the sterling area. [It was Sir Richard's intention to discuss the Marshall Plan separately in succeeding chapters. Ed.] ;

(*b*) settle convertibility, non-discrimination, and other things related to our Loan Agreement obligations;

(*c*) whether or not or when we get some US aid we must strengthen dollar position, increase productivity and reduce military expenditure;

(*d*) develop our technique for bilateral trade relations;

(*e*) 1948 dollar and non-dollar import programmes.

Convertibility

236. Our obligation to make current sterling convertible had become effective on 15 July. There had been argument whether we should seek American release, but Ministers decided against, because this would be likely to lead to Congressional argument, and in any case new conditions might be imposed. However, with the rapidly accelerating world dollar shortage, this situation could not be sustained, and on 20 August there was no alternative to telling the Americans of default. Eady did this with great skill, and Snyder was persuaded to be very helpful. Only the last four $100m tranches had to be left in abeyance.

237. Likewise with non-discrimination, it was utterly impracticable to sustain our obligations in conditions of dollar shortage – otherwise we could do no trade at all. The Americans could of course see the weight of this; their main preoccupation was that we should continue to support ITO (International Trade Organization), and they seemed to be favouring a transitional concept. However, as Marshall Aid came along, some of these concepts tended to change.

Further Internal Action

238. Meanwhile, in an attempt to push the internal situation forward, further measures were announced by the Prime Minister in a State of the Nation debate. This concentrated on increased productivity, particularly coal, steel, agriculture, textiles, etc., and building resources were to be devoted to special industrial priorities such as agricultural houses. All purchases of US food were stopped.

Bilateral Agreements

239. The change to a bilateral system of trade and payments turned out to be easier to accomplish than expected. The essential was to set up an interdepartmental committee (under Leslie Rowan) drawn from the departments concerned with the particular negotiation, as a team, working very fast and only rarely requiring special Ministers' approval. There were literally scores of countries to be dealt with, each in its particular way, and the one fatal course would always be to waste time or fail to be decisive.

1948 Dollar and Non-Dollar Import programmes

240. The dollar and non-dollar programmes had to be treated separately, notably to get the dollar import decisions taken. The combined arithmetic was as follows:

Table 7. UK Current Account 1947–1948 (£m)

	American[10] Continent	Sterling Area	Rest of World	Total[11]	1947 Actual
Imports (f. o. b.)	519	603	434	1595	1560
Exports and re-exports (f. o. b.)	−275	−724	−553	−1552	−1146
Government (net)	21	86	− 10	105	149
Invisibles	17	145	38	− 130	− 121
Deficit (+) or Surplus (−)	+282	−180	− 91	+ 18	+ 442
(Rest of sterling area)	[88]	[180]	[56]	[318]	

241. The dollar programme as set out would leave gold and dollar reserves of £445 million at the end of 1948. But this assumed that the Americans would release the frozen £100 million credit and that the IMF had allowed us to draw a further £80 million in 1948; whilst the Cabinet had decided on a further £175 million dollar saving from the original total — food, raw materials, petroleum, tobacco, Government expenditure. For the food, it would be necessary to cancel the long-term contracts (e.g. Canadian bacon); to store the food for consumption later; or to sell the food.

242. The 1948 non-dollar balance of payments plan, produced in November, is more complex, but its essence was straightforward — to increase exports to, and reduce imports from, sources costing dollars; developing non-dollar sources of supply; not to restrict imports more than necessary, etc. For the year, it was expected that there would be a surplus with the rest of the sterling area and the rest of the world about equal to the deficit with the Western Hemisphere.

243. It is fair to say that the progress made in the second half of 1947, both in decisions and in procedures, was the best that had been made.

Machinery of Government

244. Throughout 1947, there had been intense dissatisfaction with the 'planning' machinery. Mr Morrison had been unable to grasp this work, and when illness overcame him in January 1947, there was strong opinion for a change. Sir Stafford Cripps took on much of the job, as for the Economic Survey for 1947. At much the same time, Sir Edwin Plowden came in as Chief Planning Officer, with a team predominantly of civil servants; and this was beginning to build up some strength. The organization problem continued, and in September Cripps became Minister for Economic Affairs, doing both the 'economy' and the new bilateral lines of policy. So the financial and economic work was divided between the Chancellor and the new Minister. This kind of division could easily be a bad failure, as in 1964, but in fact Dalton and Cripps worked well together, and there was no reason to look for trouble.

245. However, in November came the tragic end for Dalton in his Budget leak; Mr Attlee had to accept his resignation, so Cripps became Chancellor and Minister for Economic Affairs, in machinery of government which continued successfully until 1964 under eight Chancellors of the Exchequer.

Notes

1. The figures are not all precisely comparable from one review to the next, because of definition changes made for convenience in handling. The total 'actual' is taken from the Red Book, *United Kingdom Balance of Payments 1946-1957* (HMSO, 1959) so that it is strictly comparable with the 'actual' for 1947 from the same source.
2. Dalton, op. cit., p. 106.
3. [The document is dated 20 February 1946. An appendix headed 'Relevant facts on rejection' is reproduced as Document 13. Earlier minutes, including an exchange with Lord Keynes, are reproduced as Documents 10-12, and a further exchange with Keynes is reproduced in Documents 14-16. Ed.]
4. Dalton, op. cit., p. 194.
5. I hope Lord Shinwell will not regard it as improper for me to record an incident which took place in one of these. The Ministers were considering various possibilities for making better use of the national manpower, and Mr Shinwell was suggesting that more effective use could be made of prison labour. He recalled that 'when I was inside in World War I, I used to spend all my day riddling ashes'. Mr Dalton boomed out immediately 'A very suitable occupation for the future Minister of Fuel and Power.'
6. One important decision was taken at this time, which was to tell the Greeks that we were stopping our subsidy at the end of March — a measure which showed the Americans that the British were unwilling to go on accepting political financial commitments which did not clearly and obviously represent British interests. This may have been one of the first steps in creating the governmental and congressional opinion which led to the Marshall Plan.
7. [The paragraph reads:- 'Our methods of economic planning must have regard to our special economic conditions. Our present industrial system is the result of well over a century's steady growth and is of a very complex nature. The decisions which determine production are dispersed among thousands of organisations and individuals. The public is accustomed to a wide range of choice and quality in what it buys. Above all, our national existence depends upon imports which means that the goods we export in return compete with the rest of the world in price, quality and design, and that our industry must adapt itself rapidly to changes in world matters.' Ed.]
8. [The Treasury's proposals are given in the memorandum reproduced as Document 19. Ed.]
9. At a later meeting to discuss the health and nutrition implications, Sir Wilson Jameson of the Ministry of Health scored a notable success, leading me to believe that one always needed for this kind of 'expert' work in public life a Scottish pipe-smoking doctor. I had some doubt that his nutrition figures were wholly consistent with the import figures but it would have been unwise to make a controversy, for he was carrying all before him with his pipe.
10. This was now used instead of 'dollar area', to simplify the geographical definitions for the Marshall Plan work.
11. Including certain items which could not be geographically allocated.

DOCUMENTS

Table of Contents

I Wartime Documents

1. Letter on the planning of weapons production from Jean Monnet, British Supply Council in North America, to Hon. T. H. Brand, War Cabinet Offices, London, 1 July 1941

Dear Tommy,

The aim must be that plans be laid down now for the production some time by the end of 1942 of sufficient weapons, tanks, planes etc. to exceed the German material strength without any doubt whatsoever.

I.   This requires:-

    (a) knowledge of the production now planned in the U.S.A. and Great Britain until the end of 1942

    (b) estimate of what is the "matériel", planes, tanks, etc. that it is necessary to produce by the end of 1942 to exceed the German "matériel" strength.

A new programme of production will be deduced from these two statements.

II.   This new programme will necessarily depend on U.S.A. production, since we must assume that Britain's production is already geared to a maximum.

This new programme to be achieved in the U.S.A. will require:-

    (a) that adequate dollar appropriations either Army or Lease-Lend be obtained in time

    (b) that adequate steps be taken to lay down effectively now the production plans necessary.

III. The allocation of the weapons to the U.S.A., Great Britain or such other as will have to man them will be planned later, in the light of the strategic and other circumstances.

It is essential to note that the problem is approached from the point of view of "What is the matériel necessary to have by the end of 1942 to exceed Germany's matériel strength?", and not "What is the matériel that can be manned by England or the U.S.A.?".

It is essential to keep the whole question on this basis, as no proper answer can be given at this time to how and who will man the weapons.

We assume and believe that the U.S.A. will be in the war in 1942, and thus will have as their objective to defeat Germany, while for the moment the U.S.A. General Staff make their plans not on that assumption, but in compliance with the instructions given to them by Congress and the President that they must plan to arm X men. Thus, the weapons are now planned to be produced to arm X men, and not the weapons that need to be produced to defeat Germany.

The question of who will man and how will the weapons be manned will certainly find its answer from the circumstances in the course of the next few months, but to try to answer it now is to defeat the objective in view. Also, since weapons take so long to produce, it is vital that plans for production be made and begun now so that weapons are available when circumstances will force an answer to the question of who will man them.

Therefore meanwhile, the only question to debate now is "What is the production of weapons, tanks, planes etc. necessary by the end of 1942 to exceed the German matériel strength without any doubt whatsoever?", and when the answer has been given to this question the job is to set the U.S. industry to plan producing what is not already planned for in England and here.

. . . .

With a view to ascertaining the programme of deliveries of weapons between now and the end of 1942 as now planned to be produced in the U.S.A., England and Canada, Secretary Stimson has asked that a consolidated balance sheet be drawn up promptly. Copies of his instructions to the U.S.A. administration and his request to us have been telegraphed to London. The work is in progress here and, given a fairly prompt answer from London, a full statement should be at hand very soon.

As regards the estimates of what weapons are necessary to exceed by the end of 1942 the matériel strength of Germany, I understand that it is Secretary Stimson's intention to request us to obtain it from the British Government. In anticipation of this, our intention is to hold to-morrow a joint meeting of the Strategic Committee with adequate members of the Supply Council for the purpose of setting on foot a preliminary study based on the material at hand, enabling us to make to London a recommendation promptly after Stimson's request is received.

. . . .

How are these requirements going to be financed? Obviously, by new Lease-Lend and/or Army appropriations.

As far as new Lease-Lend is concerned, we have been asked by General Burns of Hopkins' office to prepare the list of requirements that we wish to have financed under these new appropriations.

We have deliberately delayed passing this request to London because we knew of the developments sponsored by Stimson and explained above, but were not in a position to inform you officially. We con-

sidered that if we asked London simply to express their new requirements for inclusion in a new Lease-Lend, we would only put to them a
part of the picture, since Stimson's new demands change completely the
basis on which London is asked to consider its new requirements; also,
that what part may be financed by Lease-Lend and what part by Army
appropriations will, we hope, be determined by the Americans themselves.

Also you must bear in mind that the amount that the Administration
will apply for under Lease-Lend will not necessarily reflect the dollar
value of the full programme we shall put forward.

Any new Lease-Lend application is a political move, and thus subject to all the limitations inherent to such move. The programme of
weapons necessary to defeat Germany must not be subject to limitations
coming from such considerations. That is why we are encouraging Mr
Stimson in his approach to the problem. If he succeeds it will result
in defining a programme the production of which is vital, and which will
then not be limited by Lease-Lend considerations. It should, and I
believe will, then be financed partly by Lease-Lend and partly by Army.
In other words, this procedure should disassociate Lease-Lend
appropriations from our real needs. On the one hand there will be a
programme of full requirements <u>not necessarily</u> British – but of requirements necessary to <u>defeat</u> Germany. On the other, will be new Lease-
Lend appropriations with which the U.S. Administration will finance
such part of the requirements as they consider politically possible.

It is along these lines that we are working. You have in London
Campion and Vogel; each know a great deal of the background and
understand fully our objective. Will you please show them this letter
and advise me as soon as you have received it so that from then on we
can discuss the matter on the telephone.

Morris Wilson will telephone privately to the Beaver[*] advising him
in advance of Stimson's request for the balance sheet, so that the
Beaver understands and appreciates that it is not to satisfy an
administrative statistical mania, but a way to obtain promptly the
increase in tank production which he wants.

Purvis is away for a few days which he badly needed, but will be
back on Monday.

I will write further on the production aspects of this new enlarged programme. But for the moment let us concentrate on defining
our goal.

Yours ever,

(Signed) Jean /Monnet7

---

[*] i.e. Lord Beaverbrook.

2. The Treasury View on Sterling Liabilities in 1944

[This note is taken from the briefing prepared in advance of the Stage II negotiations in Washington in the autumn of 1944 and formed part of Annex A to British Requirements for the First Year of Stage II (Gen 43/40, 23 October 1944). The full detail of sterling liabilities by country has not, however, been reproduced. The note develops the reasons why 'we cannot agree to borrow outside currencies in order to make sterling war indebtedness available to buy exports from outside'. Ed.]

1.   The grand aggregate of the net liabilities (i.e., after deducting similar British assets abroad) amounted to ₤11,223 million at the 30th June, 1944, compared with ₤8,588 million a year earlier. This can be broken up into the following main groups, certain of which are clearly much less burdensome in the near future than others:-

₤ million

(a) United States and Canada (including governmental
     loans)   1007.2

(b) The Special Account Balances owing to South
     America and Neutral Europe (including Portugal)   737.2

(c) The Balances of the Sterling Area Dominions
     (Australia, New Zealand, South Africa)   633.2

(d) The Balances of the major Sterling Area countries
     the currency reserves of which we hold (India,
     Egypt, Eire)   4939.2

(e) The Crown Colonies and Mandates the currency
     reserves of which we hold   2376.0

(f) Certain Allies and others which do not normally
     keep substantial balances in London (including
     Iraq)   1390.4

2.   The chief difficulties in the early post-war period are likely to arise from the last three categories above. All these countries will seek to spend their sterling balances on a considerable scale as soon as goods and shipping are freely available, in so far as they are free to do so. Under the existing arrangements, the countries in the sterling area are free to spend their sterling balances anywhere in the Sterling Area without restriction, and to obtain external currencies on condition that they are required for essential goods which cannot be obtained from the Sterling Area. It is only the shortages of goods and shipping which have made it financially possible to continue these arrangements unchanged during the last three years, and it is not anticipated that a similar latitude to spending sterling balances outside the Sterling Area can be continued much longer. On this assumption, and provided the Sterling Area countries are prepared to continue to sell their exports to the United Kingdom on the present basis, no acute financial problem will arise in the early period. The balances will have to be repaid, as and when it becomes possible, through British exports. Thus the existence of the above large volume of sterling balances affects the financial position of the early post-war period much more because they affect the amount of the further sums

which the United Kingdom can afford to borrow, than because the United
Kingdom can be called upon to repay these monies immediately, since in
the nature of things this is impossible.

3.   Nevertheless, there must be some exceptions to the restriction of
the use of the abnormal balance. The members of the Sterling Area have
placed at the disposal of the London Exchange Control all their earnings
of external currencies, more particularly dollars. Moreover, the
majority of them have entrusted the whole, or nearly the whole, of their
currency reserves to London, thus enabling the British Government to
pay their way over a considerable part of the world in terms of paper
backed by sterling Treasury Bills in London. When the holders of this
paper are again in a position to purchase goods, there will be a heavy
moral responsibility on the British Government to do anything which
lies in their power to operate the above system with as much moderation
and as much regard to the freedom of international trade generally as
is financially possible. Some part of the British gold reserves,
though in present circumstances it may have to be a very small part,
must, therefore, be regarded as available for the use of the rest of
the Sterling Area. Equitable and satisfactory means of allocating the
amounts, if any, which may turn out to be available when we know the
size of our reserves at the end of Stage II have not yet been worked
out. Those Colonies which are not themselves substantial dollar
earners, and the entire currency reserves of which have been accumulated in London, would seem to have a particularly strong claim to any
ration of gold or dollars which can be spared.

4.   It is not the purpose of this memorandum to offer, or to debate,
the ultimate solution. Nevertheless there are certain general
principles to which we must hold henceforward with the utmost resolution, if we are to face realistically the consequences of the overseas
financial policy which we have adopted during the war. We do not
intend to seek outside assistance in meeting the war debts which we
have incurred to the other Sterling Area countries and to neutrals.
We propose to meet these over a period of years in the shape of British
exports and perhaps, to a small extent, by a further disposal of our
pre-war investments in their territories. But we shall ask those
concerned to agree that, in view of the origin of the debts, the
interest element shall be reduced to a minimum or altogether exting-
uished. That is to say, it is the capital sum which we shall endeavour
to repay. Furthermore, subject to only minor exceptions, repayment
must take the form of direct British exports, additional to what we
need to pay for necessary imports, and cannot take the form of free
exchange, of which we see no prospect of possessing a sizeable surplus
in the foreseeable future. The abnormal war balances can be made
available to those who own them only by instalments and only subject
to these conditions. During the transitional period we hope to be able
to allow certain transfers of indebtedness between our creditors within
the Sterling Area. But in general we cannot agree to borrow outside
currencies in order to make sterling war indebtedness available to buy
exports from outside. For we should have no sufficient expectation of
being able to repay such loans. All this is rooted in the inescapable
necessities of the case.

5.   It has been indicated above that the willingness of the United
Kingdom to borrow will be a limiting factor, as well as the willingness
of other countries to lend. The United Kingdom have already entered
into obligations for the purposes of the war on so vast a scale that

their capacity of repayment even over many years will be gravely
strained. It is not the intention of the British Government to enter
into further obligations on a scale or on terms which might jeopardise
the security of ultimate repayment of the capital, either of existing
or of subsequent loans. Even if the interest element can be kept down
to an insignificant figure, this consideration may well impose a
narrower limit on the aggregate of future credit facilities than is
set on the other side of the account by the willingness of lenders to
lend. The British Government are determined not to borrow more or on
more onerous terms than they have a reasonable expectation of being
able to repay over a term of years.

---

3. Towards a Balance of Payments

[This memorandum by Sir Richard is headed First Draft but does not appear to have
been revised subsequently. Its preparation before the end of the war in Europe was a
remarkable *tour de force*. In the light of after events Appendix B is of particular
interest. Ed.]

We must become able to pay our way by the end of the transition.
Between now and the end of Stage III we shall require to borrow heavily
from North America and from the sterling area. But if we have not
restored our external financial equilibrium by the end of this
breathing-space, we shall be on the slippery slope which leads either
to open and humiliating dependence upon the United States or to a
desperate and terribly costly last-minute attempt to wrench our
economic structure into an entirely new shape. We have three or four
years in which to mould the economic structure so that it will stand
in the post-war world. There is no reason to suppose that the normal
working of events will bring us back to equilibrium; decisions are
being taken daily by Departments which may make the whole task much
more difficult.

This paper is a tentative attempt to set out a programme for
reaching the objective. It begins with an appreciation of the main
elements in the post-war world economy; it continues with an analysis
of the United Kingdom's position and prospects in that background; it
concludes with suggestions for long-term and immediate policy
accordingly. Much of this paper may appear speculative, but if we
stick to solid audited fact we cannot begin to think about the post-
war world; we really have to decide now what is possible and what is
impossible, and this involves some intelligent guessing. There are
pitfalls in this, but they are nothing compared with the danger of
working on implicit and unstated assumptions which are in fact wholly
impossible.

I - POST-WAR VOLUME OF WORLD TRADE

1. The first task is to get the most realistic picture possible of
the world background in which the British economy will have to work.

There is considerable division of opinion on this. The Americans are
very bullish. At the Inter-American Conference in Mexico in February,
Mr Clayton committed himself to the statement that within a few years
after the end of the war the volume of international trade would
"expand considerably higher than pre-war levels". Others, however,
expect that the autarkic development of the pre-war decade will be
resumed in the post-war period, perhaps even with greater intensity
than before. This depends only partially upon policy decisions which
are still unknown and it should be possible to narrow down the possible
range of alternatives quite appreciably.

2.   The experience last time is of some limited use. World trade began
again in 1920 and 1921 at a level about 25% below 1913. A rapid
expansion followed; the 1913 level was regained by 1925 – six years
after the Peace – and trade swept on to a peak in 1929, some 25% above
pre-war. During this period trade increased fully as fast as world
production and its rate of growth was literally unprecedented. In the
slump the volume of trade fell momentarily to 5-10% below 1913, but
there was very marked recovery and the level of trade in 1937 was, in
fact, better than in any year in history except 1929. In the period
between wars as a whole, trade was never better than 25% above 1913
but it was never as bad as 10% below 1913. The increase in the
'twenties was extremely good; the 'thirties, in terms of volume of
trade, were by no means as bad as they are frequently painted.

3.   In this post-war period there will be four fundamental determin-
ants of the volume of world trade which are related but which are,
nevertheless, independent in the sense that they depend upon different
types of decision by different groups of people:-

   (a)   Level and stability of U.S. national income.

   (b)   Rate of economic growth of middle and low-income countries.

   (c)   Rate of recovery of the European economy.

   (d)   Extent of restrictions and autarkic practices.

No other factor affecting world trade – apart, of course, from political
security – is in the same class as these. The first three are the
springs of world trade; the fourth determines whether the channels are
clear or blocked.

4.   The level of U.S. national income determines the volume of U.S.
imports and is related to the volume and stability of U.S. foreign
lending. The Americans will certainly have grave difficulties in
maintaining a high level of income. But they must have learnt something in the last few years and it is unlikely that in any circumstances
they will have worse unemployment than they had in the late 'thirties,
say 1935-1938. At the other end of the scale they are unlikely to have
more than momentary full employment. The Department of Commerce
defines full employment as a gross national product of $175 billion
(the present rate is $200 billion). It seems safe to assume that their
G.N.P. will fluctuate between $100 and $150 billion and there will, of
course, be a secular upward tendency as their productivity and working
population increases. Translating this into imports by a Department
of Commerce formula we find that their volume of imports will not fall
below 1937 (i.e. $3.6 billion) and may be $1.8 billion above 1937 (all

at present prices). It is perhaps worth noting that the Department of Commerce estimates that sweeping tariff reductions could increase imports by about one-sixth (i.e. by between $0.6 and $0.9 billion). The size of the U.S. national income, therefore, means much more for world trade than the height of the U.S. tariff.

In order to get a high national income the U.S. will have to lend abroad; I cannot see how they can modify their economic structure to the extent needed to mop up their whole productive power for the home market. The Department of Commerce reckons that they can lend abroad $3 billion a year; private estimates of the amount of foreign lending they will have to do to keep a large national income, are higher. The $3 billion figure would mean about the same size of lending in relation to the volume of world trade as that of Britain, France and Germany, in the golden decade before the last war. Lending on this scale is all to the good, but when one remembers the results of the sudden cessation of U.S. lending (only half a billion dollars a year) in 1930 and 1931, one's feet tend to freeze. However, this is a risk which has to be run; the Americans have got to work on the principle that if they ride their bicycle fast enough they will neither fall off themselves nor throw off all the others who are riding on the step.

5. The rate of economic growth of middle and low-income countries – i.e. the whole world outside North America, U.K., Western and Northern Europe and Australasia – is of rapidly growing significance. Industrialisation and capital development is in the air; the example of Russia (and Japan) is irresistible. Southern and Eastern Europe are due for rapid development, but Russia's attitude to this (which will be largely decisive) is yet unknown. Latin America and Middle East will develop their resources and India and later China will not be far behind. This urge for capital development is becoming a sociological fact, greatly stimulated by the war. The populations in all these countries are increasing fairly fast and the countries are getting a sufficient degree of political coherence to enable capital development to take place. There are large dollar (and sterling) balances which these countries hope to use for this purpose and in any case there will be U.S. foreign loans.

The effect of this upon world trade depends upon how the development is done. The Russian development has, of course, increased trade very little; the Japanese, on the other hand, increased it tremendously. In any case it is likely to lead to increased world trade in raw materials and capital goods but it may easily choke off world trade in manufactured goods very considerably. This depends upon the policy of the development. If the right balance can be maintained between finance from home and foreign sources and if these countries can be persuaded not to tilt their development in directions where there are great world surpluses of industrial capacity, the scale of possible expansion of world trade is really stupendous. Many of these countries, however, have a passion for self-sacrifice; the Birla plan for India, for example, aims at capital expenditure of £7,500 million in 15 years of which only £2,000 million would be derived from abroad – a lay-out which would probably force the unfortunate Indians into quite unnecessary sacrifices equivalent to those of the Russians and Japanese. This is not a problem of trade restrictions in the normally accepted sense; it is a question of guiding capital develop-

ment and of persuading the leaders of these countries of what is the
best thing in the common interest.

It seems probable that by the end of Stage III these countries will
be importing appreciably more than they did before the war; in general
they have the money to do so. It is possible to put an upper limit on
the extent to which they will be able to go on increasing their
imports. Since the beginning of this century Japanese imports have
increased in volume at a very steady rate of 5% per year - i.e.
doubling every 15 years. This is also the same rate of expansion as
that of U.S. imports in the great period between the Civil War and the
end of the last century and of Swedish imports during the Swedish
industrialisation from the 'nineties to 1914. It is most unlikely
that any country will expand its imports faster· than this however
rapidly it develops, and if the capital development is on autarkic
lines there will be a much less spectacular expansion.

6.   The rate of recovery of the Western European economy is highly
important in the short run. Western and Northern Europe and Germany
before the war imported from outside Continental Europe more than
North America - which shows the weight of imports depending upon their
recovery. Experience of the last war is of little value here but we
can get a line on the worst possibilities from the greatest economic
collapse of all time - that of Russia in 1918-1921. In this awful
period industrial production fell to 20% of pre-war; agricultural
production to 50%; the transport system was literally destroyed,
making communication between different parts of Russia impossible;
millions starved to death; the collapse was total. Yet within five
years the pre-war industrial and agricultural production had been
exceeded, in spite of the fact that the Russians received very little
external help and indulged in fantastic administrative muddle and
experimentation. Western Europe will get a lot of help and the
experience even of the last six months suggests the recovery will be
reasonably rapid. By the end of Stage III indeed one would expect
Western and Northern Europe to be producing and paying for imports at
the pre-war rate and even Germany may recover more quickly from total
breakdown than she did in the protracted process last time. Partition
of Germany could lead to greatly increased food imports to the western
and central segments from outside Europe - provided that these segments were allowed sufficient industrial exports to pay for them.

In the longer view it is difficult to see any spectacular
expansion in the imports of this area. Its population will never be
as great as it was before the war, and although employment is likely
to be reasonably good the course of economic development is not likely
to lead to much increase in imports.

7.   The extent of restrictions and autarkic practices is obviously
important but probably less decisive than the Americans claim.
Certainly in the pre-war decade there was a big reduction in the
proportion of world production which entered into foreign trade. It
is estimated for example, that in 1937 only 12% of the world's production of manufactured goods were exported compared with 17% in 1929.
Much of this decline was attributable to increase in trade barriers
in the generally accepted sense. But much of it also represented

genuine changes in the world economic structure - Russian development, technical changes, altering specialisation, etc. It is difficult to visualise what would have been the effects of a commercial convention on the lines which have been discussed but it is hard to believe that the trade:production ratios would have been maintained at the 1929 level. The Department of Commerce estimates that the most sweeping tariff reductions could increase U.S. imports by about one-sixth. The increase in U.K. from similar action would surely not be anything like as large; no doubt there could be increases in Europe though probably largely in trade between European countries rather than between Europe and the world as a whole. I find it very difficult to believe that the maximum feasible reduction of trade barriers could conceivably yield an increase in world trade of more than about 10% at the outside. Some corroborative evidence is to be found in the fact that if the expansion of world trade had continued at the same rate as in 1900-1913-1929 - a straight line trend - the volume of world trade in 1937 would have been 10% above 1929, whereas in fact it was a trifle below 1929 - a reduction which could be only partially attributed to autarkic practices.

It seems clear, moreover, that whatever commercial conventions nations may sign they will insist upon a prior claim to:-

(i)   Internal employment (high income countries)

(ii)   Industrialisation (middle and low-income countries)

(iii)   National defence and balanced economy

(iv)   Freedom to take action to right major deficits in their balance of payments

This applies, of course, to U.S.A. and U.K. equally with everyone else; hosts of exceptions have already appeared even in bilateral negotiations between U.S.A. and U.K. and it is arguable that in quantitative terms these exceptions already represent the rule. No commercial convention will stand up for two minutes if 3(a), (b) and (c) above do not develop favourably, and we are deceiving ourselves if we think that it will. I am inclined to the opinion indeed that the big dividends in world trade lie in the development of means to bring international influence to bear on internal Governmental decisions on employment policy in the high income countries and capital development in the middle and low-income countries. This is more difficult but may be more profitable than attempts to provide rules for commercial practices where these practices are, in fact, governed quite largely by social and military considerations rather than by pure doctrines of economic cost. This may be a heretical view but it does not, of course, deny the desirability of getting the maximum reduction of trade barriers of the conventional kind. But I would regard any increase in world trade which resulted as a bonus.

8.   From these considerations it is possible to get some idea of the limits within which world trade is likely to develop. The 1937 world imports were as follows in billions of present dollars:-

	⊄ billions
U.S.A.	3.6
Canada	1.0
U.K. and Eire	5.8
Australasia	0.9
*Western and Northern Europe	3.4
*Germany	1.4
U.S.S.R.	0.3
Japan and Colonies	2.0
*Southern and Eastern Europe	1.2
Middle East	0.7
Latin America	2.3
India and Ceylon	0.8
Far East (except Japan and Colonies)	1.5
Africa (except Egypt)	1.8
Total	26.7

*Excluding trade with other Continental European countries.

9. At the end of Stage III – say, 1949 or 1950 – it seems unlikely
in the light of what has been said above that the total trade will be
less than it was in 1937; the main potential negative factors are the
destruction of the imports of Germany and Japan and these should be at
least offset by increased imports into the U.S.A. and Canada. On the
other hand, even on favourable assumptions both of North American
employment, European recovery and the development of importing by Latin
America and other middle and low-income countries, it seems unlikely
that the volume of trade will exceed, say, 15% above 1937. This would
postulate a more rapid recovery than that after the last war – in which
the pre-war level was not regained for six years – and can hardly be
regarded as pessimistic.

10. When we look farther ahead to the end of the first decade after
the end of the Japanese war it is impossible to envisage world trade
at a higher level than 50% above 1937; this would assume very good
employment in U.S.A., something like the maximum possible growth of
imports of the middle and low-income countries (assuming that they
have a large capital development directed in favour of world trade)
and some considerable reduction in trade barriers generally. On the
other hand, it is equally difficult to envisage such bad trade
conditions that by that time world trade will be less than, say, 10%
above 1937. This is the possible scale of development; it does not
narrow the possibilities to anything approaching accuracy and I believe
it would be possible by considerable effort to get a closer picture.
But I believe it does distinguish between what is possible and what is
impossible.

II – THE BALANCE OF PAYMENTS IN 1950 AND AFTER

11. Britain's competitive power has been declining since before the last war – for twenty years before that it was causing concern. The more far-sighted people have been crying "Wolf" for so long that they now have difficulty in getting a hearing. But the facts remain:-

	1913	1924	1929	1937
Volume of trade				
Exports	145	111	120	100
Retained imports	74	80	92	100
Value as % of world trade				
Exports	13.9%	13.0%	10.8%	9.9%
Imports	16.5%	17.9%	15.2%	17.0%
Terms of trade				
Prices of imports in terms of exports	132	107	109	100
Balance of payments (£ millions)	+194	+72	+103	–56

The record is not discreditable. We maintained our share of world imports, and can certainly be acquitted of the charge of restricting imports and exporting trouble. We got our essential imports at a progressively cheaper cost in exports. Admittedly the swing in the terms of trade in industrial countries' favour saved us from acute difficulty; admittedly by 1937-38 we were continually on the border-line of living on external capital. But we had solid assets in social progress to show for our imprudence.

12. Since before the last war, imports have steadily risen while exports have almost steadily declined; in 1937 we had half as much exports in relation to imports as we had in 1913. This has really meant that exports have become a side-line; before the last war, we exported between one-third and 40% of our industrial production, but in 1938 we exported less than one-sixth. The most active and energetic management was devoted to the home market, and as less and less effort and enterprise was devoted to exports, so we got left further and further behind in export design and ideas. Thus our position cumulatively deteriorated, for our imports (particularly of food) were increasing all the time.

Competitive Power

13. Our post-war competitive position will depend upon (i) our real physical efficiency and productivity, (ii) the exchange rate and (iii) the will to export.

(i) The real efficiency and productivity of British industry is surely greater than it was before the war; if the war-time techniques (e.*g.* standardisation) can be held and if the coal, steel and cotton industries can be thoroughly re-equipped, we need not fear. British industry has not improved faster than American, but it has almost certainly improved faster than that of our other competitors. The present criticisms of British industry were as true before the war as they are now. Awareness of the deficiencies is a positive gain, provided that it is translated into action.

(ii) The evidence about <u>exchange rates</u> is inconclusive. During the war, prices of manufactured goods have risen by 25% in U.S.A. and by 47% here, bolstered by subsidies; on paper, the $4 exchange rate should give the same competitive positions as pre-war. But we know that steel prices will be 47s. a ton higher in U.K. (allowing for the latest increase in coal prices), and the removal of subsidies would appreciably raise the British figure. Comparison of changes in hourly earnings, however, gives a "parity" of $4.38. All one can say now is the $4 rate is not yet obviously out of line with the 1939 rate of $4.68.

(iii) <u>The will to export</u> (or lack of it) may swamp the other factors. The decisive question is whether firms are going out for export business or not. In U.S.A., about 40% (sometimes rising to 50%) of the selling price of custom-made machinery and equipment represents overhead and profit; in mass-production industries it is around 30%. These highly capitalised producers can profitably quote for export at 60-70% of the "normal" price. Even if costs are perfectly adjusted to the exchange rate, there may be a 50% difference between the quotation of a firm that wants the business and that of a firm which does not care much. If we have full employment and U.S.A. does not, the implications are rather staggering (cf. the New Zealand hydro-electric contract). This factor has always been more or less present, but it becomes decisive as industry becomes more capitalised and as full employment policy provides a permanently stable home market. The task is less one of making costs (in general) competitive than one of influencing the deliberate policies of large industrial undertakings, making them become export-minded.

My own view is that (iii) presents much more difficulty than (i) or (ii).

Post-War Export Requirements

14. Last July, Mr Meade calculated the required level of exports in 1950. I have amended these to allow for military expenditure overseas, debt service on Lord Keynes's plan, and extra imports resulting from concessions in commercial policy. At prices 60% above 1938, our imports will be about £1,500 millions, our net invisible exports £250 millions, leaving an export requirement of £1,250 millions - two-thirds more than 1938 or 50% above 1937. This calculation gives us the benefit of nearly all the doubts. (Appendix A).

15. It is assumed that the terms of trade will be the same in 1950 as they were in 1938. Last time, there was a big movement in favour of manufacturing countries, followed by another great swing against primary producers during the slump. Certainly during Stage III prices are

likely to favour manufactured goods, but the terms of trade will swing back, and it is difficult to say where the pendulum will be in 1950. This is highly important, for a 10% movement against us would raise export requirements to 66% above 1937, and a 10% movement in our favour would reduce them to 35% above 1937. It turns basically on the relative expansion of output of primary and manufactured products, and it is impossible to assess this yet.

16. At the end of the 1950's, our imports will not be much larger than in 1950; as the national income grows, we shall not buy much more food, and expansion of the big import-consuming industries is unlikely. The increased cost of debt service should be offset by a rise in invisible exports and some fall in overseas military expenditure. On the other hand, if world trade is good, an adverse movement of the world terms of trade is practically certain. By concentrating upon high-quality exports we may avoid the worst effects of this price movement. But it is hardly deniable that we shall require a steady increase in the volume of exports – unless world trade is so bad that the terms of trade move in our favour, in which case we shall not get the increased exports anyway.

17. There should be no difficulty on supply grounds in raising exports by 50% above 1937. Before the war, we exported one-sixth of our industrial production; exports of one-quarter of industrial production (the proportion in the late 'twenties) would be ample. Put another way, it means that only <u>half</u> the increase in industrial production from 1938 to 1950 arising from full employment and increased productivity need be devoted to export. In global terms of manpower and industrial capacity, the quantities involved are comparatively small. There are some difficult spots; we shall never again get near our pre-war coal exports, so that in order to get a 50% overall increase over 1937 we shall require to increase exports of manufactured goods by 60%. Cotton textile and steel exports will be slow to increase until major reconstruction has taken place. Some sections of industry will have to expand capacity furiously, and there may be clashes between the claims of re-equipment of British industry and those of export. But the problem is basically one of producing the right things and selling them.

Our Share of World Trade

18. The pre-war shares of the world's <u>manufactured</u> exports were:-

	% of total	
U.K.	20	
U.S.A.	17	
Germany	17)	mostly intra-European trade
Other Europe	30)	
Japan	7	
Other countries	9	
	100	

We were still the largest exporters of manufactured goods, but in the pre-war decade our share fell from 22% to 20%; the U.S.A. share remained unchanged; the European countries' share fell slightly, and Japan's doubled.

19. We shall draw short-term advantage from the temporary reduction of German and Japanese exports, especially as most other European countries will not be able, even by 1950, to do much extra business. The corresponding loss of German and Japanese imports cuts the other way. The gain may be 10-20% according as the enemy countries' economic revival is fast or slow. In the longer view we cannot hope to hold the bonus. We can properly allow for it in 1950, but we should be unwise to bank on it in the farther future.

20. Except for this temporary gain, we cannot expect to increase our share of the world's manufactured exports. Our share in the world's population and productive power is necessarily falling, and we shall have to work very hard to hold our own. The Americans will be exporting hard, backed by foreign lending and stimulated by the big corporations' desire to keep their vast productive capacity fully occupied. The Western European countries' share will no doubt diminish; their competitive power can hardly be as strong as pre-war unless they re-equip their industry on the most modern lines. Germany and Japan will literally have to export or starve, and will no doubt set a hot pace. Countries which are not now large exporters of manufactured goods (e.g. Canada, India and perhaps even Russia) will want a share.

21. We shall need all the competitive power we can exert in order to hold our share. We have certain advantages. We are well-equipped to supply semi-luxury goods to the expanding North American market and capital goods to the middle and low-income countries; we have unique world-wide export contacts; our distribution of markets is a particularly favourable one for taking advantage of an expanding world trade. On the other hand, one-third of our pre-war manufactured exports consisted of textile products - the first things which industrialising countries produce for themselves and industries which Germany and Japan, kept out of engineering, will develop intensively for export - and one-half consisted of metal and chemical products, in which there will be excessive world capacity unless the rate of world economic expansion is very great. The industrial and geographical structure of our export trade is favourable in a world of rapid economic expansion unless this is highly autarkic. But it is highly unfavourable if world trade is stagnant. Our exports will depend increasingly upon the U.S. national income and the middle and low-income countries' demand for durable goods, both of which are highly vulnerable to depression.

Possible Export Level

22. In the previous section, we estimated that the volume of world trade in 1950 will be at best 15% above 1937 and in the late 'fifties 50% above 1937; on an unfavourable assumption trade will be about the same as in 1937. The trade in manufactured goods may be expected to be better than this in good times and worse in bad; it is more sensitive than trade in food and raw materials. Holding the pre-war share, and allowing for Germany and Japan, we shall at best achieve in 1950 an increase of 40% in manufactured goods and at worst an increase of 15% above 1937. In the longer view to the late 'fifties we may increase our manufactured exports by 60% in very favourable conditions, but in unfavourable conditions we may hardly increase them at all.

23. Relating this to the required 60% increase of manufactured exports, and allowing for consequent changes in the terms of trade after 1950, we find that on the most favourable assumption about world trade our deficit from 1950 onwards would be £125-150 millions a year, whilst on the assumption of stagnancy the deficit would rise to £250-300 millions a year. To better this, we should have to wrench from other countries a larger share of world trade, and I very much doubt whether this can be done without reducing the size of the total trade and thus giving us a larger share of a smaller market. One cannot.be dogmatic about this, but I believe that in the most favourable world conditions we cannot push up our <u>total</u> exports by more than 35% above 1937 (or 50% above 1938), which leads to the deficits above. It is sheer self-deception to pray that we may do more; we shall do brilliantly if we achieve as much.

<u>Reduction of Imports</u>

24. Mr Meade's estimate of 1950 imports, plus an addition for concessions on commercial policy, is £1,525 millions, or £150 millions above 1938 imports. If we could cut our prospective imports by 10% - i.e. reduce them to the 1938 level - we should be balancing our books on the most favourable assumptions about world trade, and we should have gone half way to meet the problem in conditions of stagnant world trade. We should seek to do this by methods which permanently reduce the demand for imports rather than by restrictive practices which would recoil on our own heads.

25. The following are possibilities:-

(a) <u>Food</u>. The Ministers of Agriculture and Food estimate that the maximum expansion of home agriculture would permit the required expansion of food consumption without increasing imports above the 1938 volume. This would save £75 millions on Mr Meade's figures. We must be careful in cutting food imports, for other countries' entire economies depend upon our market; but if we still import as much as in 1938, our suppliers cannot complain.

(b) <u>Petroleum</u>. We could make big economies by tilting the transport structure in favour of the railways - e.g. by letting the railways compete with road transport on even terms. There are also possibilities (not yet, I hope, dead) of refining here, which could save all or part of £30 millions and improve the chemical industry too. Also further development of synthetic oil.

(c) <u>Industrial Products</u>. Imports of raw materials and semi-manufactures were falling fast in relation to industrial production before the war; imports of finished goods changed very little in volume from 1929 to 1937, but a reduction in the tariff would increase them unless the exchange rate was correspondingly adjusted. Certain special structural adjustments are possible:-

(i) Filling gaps in war potential (e.g. a wide range of chemicals, clocks and watches etc.).

(ii) Creating production of other products (e.g. office machinery and others in R.(I.O.)(45)12) which for some reason

have not been developed here. We should welcome foreign
capital and knowhow in these fields, and these industries
should have a specifically limited period of protection.

(iii) Develop U.K. sources of raw material (e.g. timber).

(iv) Discourage relative growth of industries which are
large import-users. The metal and building industries, for
example, import about one-half as much raw materials per
worker as the textile, leather, clothing, paper and printing
industries. This type of consideration should be taken into
account as the structure of post-war industry is moulded
(see Appendix B).

(v) Agreement on specific economies (e.g. agreement with
N.P.A. permanently to limit size of newspapers, very profitably for them).

(vi) Maintain war-time salvage collection, which was very
profitable pre-war for the few enterprising local authorities
who did it.

(vii) Restrict home production and imports of obvious non-
essentials, either by prohibition of certain material uses
(and corresponding imports) or by heavy purchase tax.

26. We could cut off the £150 millions fairly easily without restrictive practices which would be forbidden in any practicable commercial
convention. It is hopeless, of course, if any interference with
laisser faire is ipso facto a restrictive practice - but nobody outside
the U.S. State Department would tolerate this for a moment. If we
acted on these lines, our total imports - now about 20% below 1938 -
would simply never rise above the 1938 level.

Conclusions

27. The upshot is that in the best world trade background imaginable,
and with full competitive power, we cannot hope to increase our
exports beyond 50% above 1938. This leaves a deficit on the post-war
import estimates of £125-150 millions. This can be filled by stabilising total imports at the 1938 volume. If the appropriate measures are
taken to adapt the structure of agriculture, transport and industry,
this is compatible with increased food consumption in U.K., with concessions on general commercial policy, and with avoidance of restrictive practices of a kind which would recoil upon us. We can therefore
reach an even keel provided that world production and trade expands
violently and continuously.

28. If world trade fails to expand, there will be a further deficit -
even after the above measures - of some £150 millions. If the failure
of world trade were attributable to general cyclical depression, this
would be the sort of situation which the Bretton Woods Fund was
designed to handle, and we could justifiably borrow to cover our
temporary difficulties. If the failure of world trade were due to a
failure of world economic growth or to the development of autarkic

practices, this would be a permanent deficit against which we could
not permanently borrow. I see no alternative in that situation to a
full-blooded use of all the weapons in the bilateralists' armoury.

III - IMPLICATIONS FOR LONG TERM POLICY

29. The figures are only illustrative but they show beyond reasonable
doubt that unless we exert great competitive power and world trade
expands with remarkable speed, we shall be forced towards a choice
between perpetual borrowing and a quite unpredictable Schachtian
adventure.

Competitive Power

30. This is not the place to deal with two of the main elements in
competitive power - an increase of physical efficiency relative to
other countries and an enhanced will to export. Both, however, can be
rendered quite abortive by an unfavourable exchange rate. A 10%
reduction of real cost takes quite a lot of getting; the proposed re-
equipment of the steel industry costing £100,000,000 would yield rather
less than this. The simple way to stimulate the will to export, moreover, is to make the relation between home and export prices such that
export business is profitable. We can make stupendous efforts to
increase efficiency and to make industry export minded, but if we have
over-valued sterling - in terms of European currencies and sterling
area currencies as well as in terms of U.S. and Canadian dollars - we
shall not get very far.

31. It is vitally important, therefore, that we should enter the
multilateral world with an exchange rate which at least gives us the
benefit of the doubt. It is against our interest to aim at an under-
valuation of sterling; after all, the lower the exchange rate the
greater the tendency for the terms of trade to move against us and the
harder our physical task. But we must avoid over-valuation. This is
of particular importance because once the rate is fixed we should be
very loth to change it. If we had made any significant part of the
sterling balances convertible before, devaluation would unfairly
penalise those creditors who had continued to hold sterling. Moreover,
it will be very difficult to get multilateral order and to get the
exchange rates of the liberated and enemy countries on to a sound long-
term basis if the sterling-dollar rate is fluctuating at the same time.
We shall be bound in practice to a stable sterling-dollar rate as soon
as we allow convertibility.

32. The difficulty is, of course, that we shall not be able to tell
what is the proper rate until we are well into Stage III. At present,
as we have seen, the $4 rate gives a parity of industrial prices with
U.S.A. which is very much the same as pre-war. I would expect U.S.
internal prices to increase less than ours between now and the end of
Stage III, for our present price level contains a tremendous element
of subsidies and we are much more likely to have full employment in
1950 than the United States; I should think also that our budgetary
problem may be more difficult than theirs. I admit, however, that one

could make an equally strong case for the alternative point of view.
This uncertainty increases the danger that we shall find ourselves
saddled with over-valued sterling. The danger becomes even more real
when we consider that concessions on commercial policy will inevitably accompany convertibility; as a founder-member of the Commercial
Club I doubt whether we could at the outset invoke the escape clause
by which we are allowed to impose import restrictions when our balance
of payments is adverse.

33. I feel very hesitant to suggest what we should do in these circumstances. But we should be a good deal better placed to take these
risks if the rate was $3.50 than we are with the rate of $4. At least
we should surely not leave the Americans under any illusion that the
$4 is something fixed and immutable.

34. It is of course equally important to ensure that rates of
exchange within the sterling area are appropriate. While anything like
a sterling area exists, over-valuation of the Australian £ against $
is nearly as bad as over-valuation of £.

Expanding World Trade

35. What measures can we take to stimulate the growth of world trade?
I am rather sceptical about the possibility of securing the extremer
form of agreement on the rules which shall govern international trade.
In their extreme form these rules run the risk of throwing out the baby
with the bath water. We would surely prefer tied loans to no U.S.
foreign investment at all. The growth of world trade requires great
economic development of backward countries, but few countries in the
past have been able to expand productive power and national income without considerable protection. It is very well to clear out the
channels through which world trade flows but this process does nothing
to create the springs from which world trade is generated, and may
indeed dry them up. In any set of rules, there must be hosts of
exceptions and escape clauses. These might at best nullify most of
the positive gains from agreement; at worst they might lead through
Geneva-like sophistries to an actual increase of trade barriers.

36. At the same time, of course, there are specific benefits to be
gained from hard trading to reduce the U.S. tariff. It is difficult
to know how much we should concede to secure a worthwhile U.S. tariff
reduction; it is possible to get quite a good idea of the additional
exports we could hope to secure from the deal but as far as I know we
have no statistical estimate of the worth of preferences and of
general protection. It seems to me important to think of the exchange
rate in connection with this, for it would obviously be ridiculous for
us to do a deal with the Americans which reduced our tariffs and theirs
and which was followed almost immediately by an increase in our
tariffs - probably above their previous levels - in order to right our
balance of payments. The American public would assuredly claim, in
such circumstances, that they had been sold a pup.

37. Apart from what can be done to reduce trade barriers in the conventional sense we must seek to secure full employment in the advanced
countries and a rapid and non-autarkic economic growth in the middle
and low-income countries. These are the elements upon which world
economic expansion really depends and we cannot afford to leave them

to chance. Something can be done to ensure stability through the proposed International Commodity Organisation and through the I.L.O. The real difficulty, however, is that both full employment and rapid economic growth depend primarily upon decisions on internal policy in the countries concerned. If we are to do anything effective in this very important field we have to devise techniques for bringing influence to bear upon other countries' internal decisions.

38. This kind of influence cannot be brought to bear through international bodies such as the Social and Economic Council. Bodies of this kind are best engaged in the sort of work which was done by the Economic Section of the League of Nations - mainly surveys and fact finding by international officials. The secretariat of the Social and Economic Council will no doubt work on these matters but the result is more or less bound to be a series of academic studies by international officials which will influence the various brains trusts but can hardly do more than that. If a serious attempt were made by the Social and Economic Council to interfere with internal policies this would certainly be treated as interference with national sovereignty. One cannot very readily imagine, for example, discussion at high level on the Social and Economic Council about the measures which the U.S. should take to maintain full employment or about the propriety or otherwise of an Indian plan for economic development.

39. If we are to influence these matters at all we must surely find a new technique for doing so and this will have to be by intimate and informal discussion rather than new constitutional machinery.

40. We seek to ensure that rapid economic growth will take place in the world's backward areas and that this growth will be of a nature which will increase world trade. We could usefully begin with parts of the world in which we already have great influence - the Colonial Empire, the Middle East and India. In all these countries we have large debts and considerable administrative influence and contacts. If we accept the principle that we want to see rapid economic development there we should be able to exert a very great influence upon the structure of that development. We need not overtly use the sterling balances as a weapon; but the fact remains that if those countries want to be repaid in goods they will be very well advised to accept our advice on the general course of their development.

41. We should place great emphasis in all those countries upon the increase of agricultural efficiency and upon the development of transport and electric power. We should tend to deprecate industrialisation for its own sake where adequate world capacity already exists for meeting all conceivable demands. A considerable measure of industrialisation is, of course, necessary and we must, of course, thoroughly endorse the principle of Indian industrialisation. But we should seek to drive from the minds of those who are fascinated by Russia the idea that industrialisation by itself is a panacea. In countries where anything up to 75% of the population is at present engaged upon agriculture the quickest way to increase the national income is to increase agricultural productivity, drawing off the surplus agricultural workers into local industries (e.g. building and development of local material resources) and services (e.g. transport and distribution). We should also seek to dispel the illusion common among

leaders of backward countries that there is some intrinsic merit in
sacrifice; we shall not succeed in this, however, unless we can prove
to them that what we suggest is actually in their own interests as
independent people, and does not represent an attempt at foreign
domination. One need hardly stress the danger to us of autarkic
industrialisation undertaken for its own sake and the advantage to the
terms of trade of a real growth in agricultural efficiency; we have
to show that it is in their interests too.

42. We should aim at getting ten-year programmes for capital equipment
for these development schemes. This would give us a guaranteed export
market and thus a long-term stability in our balance of payments.
Within the Colonial Empire we could ask for schemes for doubling each
Colony's national income in 15 years; in the Middle East and India we
should seek intimate discussion with industrial and Governmental
leaders of their plans for economic development. Something is already
being done on these lines. Much of this would, of course, be paid for
through the funded sterling balances; we should derive great advantage
in addition from the movement of terms of trade resulting from greater
agricultural efficiency and from the increase in normal business
resulting from the growth in national income in these countries. This
would emerge both in visible and invisible exports. It is rather uncertain how far these countries would have to draw capital from U.S.A.
in addition to that provided by the reduction in sterling balances.
It might, however, be to our advantage to borrow from U.S.A. ourselves
and re-lend as necessary; so long as our balance of payments on
current account is in order the essential objections to borrowing from
U.S.A. would not apply and this might be a way round the difficulty
that the Americans have a great deal of money to lend abroad but very
little experience and knowledge of how to lend it.

43. This raises the question of co-operation with U.S.A. and other
countries in the development of middle and low-income countries
generally. We clearly cannot ourselves invest abroad except by paying
off debt. But to the extent to which U.S.A. and other countries
provide untied loans for development purposes it would be well worth
our while to co-operate with them both in order to express our view on
the course of development which is desirable - again emphasising
agricultural productivity - and to get our share of the exports
involved. We might have fruitful co-operation with the Dutch, the
Belgians and the French on such development as they seek to organise
in their Colonial Empires. Similar considerations should be taken
into account in the Bretton Woods Bank loans. What I am suggesting
is that we should take a definite line on the desirable course of
economic development of backward areas, that we should press this
strongly in those areas where we have great influence and that we
should press the same ideas upon others who will become responsible
for such development elsewhere. If we can develop a view which is
genuinely and obviously in the interests of the undeveloped countries
as well as in our own and if we can build up the batteries of advisers
and experts which these countries need, the dividends to British trade
can be very large indeed. This is, indeed, a natural development from
our 19th century position.

44. If we worked closely with U.S.A. in these matters this would give
us an admirable opportunity for also bringing our influence to bear to

get a U.S. full employment policy. During the war we have been very successful in influencing the Americans on purely internal matters. After years of muddle they adopted, in its essentials, the British system of raw material allocation; we helped them greatly to get their regional organisation on the right lines; we had some success in impressing upon them the need for organisation linking the production people with the strategists; we got them to control textiles so that there would be a margin available for export; we have reached the stage of integration of war production programmes at which it is impossible for any item of war equipment to be scarce in one country and plentiful in the other. This was done through the combined organisation; we got our results by sitting in with the Americans day by day, housed in American offices, sending them British Officials for visits and generally by winning their confidence. For certain post-war problems, this kind of technique is already being applied, e.g. the Rubber Study Group.

45. I believe that some sort of organisation of the same kind is possible in peace conditions. It implies more intimate co-operation between ourselves and U.S.A. than some of us would like. There would not be much room for the extremer kind of business secrecy nor for the luxury of conducting a phoney economic war with the Americans. But provided that we get a just settlement of the Stage III problem and provided that we are not permanent borrowers from U.S.A. so that we work with them as equals and not as pensioners, is there any real objection to co-operation of this intimate kind? Surely our interests depend so heavily upon U.S. internal prosperity and a wise use of U.S. external economic power that we should do all we can to influence them, even though this may involve frank discussion with them on matters which we might sooner keep secret.

46. The danger of U.S. depression far exceeds that of failure to maintain full employment elsewhere. But there is considerable advantage to be gained from similarly intimate relations with the Dominions and possibly also between U.K. and Western Europe. Matters of internal and international economic policy impinge upon one another so directly that I cannot see how international organisations to deal with international economic affairs can possibly succeed by themselves. They must be reinforced by a network of much more intimate relationships between the chief Powers concerned. They surely depend upon a close understanding by the chief countries of each other's total economic position and this is possible only in the background of intimate co-operation and interchange of information and ideas which has developed between ourselves, U.S.A., and Canada during the war.

47. These suggestions are tentative, and detailed proposals would require close examination. But I believe that movement along these lines is imperative. The multilateral system can work (from our point of view) only if there is a high U.S. national income and a rapid and non-autarkic economic growth of the undeveloped countries, and we must manifestly do all in our power (even at some inconvenience to ourselves) to secure these. If we are forced into bilateral working, moreover, the need for relations of this kind with the countries in our bilateral system will be even more pressing and urgent.

IV - POLICY IN THE TRANSITION PERIOD

47. If these are the considerations which should govern our long-term policy, a number of fairly clear conclusions emerge for the transition period. Our objectives are to balance our payments on current account and to secure the convertibility of sterling on current account. But our ability to secure the second of these objectives depends upon the willingness of the United States to make a just settlement and upon our collective ability to secure an expansionist framework for world trade. We hope to be multilateral but we cannot be certain that we shall be able to achieve it. It is highly necessary, therefore, that we should maintain the power and apparatus to enable us to be bilateral if events prove this to be necessary. We should do nothing to make a multilateral solution more difficult. But we should also do nothing to destroy our own ability to be bilateral.

48. The most serious danger is the acceptance of convertibility before we have balanced our current payments - or at any rate before we are satisfied that the structural changes in our economy are being made which will enable us to achieve a balance of current payments. This would, indeed, be the slippery slope, for once we give everyone the impression that the exchange problem is solved when, in fact, our economy is under-pinned by North American loans, we shall never be able to get the action which is needed to achieve a balance in our own right.

49. In my view we should concentrate in the next three or four years upon the ultimate objective. During this period we cannot conceivably balance our payments; it would be very optimistic to suppose that in the three years of Stage III we shall get nearer than £1,000 millions to a balance on current account. I cannot see that it makes very much difference whether our borrowing over this three year period is £800 millions, or £1,000 millions or £1,200 millions. The main thing is that at the end of the period we should be in balance. We should surely be unwise to limit our spending abroad during that period if such expenditure would improve our prospects of getting a balance in 1950. We need these years to get the economy into a shape in which it will stand in the post-war world and our policy on day-to-day issues should be determined by that.

50. The basic problem is one of our <u>total</u> overseas economic position; we should, therefore, think less in terms of hard and soft currencies than in terms of imports and exports as a whole. If we are able to balance our overall current payments in 1950, the question of hard and soft currencies will look after itself. Discrimination on currency grounds, both in imports and in exports should therefore be avoided as far as possible. This practice is, in any case, forced upon us by the views of the United States and Canada, for we can hardly hope that they will help us over our immediate difficulties (as they must if we are not to go bankrupt altogether) if at the same time we discriminate against them. We should retain the machinery which would enable us to discriminate, for this is fundamental for keeping prepared for ultimate bilateralism. This means in particular import control, without which exchange control (except on capital transactions) surely becomes impossible. We should be very careful to avoid using this machinery in a discriminatory way. If bilateralism is ultimately forced upon us

it will have been greatly to our advantage to have a clean record.   In
any case North American prices for primary products are perhaps as much
as 50% higher than those of our other suppliers and we shall, in fact,
be able to switch away from North American sources simply on price
grounds.

Import Control

51.   We should aim for balance of payments equilibrium with a volume
of imports equal to 1938. Our present imports (other than munitions)
are about 20% below 1938 in volume. We can therefore allow imports to
rise steadily. This does not mean, of course, that the imports of each
individual class of commodities should be allowed to rise to the 1938
level;   the post-war requirements, however, suggest that total food
imports of the 1938 volume would be appropriate in the total.

52.   Imports of food should be allowed to rise to the 1938 volume as
fast as supply and shipping conditions permit. Imports of raw materials
should likewise be allowed to rise to their ultimate level, (corresponding to the 1938 volume of total imports). During this period, when
we must inevitably borrow heavily, we could hardly justify any other
course either to lender-suppliers or to British public opinion. We
should confine restrictions on the volume of these imports to those
which we wish to impose permanently (e.g. the newspaper complex). When
we come to 1950 we may find that we cannot afford the 1938 volume of
imports;   then would be the time, however, to make a further cut rather
than in the time when our starved economy needs all the supplies it can
get in order to recover its strength and to permit the long-term
industrial and personal effort which will be needed. Austerity should
be exercised more by starving the home market in favour of exports –
which assists our long-term balance of payments – than by a temporary
curtailment of imports which are seriously needed and which will
ultimately have to come. Restriction of imports which we shall need
in 1950 and after serves only to make a small reduction in the amounts
which we have to borrow, may have quite considerable effect upon our
ability to borrow on reasonable terms and is a bad indication of our
expansionist intentions.

53.   In particular we should be sympathetic to imports which would
increase the productive power of British industry. It will be better
in the long run for us to export capital goods in the transition period
and fill up home needs with American machinery – especially where that
is better than ours – rather than using the bulk of our engineering
capacity to supply machinery for the home market in the hope of subsequently developing exports when the home market is sated.

54.   There seems no alternative to quantitative control of imports
throughout the period. Fiscal measures are not nearly elastic enough
for this purpose and operations of control by tariff would require
great increases of certain tariffs which would have a bad international effect. Moreover we shall, in the long run, have to reduce
imports of a number of things which are hardly protected at all,
especially in the raw materials field;   we seek to aim at structural
changes in the economy which reduce the demands for imports so that
ultimately, in conditions of full employment, uncontrolled imports
would not exceed the 1938 volume. Quantitative control is indispensable

for this purpose and, in any case, it is indispensable simply for maintaining our power to be bilateral if the multilateral attempts go wrong. In other words we need to continue import licensing right through Stage II and Stage III. This is, of course, perfectly compatible with the issue of open licences for certain commodities, but it is essential that the whole import programme should be kept under control all the time. The motto is to control imports but to exercise the import control in a manner which enables imports to expand to the volume for which in the long term we can hope to pay.

Export Policy

55. The doctrine is that every export paid for is a good export and that there is no case for discrimination on currency grounds. This certainly requires some interpretation for non-paying countries of which Italy is the most important immediate example. It also requires interpretation for export of capital goods which are not normally paid for in cash. In addition to this there is obvious need for discrimination on commercial grounds, for in a period of shortage of capacity it would be quite wrong to permit certain markets which are the manufacturers' favoured sons to be supplied in full while other potential markets were left without any goods at all. Moreover, the "Export Development Areas" - Colonies, Middle East and India - should be given good supplies of capital goods in order to develop their long-term import capacity.

56. Exports of consumption goods should in general be allowed to flow where the manufacturers can sell them best. It is difficult to imagine circumstances in which we could consider selling them on credit. Nor should we want to discriminate between markets; textiles are the chief example and for as long as they are in acute world shortage the exports will be allocated by the Combined Boards. If anything is so scarce that an allocation between markets is necessary to prevent some markets from being completely starved it is probably as well for this allocation to be done on combined basis. This at any rate saves us from the ill will which would result from a purely U.K. allocation.

57. The distribution of capital goods exports is more difficult. The only sound way to do it is to get a programme, industry by industry, which at one and the same time decides the proportion of home and export orders accepted by the industry and looks after the distribution of exports between various countries. If there is capacity available in an industry after looking after essential home demands and paid export orders there seems to me no reason why orders for non-paying countries should not be considered; a trickle of supplies of capital goods to the non-paying countries would help to get the latter on to their feet again and would keep our foot in the door. I do not suggest that we should do this on any significant scale; obviously such orders would have to rank behind paying orders. Moreover, such orders would have to be against Government or near-Government requirements programmes from these countries. But on the general principle of looking towards 1950 we cannot afford to neglect entirely markets which can ultimately take quite a large quantity of British goods and pay for them. An iron ruling against such exports if we had capacity to supply them seems to me undesirable. The important thing is surely to have a policy for each country and to weigh up the amount which we

can afford to give it, having regard to the capacity situation in the industries concerned and the possibilities of future export development.

U.K. Investment Abroad

58. We shall probably be confronted with many requests to invest abroad - mainly for direct investment by British industry. We cannot in general reject such applications; indeed, in the world-wide economic expansion which is indispensable for our balance of payments, knowhow is an important potential invisible export. If British firms do not invest abroad, the market will in many cases be lost altogether. We shall have to be rather selective, and we perhaps should not encourage British industry to develop foreign subsidiary and associated concerns. But it would be most unwise to reject applications offhand.

59. Even in the long view, there seems no obvious reason why we should not invest abroad, filling the gap in the balance of capital payments by borrowing from U.S.A., provided that our current account balances. In the shorter transition, provided that the quantities involved are fairly small, we should not mind increasing our indebtedness to that extent; this is surely a case in which we should use the transition for our long-term benefit rather than for restricting our foreign payments to the minimum possible. We must enable British interest and knowhow to get in on the ground floor.

60. Rather similar in character are credits for building up the working capital of the British export trade - servicing organisation for vehicles, assembly plants, etc.

U.S. Investment in U.K.

61. Direct investment by foreign firms in U.K. should be assessed not on financial grounds but on industrial grounds. In the long view (which is the important one) such investment is financially detrimental; the foreign-financed undertaking will want to transfer much larger profits than the service which would be required on a Government-Government loan of the same size. It is a very expensive way of easing the immediate balance of payments problem.

62. But in special cases, the advantage of foreign investment here can be very great. In principle, we could properly take the line that such direct investment should be welcomed when it introduces a superior foreign technique and knowhow (whether the industry is an export industry or not). Except in industries which are virtually non-existent in U.K. - so that the investment would effect a permanent reduction in imports - these applications should be resisted if they involved a cartel agreement which would prevent the British subsidiary from exporting.

63. We cannot very well seek to prevent U.S. direct investment in the Colonies and other British export development areas; we cannot restrict such investment if U.K. manufacturers are allowed to do it. But we should, I think, greatly prefer U.S. investment in the Colonies via U.K.; in India on the other hand, some direct investment by U.S. manufacturers might be good both for India and for U.S.A.

Commodity Policy

64. The signs point to good times for the primary producer, unless
there is a collapse of the world economy. Farmers certainly have the
bit between their teeth all over the world, and the general course of
social development will make them even more vocal. This means that in
general - except where there are large world surpluses - there is no
particular reason why we should embark upon projects to shore up the
prices to growers. At the same time, we have a marked interest in
preventing a collapse of commodity prices at any future time. From
the world point of view, prices should not be allowed to fall below
the level at which they bring out new demands, and should not rise
beyond the point at which they choke off demand. The peculiar habits
of primary producers, left to work out by themselves, result in far
greater swings than this.

65. The organisation of primary producers has come to stay (and is
not undesirable in itself). On balance, the wicket is likely to
favour primary producers. This suggests that we may need the international commodity policy to protect consumers (and especially ourselves). The conditions vary so widely from commodity to commodity
that it is difficult to establish general principles. But the
circumstances are such that we may fare better from negotiation than
from the operation of the market; and we should press ahead very hard
with measures to increase agricultural productivity wherever we have
influence to do it. The only hope of keeping commodity prices down in
relation to those of manufactured goods is to lower the costs of
agricultural production very fast.

66. The advantage of this line of approach is that it avoids the main
arguments which are used to induce us to follow the U.S. cartel
policy. If we plump for laisser faire in commodities, we cannot
logically refuse to co-operate in international trust-busting, a
procedure which is designed to perpetuate the situation in which the
export market is the "marginal" market, where cut-throat competition
is waged to the great advantage of the people with the largest home
market on which to throw their overheads, and a procedure which would
also logically prevent us from getting the advantage of U.S. technique
and knowhow.

Commercial Policy

67. In commercial policy, what is surely needed is an extremely simple
international agreement, perhaps on the following lines:-

   (a) Reduction of tariff by, say, one half, with a floor of, say,
   10%.

   (b) Fixing of maximum preferential rates at, say, 10% - i.e.
   permitting a general tariff of 25% and preferential tariff of 15%.

   (c) Agreement not to use quantitative import restrictions or
   export stimuli in a discriminatory way.

   (d) Agreement not to alter importing and exporting conditions
   without first informing other countries which are directly
   affected.

(e) Right of any nation to complain (and be heard by I.C.O.) against any commercial practice by any other nation.

This is of course much less ambitious than the American plan. But I believe that it would give the substance of what is needed. (a) and (b) would be a clear indication of intent to reduce trade barriers. (c) would prevent use of necessary import controls in a discriminatory manner between countries. (d) and (e) would be a powerful deterrent to unduly protective practices; governments wishing to adopt protective practices would have to risk having to explain their reasons in public, and this would greatly strengthen their hand against the interests which called for protection. I.C.O. would not be able to order an individual government to refrain from a practice which had been complained of; but the publicity would make it very difficult for that government to maintain its position.

68. For example, if we were developing a watch industry under agreement of this kind, we should not be allowed to increase the tariff but we could impose an import quota. We should have to inform the Swiss before we did so. They could complain to I.C.O., and there argue that there was already more than enough watch-making capacity in the world, and that this would be a frightful blow to their economy. We could carry on after hearing the argument, but it would be difficult for us to do so, and in fact we should have to square the Swiss first.

69. This general process would greatly discourage uneconomic development; it would do so without setting up rigid rules (each with its escape clause) which could not be policed or enforced. After all, during the war, even the Combined Boards could not order their member countries to do things; they could only advise. I cannot believe that an I.C.O. would have anything like the authority and super-State power which would be required to police rules and permit or forbid the use of the escape clauses. All we shall be able to do, I believe, is to get tariffs down, to prevent discrimination, and to ensure that nations whose interests are damaged by any change in commercial policy have a chance to discuss the matter with the nation concerned before the final decisions have been taken, and have the opportunity to complain to world opinion if nevertheless the change is made.

70. Meanwhile, it would obviously be prejudicial to our chances of getting such (or any) agreement if we increased our tariffs now, and this reinforces the general case for quantitative (rather than fiscal) control of imports during the transition period.

Combined Organisation

71. Finally, before the Combined Boards expire – or are exploded in the outbreak of economic warfare – it would be well to consider what sort of Anglo-North American, Imperial and Western European intimate organisations can be set up to provide co-operation towards full employment and a rapid non-autarkic economic growth of the undeveloped countries on the lines suggested in paragraphs 44–46 above.

Conclusion

72. It may be – indeed, on balance it may be most likely – that whatever we do we shall have to move into bilateral arrangements. The odds against a sufficiently rapid expansion of world trade and a sufficient

increase of British competitive power are rather heavy. But bilateral policy for the U.K. only means in fact having a U.K.-based multilateral group of less than world size, and it is only in currency and import discrimination that there is any difference at all; an expansion of world trade is as important to the bilateral policy as to the multilateral policy; we should need a still more rapid expansion of the export development areas, and still more determined attempts to check adverse movement of the terms of trade; there is a difference in kind, but most of the policy is essential in any case. And in neither event can we hope to survive unless the necessary structural changes in the British economy are made and our current payments brought into balance by the end of the transition period.

<u>APPENDIX A</u>

<u>BALANCE OF PAYMENTS IN 1950</u>

1. Mr Meade's recent estimates for 1950 – say three years after the end of the Japanese war – are as follows, assuming a general price-level 60% above 1938:-

	1938 Actual £m	1938 At 1950 prices £m	1950 At 1950 prices £m
<u>Retained imports (C.I.F.)</u>			
Food and drink	395	632	707 (a)
Materials and semi-manufactures	315	504	514 (b)
Finished manufactures	73	117	117
Tobacco	23	37	37
Petroleum products	45	72	90
Total (inc. parcels post)	858	1,373	1,475 (c)
<u>Receipts</u>			
Exports	471	754	(required 1,165)
Income from foreign investments	200		155 (d)
Net shipping earnings	100	160	120 (e)
Other receipts	22		35 (f)
Total	793		1,475

This calculation called for exports at $54\frac{1}{2}$% above 1938. The following points are relevant:-

(a) Food consumption is assumed 15% above 1938 because of full employment, nutrition policy, etc.

(b) Industrial production is assumed about $22\frac{1}{2}$% above 1938 but it is reckoned that this will have very little effect upon the volume of imported raw materials and semi-manufactures which was falling quite sharply in the pre-war decade in relation to the volume of industrial production. (This assumption requires examination in the light of changes of industrial structure between 1938 and 1950).

(c) The same general level of protection as in 1938 is assumed; if the barriers to imports were reduced to the level of the 'twenties, imports might rise by a further £100 million or so and in order to get the U.S. tariff down we should probably have to make concessions which might be equivalent to £50 million additional imports.

(d) No allowance is made for debt service either on sterling balances or on Stage III loans. At best this will be about £30 million in 1950 rising to £70 million in 10 years.

(e) If we had restored our pre-war merchant fleet by 1950 shipping earnings would be £160 million.

(f) No allowance is made for reparations or for occupation costs; we shall be lucky if these cancel each other out. But there will certainly be big military expenditures overseas the cost of which will depend upon financial arrangements with India, Egypt, etc., but which cannot be safely put much below £100 million (the present figure is £600 million). On the other hand, there is evidence that our pre-war balance of payments figures contained a considerable under-estimate of miscellaneous receipts perhaps even of the order of £50 million.

(g) Exports in 1937 were 12½% above 1938 - a particularly bad year.

2.   The following amendments may thus be made to Mr Meade's figures:-

(i) Taking (c) into account, retained imports would be £1,525 millions, or 11% above 1938 in volume.

(ii) Taking (d), (e) and (f) into account, net invisible exports would be £250 million instead of £310 millions.

(iii) Required exports would thus be £1,275 millions, about two-thirds above 1938.

APPENDIX B

IMPORT CONTENT OF U.K. INDUSTRIAL PRODUCTION

1.   An analysis has been made of the pre-war consumption of imported raw materials and semi-manufactures by various industries. This cannot be exact, but the statistical material available is good enough to ensure that the orders of magnitude are right.

2.   A word of caution is necessary about the interpretation of figures for individual industries. "Imports" in this context mean the materials which the industry imports itself; they do not include the import content of materials which the industry takes from other industries. For example, the imports of the engineering industry include copper wire

and anchors and ball bearings and vehicle parts which the industry imports, but they do not include the imported copper in the copper wire which the industry buys from the non-ferrous metal industry or the imported iron ore in the steel which it buys from the iron and steel industry. The figures for the groups of related industries are thus much more reliable than those of the individual industries.

3. The table relates imports to the employment in the industries:-

Imports and Employment 1935

	Employment ('000)	Imports (£m.)	Imports per worker (£)
Metal Industries			
Iron and steel	539	16.5	30.6
Engineering, shipbuilding, etc.	1,104	14.4	13.0
Non-ferrous metals	122	21.9	179.4
Total	1,765	52.8	29.9
Textile Industries			
Textiles	1,055	78.8	74.7
Leather	50	10.0	198.0
Clothing	536	10.1	18.8
Total	1,641	98.9	60.3
Building and Allied Industries			
Timber	195	18.6	95.4
Clay and building materials	249	3.9	15.6
Building and contracting	502	15.4	30.7
Total	946	37.9	40.1
Other Industries			
Food, drink, tobacco	521	101.4	195.8
Chemicals	194	38.6	199.0
Paper, printing, etc.	409	23.3	56.7
Mines and quarries	845	8.8	10.4
Public utilities	698	4.7	6.7
Government Departments (R.O.F.'s etc)	102	0.4	0.4
Miscellaneous manufactures	183	10.7	58.6
TOTAL ALL INDUSTRY	7,305	377.4	51.6

4. The variation is very remarkable. The capital goods industries, in particular, are very low importers, while the consumption goods industries are in general heavy importers. The differences are so wide that there is obviously tremendous scope for influencing the total demand for imports by influencing the relative size of industries. It is obvious, for example, that we should concentrate effort very heavily upon engineering exports as compared with textile exports.

5.   In particular the table completely disproves the contention that
our imports of raw materials must expand if industrial production expands; it is possible to imagine distributions of industry which would
give equal employment and net output with import requirements differ-
ing by 20% at least. It is surely possible, by tilting the industrial
structure by controls of various kinds, to reduce imports quite
appreciably while permitting importation of materials on open license.

R.W.B.C.

11 May 1945.

---

4. The Sterling – Dollar Exchange Rate: Comments by Lord Keynes on Towards a Balance of Payments

[In paras 30-4 of his Towards a Balance of Payments Sir Richard argued for a post-
war exchange rate 'which at least gives us the benefit of the doubt' and suggested a
drop to $3.50 to the £1 from the current rate of $4 to the £1. This was challenged by
Keynes and gave rise to an exchange of minutes reproduced below. Ed.]

Mr R.W.B. Clarke

I have been reading with much interest your paper on "Towards a
Balance of Payments", which you describe as a first draft. What is
going to happen to it next and what do you mean to do with it?

Generally speaking, I find myself in agreement. The only point
where I am inclined to take a decidedly different view is on the rate
of $4 = £1 as a competitive rate of exchange. I admit that we are still
greatly lacking in data, but my present judgment is that the $4 rate is
more favourable to our position than you are allowing. In particular,
I do not agree with the view you express in paragraph 32 that U.S.
internal prices are less likely to increase than ours between now and
the end of Stage III. It is quite possible that we may be in for a new
cycle of wage increases, but that U.S.A. are in for that I feel quite
sure. I say this, in spite of agreeing with you that we are more
likely to have full employment in 1950 than U.S.

In regard to the rest of the paper, I am, as I have said, in
general agreement. My main criticism would be that one needs to make
a sharper and clearer distinction between the two alternative worlds,
in one of which we shall find ourselves, without, at this point of
time, knowing which one. Or perhaps one should say three alternative
worlds:- the first one, if we have good success in Stage III arrangements with U.S.; the second, if we have some arrangements, but not
fully satisfactory; and the third, if we are unable to secure anything approaching adequate arrangements and have to move, at any rate,
towards Starvation Corner. At present it is often far from clear
which hypothesis you are going on.

In particular, I share your view that in any event we must not be too scared or control too tightly anything which involves foreign currency. We must be prepared to import any up-to-date machinery we need, and we must be prepared to let industry invest abroad in the interests of general expansionism. I am not afraid of this, since these types of expenditure do not come to big money. Our foreign investment in the past has mainly consisted in large-scale loans to governments, where nothing but cash is involved, and a relatively low rate of interest. It is these which we must remorselessly cut out. Industrial and mining ventures and the like and finance associated with exports should be on a different sort of scale altogether. I agree with you that it would be good business to borrow enough abroad, even if the terms are not favourable, to balance such outgoings, rather than to aim at a policy of avoiding such outgoings wherever possible.

(Signed) Keynes

7.6.45.

---

5. Reply by R. W. B. Clarke to Lord Keynes's Comments

Lord Keynes

"Towards a Balance of Payments"

My general intention is to revise it first in the light of comments. If there is agreement on the general line of approach, I shall try to work it into a series of practical things to be done. These would then be taken up with the Departments concerned, preferably via an appropriate inter-departmental body which would be responsible for foreign economic policy as a whole. My own feeling is that it would probably be better to push it this way rather than to circulate it to other Departments in its present form, though there are a number of people outside the Treasury who, I think, could usefully have it when some revision has been done.

I agree that the present draft is too pessimistic about the exchange rate. Some new evidence is available about U.S. unit labour costs which is on its way to you and broadly supports your view about the current position. Coal and steel may be black spots in an otherwise reasonably competitive structure rather than typical items. But one has to be rather agnostic about engineering. On the longer view, I suppose U.S. prices will rise more than ours; of course ours contain a bigger subsidy element than theirs, but it is hardly conceivable that we shall relax controls as quickly as they. But looking ahead to the position when we have made £ convertible, I find it difficult to weigh the long-term relative inflationary tendencies here (with full employment and high taxation) against the under-valuation of £, at the $4 rate which will exist after the initial post-war inflation in U.S.A. The point I was trying to establish was that we should try to have something in hand in the exchange rate when we make £ convertible. You would argue, I presume, that as far as we can now see, the $4 rate will give us this something in hand in, say, two years' time, and I agree that the present evidence points that way.

The present draft does blur the difference between the two (or three) alternative worlds. There is a genuine difficulty of presentation, because there are different sorts of alternative worlds. My criteria of a "good" or "bad" world was the volume of world trade. I took the line that "multilateral" or "bilateral" arrangements were only one element in making a "good" or "bad" world, and that a great many of the things one has to do both to make a "good" world and to give U.K. a favourable place in it, are completely independent of whether the general commercial and financial arrangements are multilateral or bilateral. I argued that multilateralism would help towards the "good" world, but that it was not the "good".

But the draft really takes very little account of the basic U.S.-U.K. problem and the Austerity-Temptation-Justice complex, which is a great deal more radical than the difference between "multilateral" and "bilateral" in the previously accepted sense. I think I shall have to re-examine my draft to make it show clearly how we should proceed towards "good" if we got a reasonable arrangement with the Americans, and how we should proceed to make the best of a bad job if we did not.

R.W.B.C.

11 June 1945.

---

6. Further Comments on the Sterling – Dollar Exchange Rate by R. W. B. Clarke

[The minute reproduced below was addressed to various Treasury officials (Mr Harmer, Mr Rowe-Dutton, Sir David Waley, and Sir Wilfrid Eady) and to Lord Keynes. It appears to have terminated the controversy which, however, re-opened early in 1948 when the Treasury began to prepare a contingency plan and Sterling War Book. Although Sir Richard again expressed his conviction of the desirability of devaluation, the Treasury abandoned all work on the contingency plan in June 1948 and the issue did not come to the surface again until the spring of 1949. Ed.]

Lord Keynes raised the point of the $4 exchange rate on my Balance of Payments memorandum, taking the view that the $4 rate was much less unfavourable to us than I was contending. Mr Rowe-Dutton raised the same point strongly. Sir Wilfrid Eady asked for some more evidence.

The evidence either way is rather scrappy, and it can be interpreted according to choice. Comparison of changes in wholesale prices of manufactured goods suggests that the $4 rate gives about the same parity as pre-war. Comparison of changes in hourly earnings indicates a "parity" of $4.38. For munitions, the relative prices suggest an exchange rate of somewhere between $6 and $7, but this evidence should be disregarded because of the tremendous profit allowed to U.S.

munitions manufacturers. U.S. steel prices are certainly cheaper than ours - 47/- a ton cheaper.

Mr Bareau has sent from Washington some new and very useful evidence - official figures of the course of unit labour costs in 26 manufacturing and mining industries, covering a wide field of non-munitions industry. I have spliced this with U.K. figures for the same industries, and the results are set out in the attached paper.

I think this new evidence supports Lord Keynes's view. It suggests that since 1938, relative unit labour costs have moved in U.K.'s favour by something like 10%, taking account of the change in the £/$ rate. But this excludes the whole metal and chemical field, for which there is not much clue. And our relative coal labour cost has deteriorated by 23%.

As things stand now, I would say that our general industrial cost structure is not unfavourable vis-a-vis the American, at a $4 rate. But there are important sectors - notably coal and steel - which are seriously out of line, and the realities in the decisive engineering group of industries are obscure.

How the relative cost structures will move in the next period is anybody's guess. I suppose in the next two years, the decisive factor is the relative propensity to remove controls on wages and prices (and internal subsidies), and after that the relative propensity to full employment. The former will presumably operate against the $, and the latter against the £.

I think the danger is that we ultimately stabilise at a rate which seems appropriate at the time, but which will over-value £ when U.S. loses full employment while we retain it.

R.W.B.C.

11 June 1945.

II The US Loan Negotiations

7. Financial Policy in Stage III

[This paper by Sir Richard Clarke, circulated in June 1945, before the General Election, needs to be read in conjunction with Keynes's Memorandum on Overseas Financial Arrangements in Stage III the first version of which was circulated on 18 March 1945. Two later versions were circulated in April and May but it was the March version that went to the Cabinet in May. Further modifications were made in July and August and it was the later versions that formed the basis of the discussions and instructions for the Loan Mission in September. I am indebted to Professor L. S. Pressnell for this clarification. Ed.]

This paper is an attempt to make a balance-sheet, rough and ready and incomplete, of the considerations affecting the content and timing of our approach to U.S.A. In particular it considers the outline of a Plan II – not so much as a policy in opposition to Plan I (Keynes' plan), but as a fall-back. Plan I is very closely integrated; if any important part of it fails or is largely modified, the balance is broken; this is both a merit and a weakness. There is a real risk that negotiations of this kind and importance, and for this purpose, conducted in the present circumstances of the two countries, and in the atmosphere of secrecy and leakage which will be inevitable in Washington, must proceed to an inexorable conclusion – like an inter- view between a Bank Manager and a client with a continuing unsecured overdraft. The task of our negotiators will be difficult enough, but they would be under a grievous handicap if they felt that, unless some outrageous condition were introduced, they must in the end sign what was put before them, for the affair was of bitter urgency and there was no alternative plan in sight. They must be in a position to suspend negotiations, or to break off, knowing that there was some Plan II, which could be used to keep us going, and to which indeed we might make public appeal if we had tried Plan I and had failed.

There is also a discussion of the relation between these negotia- tions and the wider field of economic relation with U.S.A., and a brief comment on the preparation of our public opinion for what is involved.

I. Roughly the ingredients of our overseas financial affairs in Stage III are:-

(1) Possession of say £500 m. in gold and dollars – mainly gold. This is our reserve and the reserve of the whole Sterling Area. £250 m. of this must be considered as a War Chest, only to be used in the gravest emergency. Some of the remainder will certainly be used for various purposes. Apart from such possibilities that South Africa will under Plan I give us £50 m. in gold, we may get some offsets to reductions

in the amount, e.g. under the working of the French payments agreement. But we shall be lucky if at the end of the third year of Stage
III, we have £150 m. in addition to our War Chest. We can only
increase this reserve rapidly by selling out to the Americans, either
direct investments in U.S.A., or assets like our half-share in the
Kuwait oil fields.

(2) An estimated deficit on current account at the end of the third
year of Stage III of £1,500 m., of which perhaps £500/600 m. will be
owing to U.S.A. and Canada for supplies during that period. (This is
subject to what is said below about import policy in Plan II.) The
remainder will be an additional debt to the Sterling Area, and to some
non-Sterling Area countries outside North America. (Our debts to other
non-Sterling Area countries are somewhat larger than had been allowed
for in Lord Keynes' paper - but the increase is not likely to be
specially troublesome.) This estimate allows for a substantial
reduction in our overseas military expenditure during the whole of the
3-year period. In paragraph 47 Keynes itemises some of the sums which
are outside his general Plan, and for the present it can be assumed
that they will be taken care of on the lines suggested.

(3) A pre-Stage III Sterling indebtedness of at least £3,000 m. (for
distribution see paragraph 49 of Keynes' paper).

(4) Less measurable but on the horizon, a group of possible claims
from U.S.A. and Canada under Lend-Lease and Mutual Aid, including
stocks in U.K. and other Sterling Area countries, Lend-Lease equipment
with post-war use, and conceivably some "wipe-up" financial payment as
a clearance of "consideration for Lend-Lease". It must also be
assumed that all questions of final adjustments of Lend-Lease finance,
including "consideration", will be covered by Plan I. We ought to
include with this the disappearance of our debt to U.S.A. for the last
war. Probably the U.S. Administration would only seek to make all
these items bargaining counters, but Congress and public opinion in
the U.S.A. could be roused to a more intransigent attitude. It must be
an essential part of Plan I that it wipes the financial slate clean as
between us and the U.S.A.

II. On this basis we can now turn to Plan I. It must first be
stripped of its argument. This is not a wrecking comment. Much of
the grandeur of the Plan is in the argument and its all-round application; it might indeed be grand for us if we can get it all, and just
like that. But we must look at it as it might appear to the U.S.A.
from the other end of the telescope, and also to some of the Sterling
countries.

The first ingredient is a gift from the U.S. Government to the
U.K. Government of £750 m. in dollars or gold, a gift we ask in
justice and they give in justice. Brand thinks we are unwise in relying on the appeal to justice; it might imply a charge of injustice;
he thinks we should appeal to the generosity of the Americans, who are
indeed generous in big things. This is almost the crucial point of
the argument, and on this I am on Keynes' side for four reasons:

(a) It is because any other basis will seem "unfair" to our successors
who in the years ahead have to take up the burden of payment that it

would be dangerous.

(b) Generosity between nations connotes its obverse gratitude; these
are emotions of explosive content to introduce into the relations
between our two Governments over a long period of years - especially
on an affair of money arising out of a joint war.

(c) It is essential to an understanding in the U.S.A. of the facts
of our position and of its development, that we should produce a shock
upon the first impact. Otherwise we will slide at once into the
atmosphere of a loan.

(d) We shall be in a much weaker position in any subsequent negotiations with our Sterling creditors if we are simply discussing an
accommodation, without some principle which has been accepted by the
U.S.A.   .

     If we get the gift, Keynes proposes that we should try to secure
a cancellation of our Sterling debt by about a quarter, the proportion
that $3 billion represents to the total of our Sterling debt, in return
for a grant of convertibility on current account /in respect/ of a
further quarter. He recognises that this formula cannot apply equally
to all the creditors. Waley doubts whether on merits we ought to
extend the formula for cancellation on this scale to any countries
beyond India, Egypt and Iraq. Rowlands advises that we would be unwise
to talk about justice to the Indians because we shall never get past
that point. My own view is that if we got the American gift proposed
by Keynes we should try for its application to practically all the
Sterling creditors starting with the principle of the quarter cancellation as a proper contribution to the war effort, and not much less
important to many of them, towards the restoration of the international
financial strength of the U.K. on which they depend, and then modify in
particular cases as required.

     Despite this, is there any chance that the U.S. Government would
accept the idea on this scale? They would have to go to Congress for
an appropriation - and every piece of muck-raking imaginable would be
on show. Why should we not sell some of our investments? or trade
bases? or anything else. Have not the Americans given us enough, of
life as well as treasure? The arguments can easily be imagined, and
unless the President cuts them all short in advance, they will all be
produced by the familiar timid souls of Washington - the Mr Milquetoasts
of their comic strips, whose family is in every Department in Washington. As against all this - (1) Men who think financially and not
politically, like Aldrich, know, and are publicly saying, that what we
shall need is cancellation of all past indebtedness including Lend-
Lease consideration, a large grant-in-aid, and power to borrow on easy
terms. It may be that as the economic realities of the post-war world
are recognised, the U.S. will want a peg on which to hang some act of
this kind.

(2) If we get it, we make an offer to bring the transition to an end
in a year (I am rather doubtful whether we could safely manage it
under 2 years - mainly for trade reasons) and to make Sterling convertible on current account thereafter. The transition period and the
blocked balances are getting on the nerves of the U.S.A. in the

Treasury, still more in the State Department. This is all to the good, for the relief created by our offer might dispose them to say yes.

III. But supposing it is too simple and too bold for the U.S. Administration, where are we? Straight, I think, in the temptation of paragraph 34 of Keynes paper, modified, as might well be managed, as suggested in paragraph 39. I think we must examine this as a probable development, occurring at an early stage in the negotiations, and made public so as to confine our negotiators to that issue.

We could have £1,250 millions - possibly £2,000 millions - on easy terms, as a loan between Governments and probably unsecured, i.e. resting on mutual good faith.

What should be the attitude of our negotiators?

The consequences of refusal will be serious, and the risks to much of what we might otherwise hope to have and do will be great. As is suggested in discussing Plan II below, we land ourselves in all manner of political difficulties internally as well as externally, if we have to set out on the journey towards recovery on our own resources, including our own will. For at least two or three years we shall have to disappoint our tired and undernourished people of much of what they expect, and have been led to expect, and believe is about their due. But I have little doubt that we ought to refuse - contenting ourselves with such credits as we shall need for the purchase of essential U.S. supplies which we cannot obtain elsewhere. We ought of course also to refuse any burdensome settlement of Lend-Lease, and to go on refusing, with resolution. This heavy conclusion is reached not only because, as Keynes points out, the deal would start all wrong, but also because it would go on becoming more and more wrong. Even at 1%, even if we take only $5 billion - though this would not allow us to do all that the Americans would expect us to do - the annual burden might well be too heavy. Indeed if the world's economy were disturbed by an American setback it would be almost unmanageable during that time. We should carry forward to future years increasing obligations of interest and amortisation which might sink us just when we were recovering. I do not believe we dare risk a loan transaction with one creditor, of this size, and for such a long time. It would be a leap into the dark, economically and politically, which, in our present condition, we dare not take.

IV. Well, what then? Plan II - of which this can only be a sketch, attempting to include the main features. (It may be said straight away that fundamentally it is not new - it is only an effort to put together previous lines of thought and to give them their colour.) Any Plan II must fulfil one condition. It must not be conceived in hostility to the U.S.A., either to the ideals of economic cooperation which they hold, or politically. Nor must it be operated as an economic fight, for such a policy would not only be wrong but stupid. We should at all times be ready to explain how and why we are doing things; we should be ready to support the early establishment of international organisation in the economic field at which all that is involved could be examined and discussed. It cannot be bilateralism or barter or a closed economy, for their own sakes. Keynes, in his earlier paragraphs was attacking a point of view with which I also have no sympathy. Nor is

restrict imports more or less – and probably dollar imports more.
There is no evidence that the U.S. intend to import – at least on the
scale that would be required to produce early equilibrium in the international balance of payments. She may reduce her tariff, and some more
goods, chiefly materials, may go in, but her Government has no intention
of a large import programme. And her people have no sense of the need
for imports. They are almost self-sufficient as they stand – or think
so. Nor does prosperity in the U.S.A. really depend – at any rate in
the short run – on prosperity in the rest of the world. The U.S.A.
will lend dollars, and in large amounts, and no doubt on terms that
many countries will accept. But that process, if unaccompanied by
buying for dollars on a large scale, can only have one end; the U.S.
will suddenly grow sick of it as they have done in the past.

VI. But the working of the Dollar Pool in the Sterling Area – the
dollars from the pay of troops corresponding perhaps functionally to
"dollar lending" in ordinary times – has shown that if the area
working together can be large enough, and the dollar earnings of the
area are pooled, a very substantial dollar purchasing power can be
currently distributed according to need, and that, if things are
reasonably favourable for the reserves of the country operating the
pool, all dollars put into the world by the U.S.A. will in fact be
spent. If we do not succeed in obtaining the assistance from the
U.S.A. which we seek, we have, in the first place, no alternative but
to try to hold the Sterling Area together, and to work it as nearly as
possible in accordance with war-time arrangements. I do not discuss
here the question whether we should easily persuade all the members to
remain in. It is enough to say that if they go out, they will leave
their balances behind them. The value of Sterling will rest on confidence, if we have a plan, and not otherwise. We would then seek to
extend it – by associated arrangements such as the various payment
agreements already existing. Could we not consider something more far-
reaching – the possible inclusion of the French, Dutch, and Belgian
Empires within the Sterling Area on the basis of a Dollar Pool and an
Import and Supplies Policy Organisation in London, working on the
analogy of the Combined Boards?

At first glance this will seem, as Keynes would say, "plain barmy".
Perhaps it is also at second glance, but let us see.

The purpose of the Plan is for the Transitional period, to start
moving trade and supplies as rapidly as possible over the widest area
possible, and getting round a series of financial difficulties which it
is clear are going to choke trade in the next two or three years, and
secondly to make the widest possible use of the net Dollar earnings of
the area. Keynes demonstrated in Washington that on balance the pooled
use of Dollars is more beneficial to United States trade than the use
by each member of the Dollars it earns and wishes to spend; the Dollar
Pool ensures, other things being equal, that all the Dollars in the Pool
are spent.

Would these three countries accept this? If, as seems now quite
possible, we are going to work towards a regional Western European Pact
within the San Francisco framework, a pact which these three countries
are anxiously seeking and which is of value to us when we have to face
the economic and political problems of Western Germany after the
Americans have cleared out, then an arrangement of this kind could be

that point of view made any more real by calling it the application of
planning to international economics. The "plans" are directed against
the U.S.A. either for fear of her dominating power, which is a fact we
cannot eliminate but may sting into action, or for fear that if we are
too closely linked to her and she fails in her efforts to maintain her
own economy, we shall be swept down in the whirlpool. There is no
planning of international trade which we can arrange which would not
be brought nearly to disaster if the U.S.A. had a major collapse.

Therefore Plan II starts from the conception that the kind of
world the Americans want would, in the long run, suit us also, that we
have to gain, both financially and in political influence, from a
liberalised economy and from an effort towards expansion and multilateralism. To make this clear, I suggest that, as part of the
financial negotiations, and if possible before they begin, we should
indicate clearly that we are prepared to cooperate in the early
establishment of an International Trade Organisation, and to support
the U.S. Government in securing the acceptance by international procedure of a well-defined Statement of Principles covering commercial
policy, commodity policy and international cartels, to whose application we and others joined with us would work progressively, in the
hope that after a period of about 5 years, they would be in full
operation.

My own opinion is that in any paper or statement made to the U.S.
on the financial negotiations, we should begin with this declaration,
and put our financial proposals second. The acceptance of our
financial proposals would be a condition precedent to our unreserved
acceptance of the trade agreement, and of course to any shortening of
the period before we can accept convertibility and thus release the
international purchasing power represented by our Sterling balances.
I should also suggest that at the beginning of the financial negotiations we should make it plain that we shall recommend to Parliament
adherence to the Final Act of Bretton Woods. I do not think we can
successfully "trade" our attitude on such matters for any major part
of the financial settlement. It seems preferable that we should display this forthcoming attitude in the hope that it will produce a more
favourable atmosphere for the financial talks, and that if the financial talks fail, we can go to our own people, and – more important in
this case – the Commonwealth and to other countries with a statement
that we tried fully. Unless we do this, we must expect very considerable reservations on the part e.g. of Canada and of some other
countries whose part in Plan II is discussed below.

V.   In saying that Plan II must not be conceived in hostility to the
U.S. this does not mean that it will not be "discriminatory". Of
course it will discriminate against the dollar. Not out of wickedness,
but because the basic fact is that a large part of the world will be
short of dollars, and will for some time remain short of dollars,
except on unacceptable terms. Even if Plan I were accepted completely,
we in the U.K. would be discriminating against dollars; Plan I only
gives us breathing space; it does not automatically produce continuing equilibrium in our balance of payments. If we had it we might find
it possible to produce equilibrium more by exports, and less by import
restrictions. But for some years, and in any event, we shall have to

one of the bargaining factors in the Pact.

Of course it will be difficult to work and there will be friction. But we have to consider all these things against the difficulties of a debtor position to the United States, and the difficulties of going on without a loan and with a Sterling Area arrangement where it is quite evident that the problem of import policy and supplies is going to make the financial arrangements difficult to maintain.

So far as we are concerned the main question is whether the inclusion of these three countries and their Empires, on proper negot- iated terms about the use of reserves, import policy and supplies policy, adds to our liabilities. This is partly a matter of guess work, partly a matter of the way in which the policy is worked out. But it seems to me that we cannot assume that a wide extension of the Area over which trade can move through a proper financial mechanism would be to our disadvantage.

Now as for the American attitude. They would of course at first be highly critical. We would reassure them however, partly by the declaration of economic policy I have suggested above, partly by ensuring that apart from such preferences as are permitted by the trade policy, e.g. the French Colonial Preferences, and the Residual Imperial Preferences for sentiment sake, there would be no internal trade preferential system within this Area, except of course the Preference that follows from the fact that over that area as a whole, Dollars are likely to be in short supply and that while we can ensure that the area spends all the Dollars it acquires it must manage its Dollar resources so that those Dollars are used for goods and supplies which are essential and are most advantageously obtainable in the United States.

If the United States were definitely hostile to such a scheme no doubt they could prevent it by putting pressure on some of the con- stituent members. But if they do they are embarking upon a slow and complicated process of credit assistance to the various component members which will certainly delay the restoration of international trade.

There would be nothing in the arrangement which would prevent any country borrowing Dollars in New York for capital purposes any more than there is anything now to prevent Australia doing this.

VII. Internal consequences of Plan II. These are really troublesome. If we have to live without a possible indebtedness to the United States, we must restrict Dollar imports to the utmost and switch to other sources of supply as rapidly as possible. Owing to the supply position the Ministry of Food's first reaction on switching is that during 1946 and 1947 we could probably not improve our present standard of living appreciably. The improvement would begin in 1948 and be sub- stantially progressive thereafter, as the stimulated production from other sources of supply comes into operation.

But it means more than this. We shall have to import some things from the United States, but we cannot afford to import all that we want. That means that imported supplies of some essential things, e.g. hard wood for furniture-making will be short and if we are to make any sense of that situation we must maintain a controlled allocation of short raw materials. The present raw material allocation controls are being wound up and will be out of existence by the end of the year, a situation which seems to us at the Treasury a desperate one.

We might also have to consider other internal consequences, e.g. compelling Lancashire to make do with raw cotton of a type different from that which they hope to get from the United States. They can do this but only if they are bullied.

It is necessary to emphasise that whether we get the financial assistance from America as Keynes proposes or not, this problem of controlling Dollar imports arises in any case, and this may involve retention of controls. As said before, the American assistance would only give us a breathing space. We cannot accept it without a resolution to move to equilibrium as early as possible, and this means not only forcing exports at the cost to the home consumer, but also restricting imports. There is too much evidence in recent weeks that this fundamental part of our problem is being dodged.

VIII. It is obvious that Plan II is in terms of comfort only second best. It is full of chances and has internal political difficulties which do not arise immediately from the nature of Plan I. Among other difficulties, it cannot, like Plan I, be handled largely, if not entirely, by the Chancellor and within the Treasury competence. It embraces not only the Chancellor, but particularly the Foreign Secretary, the President of the Board of Trade, as well of course as the Prime Minister. It is like planning the Normandy invasion. It would be based upon a directive and everybody concerned in their own sphere would have to work it out with an intention to make it succeed if it took place, and while not disregarding obvious improbabilities of success, not accepting an improbability as a certainty of failure. It is complicated, while Plan I is simple. On the other hand, and this is the essential point of this paper, the simplicity of Plan I starts from one proposition – the gift of $3 billion from the United States. If that proposition disappears, then the difficulties of the rest of Plan I, though not so complicated, are not much less serious for the Government and for our people.

IX. In the preliminary paragraph I mentioned the question of the handling of public opinion. I do not think we can let our negotiators go out on their Argonaut voyage in search of this Golden Fleece without considering the problem of educating the public both on what is involved if we succeed, and what is involved if we fail, that is if "failure" is the way to describe our inability at the first round to get what we seek.

It is not easy, especially at the present moment, to see exactly how this should be done, e.g. by a speech by the Chancellor or otherwise. But one technique should, I suggest, certainly be employed; the collection by the Chancellor of an Editors Conference to whom the whole situation could be disclosed in confidence. (This technique used to be employed before the war on major issues and was found to be of immense value.)

The purpose of the Conference would be to have the general situation firmly in the minds of Editors so that either we could stimulate them to comment if we thought it desirable, and more particularly that they should be ready with informed comment if the negotiations had begun in Washington and the news breaks or there is a leakage.

At the Editors Conference I should assume that the lines of the proposal we are going to make to the United States, as well as the lines of a possible alternative, should be given. Whether we could make the alternative work would depend upon our will to do so more than on the intrinsic facts of the situation, and it is possible that the comments of some of the Editors would be valuable. Crowther, for example, in a series of articles some weeks ago in the "Economist" was obviously playing round with a plan of this kind, and of the outsiders Crowther is about as good a judge of the possibilities of such a scheme as anyone we could find, though of course only as an outsider.

X.   I have left the question of timing until the end because timing will obviously be affected by some of the decisions taken. Keynes has pointed out, and it is a serious warning, that we ought not to be too late because if the Japanese war took a sudden turn to the finish there would be a scramble in Washington to make arrangements for the disposal of all the Lend-Lease questions, all sorts of plans would crystallise in the heads of F.E.A.* etc. and we should find ourselves having to deal with a situation in which the initiative was in American hands. This must not be under-rated.

On the other hand a premature entry upon the negotiations, which I am certain must range over a wider field than is contemplated even in Keynes' paper, including the field of economic cooperation, might be disastrous.

We gain nothing, however, by postponing consideration or not working to a target date.

But unless a decision is taken to try Plan I by itself to see what happens, a decision which as suggested above, I do not think we should take, I do not see how, in the present political situation, we can expect to start negotiations early in September. I believe that it would be wiser to fix early in October. Even to secure this will not be too easy, especially if we have to work out the lines of an alternative plan. (I must emphasise the need for work on Plan II if it is to be thought of at all.) The major disaster we have to fear is that Plan I will be fobbed off by some Ministers with some easy declaration that it is quite unnecessary and that we can get by somehow by charm and dexterity. We shall need both, but they won't take us home, at any rate in a fog.

Also we have to remember that this is a policy with such long-distance consequences that like foreign policy and security policy, the Government would probably wish to bring one or two leaders of the Opposition into consultation before a decision is taken.

---

* Foreign Economic Administration.

The first decision to take, and this could probably be taken by the Chancellor alone, is whether Departments should work out the lines of a possible Plan II with a Directive that it must be worked out on the basis that we should try and produce a viable alternative if Plan I fails.

This could proceed during July.

When the result of the Election and the composition of the new Government is known, then the Chancellor should press for the Ad Hoc Committee which he has suggested with a wish that the Committee should sit regularly and really consider what is involved in Plan I, or in a possible failure, in Plan II. It might be hoped that by mid-September at the latest a report to the Cabinet would be available.

---

8. Comments by Lord Keynes on Plan II and reply by R. W. B. Clarke

Mr R.W.B. Clarke
Sir W. Eady

What these figures show, to express the substance of what in his Plan II Sir W. Eady says in another way, is that, if a tidal wave were to overwhelm North and South America, our subsequent financial problems would not be too bad and nothing worse than starvation would supervene.

They do not help me with my essential difficulty, which is as follows:-

If, having failed to get financial assistance from U.S.A., our over-all adverse balance of trade remains as before, from which countries can we expect to borrow what we have failed to obtain from U.S.A.? Deprived of the free use of their existing sterling resources, most of the countries suggested for the sterling group cannot expect to have an over-all favourable balance after the war out of which they can lend to us. Indeed, half the problem is that they also will have a large adverse balance with the Americans.

That is why I put the essence of the situation in the following form. If we have an over-all adverse balance of trade, Plan II will not work. If we have not, any plan will work.

My next difficulty is that I see no prospect of the proposed members of the sterling group accepting membership of the club under Plan II conditions. They have everything to lose by doing so and nothing to gain. It would have to be part of the plan that they cut themselves off to the greatest possible extent from trade with U.S.A. just like ourselves. What motive have they to rupture trade relations with U.S.A. in order to lend us money they have not got?

On the secondary question of the distribution of the foreign-owned dollars, I agree that a very large part is in the Americas, though I should add Canada and Mexico to the South American countries.

Nevertheless, in the present context, what we have to think of is the total value of dollars and free gold. In addition to the American countries, France, Belgium, Holland, Switzerland, Sweden Russia and China possess very large resources. China alone, including privately owned balances, is said to hold $800 million in U.S.A. After taking account of American contributions to UNRRA, the Export and Import Bank, the two Bretton Woods Plans, etc. etc., I do not think there is any serious risk of an overall shortage of gold and dollars in the first three years.

(Signed) Keynes

9.7.45.

I do not think anyone denies that we shall have to get financial assistance from U.S.A. But I think we have some degree of freedom in stating the extent to which our whole indebtedness is canalised into a dollar loan.

Suppose we have an adverse balance of £1,500,000,000 in the 3 years from June 1946. Of this about £750,000,000 will be in respect of overseas military expenditure and will be incurred to India, Egypt, our Far Eastern Colonies, etc. We could simply refuse to allow them to take this away in dollars and the nature of the expenditure is such that they could not refuse unless they insisted that we got out altogether.

Then £500,000,000, say, represents expenditure in U.S.A. and would have to be met by borrowing. The remaining £250,000,000 would include Canada, Latin America and sterling area countries. Canada would lend us the money on fairly reasonable terms; Latin America is admittedly pretty dubious; I do not think we shall be borrowing from Australia and New Zealand though we might be from the Colonies; the amounts we require to borrow in Europe will be pretty small and apart from Sweden I should have thought we should be sending them more supplies than they send us.

I feel, myself, that there is a pretty wide difference between the scale of borrowing from U.S.A. which we should do if we worked to Plan I without the $3 billion gift and what we should have to do if we restricted our own supplies from U.S.A. to a minimum and if we made no sterling balances convertible except for financing actual purchases in U.S.A. of supplies which could not be made available in the sterling area.

I think we could get our dollar borrowing in the 3 years, including financing of the adverse balance of the sterling area down to $3 billion. In Plan I conditions without the $3 billion gift, I suppose it would be at least double this amount.

I feel that the sort of reasons which make us unwilling to embark upon large dollar borrowing ourselves would also carry weight with the other suggested candidates for Plan II.

R.W.B.C.

11 July 1945.

9. The Loan Negotiations in Washington: Minute by R. W. B. Clarke

SIR WILFRID EADY (Copy to Mr Grant)

May I play devil's advocate?

1.   We began with a great constructive conception. U.S. would give us $5 billions free (or at least interest-free). This would see us through the transition, build up our reserves, enable a favourable sterling balance settlement, rehabilitate sterling, open the door to a multilateral world.

2.   Now the poetry is prose. We are offered not $5 billion but $4 billion, at 2% interest. This is nearly commercial, apart from the waiver clause for interest (which we dislike). The non-financial conditions are obscure, but certainly include:-

(a) joining Bretton Woods (and probably making £ convertible earlier than we would like)

(b) sponsoring the commercial conference (though there is little sign of U.S. repenting their sins, e.g. shipping and agriculture). It is not clear what our commitment is if the conference breaks down

(c) handing over sterling area markets to U.S.A. (the precise commitment is obscure, but certainly we substitute dollar debt for sterling debt, and give the Americans all the trade advantages of a tied loan to India without being dependent upon India's willingness or capacity to pay)

(d) no discrimination against U.S. exports in 1946? (i.e. no help for shattered territories by taking their exports).

Our right to be bilateral, to exploit our buying power and debtor position to expand our exports, would have been well sold for $5 billions grant in cash. But not for $4 billion at 2% interest.

3.   Has not the broad conception led to an impasse? Can we not say that their offers do not strengthen our position enough to enable us to free ourselves (Clayton talks of us running down our gold to $1 billion)? Should we not leave the big questions until we see how the world is going, and confine our immediate request for accommodation to our current needs, with an offer like this:-

(a) We borrow $1 billion plus Lend/Lease settlement - say, $1½ billion.

(b) Crowley terms if necessary, probably put on an annuity basis, which would ease the load early in the period. Escape clauses on U.S. capacity to receive.

(c) We undertake to spend the $1 billion on purchases of U.S. goods for U.K. and Colonies, the orders to be placed by December 31st, 1946.

(d) We will sponsor the commercial policy conference, and the only alteration of our attitude will be a need for a longer transition

period than would have been necessary if we had had more money.
If the conference is unsuccessful, there will be no further obligation upon us under Article VII or arising from the loan.

(e) We will adhere to Bretton Woods if the commercial conference
is successful, but not otherwise.

(f) We will abstain from discrimination against U.S. exports
(both in U.K. and in the sterling area) except to the extent that
discrimination is necessitated by insufficiency of dollar earnings
and the $1 billion to pay for all the U.S. goods which would other-
wise be sold.

(g) We will enter further discussions with U.S.A. in November,
1946 with the purpose of securing an early convertibility of
sterling into dollars and of making further progress in the light
of the results of the commercial policy conference towards the
establishment of secure multilateral financial and commercial
arrangements.

4.   It would be very difficult even for Congress to refuse this
offer. As a matter of fact, they should give us much better than
Crowley terms for a small loan, all tied to U.S. exports, with important strings in (c), (d), (f) and (g). The other recipients of Crowley
money have no strings at all (no-one has suggested that the French
should abandon their preferences). A refusal of this money would be
virtually a declaration of economic war on their part.

5.   This proposition would surely go through Parliament with no
trouble at all.

6.   There are great advantages to us in delay:-

(i) the U.S. economy will be getting towards difficulties by
end-1946; the longer-sighted people will be fearful of 1947

(ii) our position will be much stronger then than now; our exports are now only 30% of our imports, but by the end of next
year they will be at least 75% of our imports and probably better

(iii) if we switch rigorously in 1946, we should by the end of the
year be much less dependent upon supplies from U.S.A. (our minimum
dollar import programme for 1947 might be no more than $500 million
compared with $1,000 million in 1946)

(iv) we should not be buying a pig in a poke, making commitments
which postulate a multilateral world without knowing whether the
world will be multilateral or not

(v) we should still have our gold and dollar reserves unimpaired
at end-1946

(vi) we should have a clear import policy for administrative purposes in 1946.

7.   On the other hand, there are disadvantages:-

(i) we should probably want to go back for <u>some</u> money for our 1947 import programme

(ii) the U.S. Administration, after an election with a new Congress, might be even worse placed with Congress than now

(iii) we should have a problem with Canada ·

(iv) we should have a difficult time with the sterling area; our financial position would be strong enough to persuade them to go on holding sterling, but they would probably want some dollars in excess of current earnings. The real problem would be the financing of overseas military expenditure, but this will probably increasingly be in "amenable" countries (e.g. Malaya)

(v) we probably should not get cancellations of sterling balances, and would have to think of methods of repayment (e.g. special exports) which did not involve transfer over the exchanges

(vi) we should have no elbow room and would face a very tricky period in the first half of 1946

(vii) our commitment for repayment might be as much as $75 million in the first year, but we could probably whittle this down, e.g. by getting the repayment and interest on to an annuity basis.

8.   This involves risks, and betting our shirt on rapid export recovery. But does it run worse risks than the big loan at 2% with its strings which even now are not very specific and may be made much worse by Congress? It might be agreed that this was much less dangerous to Anglo-American relationships than bickering about whether we were in fact honouring our pledges.

                                        R.W.B. Clarke.
                                        23 October 1945.

---

10. What happens if we do not get the US Loan? Minute by R. W. B. Clarke

[This paper, like the two succeeding minutes, was presumably sent to Sir David Waley and copied to Mr Rowe-Dutton. At the end of section 5 a manuscript note in Clarke's handwriting adds that 'a big Middle East oil development policy could probably free us from dollar oil altogether'. Ed.]

1.   This paper attempts to measure some of the possibilities if Congress rejects the loan or attaches new strings to it.

2.   I am quite certain that in the long view (i.e. 1949 or 1950) we could develop a perfectly workable multilateral system based on sterling, excluding U.S.A. This system would, indeed, have some advantages over the world wide multilateral system contemplated in I.T.O. because it would be able to insulate itself to some extent against the effects of the American depression. The difficulty would be the next three years.

3.   In considering this I would make the following assumptions:-

(a) We treat the Lend-Lease settlement as still holding good – i.e. we repay the ₤650 millions on precisely the same interest and service terms as the proposed loan.

(b) We walk out of Bretton Woods and I.T.O. We should presumably want to set up similar organisations on our own.

(c) The rejection by Congress would be dictated less by anti-British feeling than by a feeling of opposition to foreign lending. In other words, the U.S.A. would not be in a position in the next two or three years to seek to seduce the sterling area and other countries by offers of loans on favourable terms. U.S. foreign lending, indeed, would become limited to Export-Import Bank lending tied to the purchases of American goods. That is, we assume that the Americans do not adopt an active and aggressive foreign economic policy. This stage would no doubt come later as U.S. internal economic activity fell off and it is not likely before the end of 1947 or the beginning of 1948 and is thus irrelevant to the immediate problem.

(d) The U.S. administration would be in a state of frightful embarrassment and would be compelled to give us such indirect assistance as it could, e.g. in commercial borrowing. It will probably have to do this in order to avoid a breakdown of Anglo-American political and military co-operation.

(e) We should get strong support from the Dominions, perhaps even from South Africa. Canada would be in a great difficulty but would have to lend us large sums of money, perhaps on a tied basis, in order to get rid of her exports. She would be forced to control imports from U.S.A. but her gold production could go quite a long way to finance her deficit with U.S.A. We should probably have to help with this.

(f) We should get strong support (unfortunately rather worthless economically) from European countries who would see that any idea they had had of Uncle Sam as a beneficent leader was founded on sand.

(g) The allegiance of Latin America would be rather divided and this would be the territory of hottest competition from U.S.A.

(h) We should presumably cancel the sterling balance negotiations and seek to substitute for them discussion of economic co-operation. The sterling balances would continue to be spendable within the sterling area (expanded in the new circumstances).

(i) The public in U.K. would be in a state of great indignation.
As after Dunkirk there was a feeling of relief that we had got
rid of the French however, there would probably be a corresponding feeling of relief that we were no longer beholden to the
Americans.

On the whole our policy would have to be based upon the fact that
in a world of bankrupts the half-solvent is king.

4.   Our Resources

We start 1946 with gold and dollar reserves of £450 millions, of
which say £200 millions could be regarded as being disposable. The
gold production available to us in the three years 1946-48 can be put
at £300 millions. We could probably get some Export-Import Bank money
- say £150 millions. At the end of June last the value of U.S. market
securities pledged as R.F.C.* collateral exceeded the amount of the
R.F.C. loan outstanding, and in addition there were direct investments
pledged to a total of £75 millions. There are other U.K. assets
approximately estimated at something like £150 millions (the branches
of British insurance companies at £50 millions is the chief), but the
extent to which these can be realised is very uncertain.

We should probably be able to borrow commercially for some supplies
(e.g. tobacco) and, indeed, there would probably be a flood of U.S.
exporters asking us to take their stuff on credit on pretty favourable
terms. It may not be unreasonable to put the possible proceeds of such
commercial loans plus practicable realisation of securities in any but
the last resort, at around £100 millions over the three years.

We thus have:-

	£ millions
Disposable gold and dollar reserves	200
Gold production	300
Export-Import Bank loan	say 150
Commercial borrowing plus realisation	100
Total	750

5.   Balance of Payments with U.S.A.

On the present basis, assuming no easements of food from U.S.A.,
our adverse balance with U.S.A. in 1946 is of the order of £250 millions.
Food easements could add a further £25 millions. These figures exclude
Germany (which may cost us £20 millions in U.S. dollars). They also
exclude any possible dollar deficit of the sterling area - which in
these circumstances could not be large - but they include our dollar
expenditure on oil which is subsequently sold for sterling to the
sterling area and other parts of the world in order to maintain the
British oil companies' share of world markets.

---

* Reconstruction Finance Corporation.

It would, I think, be possible to work to a programme of a deficit of £225 millions in 1946, £125 millions in 1947 and £100 in 1948. This would, I think, involve something like the following:-

(a) Literally no food easements from U.S.A. and a delay in improving food standards until supplies were available from other sources (no increase in the sugar ration until we could draw it from Java and also leave Cuba).

(b) Continued intense switch from U.S. cotton and arrangements to provide semi-finished steel from Europe instead of U.S.A.

(c) Cut of 20% in purchases of U.S. tobacco involving corresponding reduction of consumption. This would probably involve rationing, but the supplies would still be reasonably sufficient.

(d) Retain basic petrol rationing. Figures for petrol are very difficult to determine because of the world wide nature of the oil companies' operations and we should probably have to surrender certain of the British companies' markets. This, however, is a separate issue.

(e) Cut films by one half. This is at present technically very difficult to do, but surely some means can be devised to do it. Probably if we went to the U.S. film companies in such a position we could make a suitable arrangement. It clearly implies, however, pressing forward very hard with the British film industry.

(f) It would probably be possible to retain a very useful flow of machinery from U.S.A. This would be necessary, e.g. for the development of the film industry.

(g) Press exports to U.S.A.

The following are very speculative figures indeed, and are meant to illustrate rather than to represent an allocation:-

	Present Plan £m	1946 £m	1947 £m	1948 £m
Food: basic	107	100	55	40
Raw materials	49	50	50	50
Machinery	25	25	30	30
Tobacco	37	35	30	30
Petrol	50	35	20	10
Films	18	15	10	10
Shipping	15	15	--	-
Total	300	275	195	170
Exports	50	50	70	70
Deficit	250	225	125	100

Detailed work with the Departments could, of course, yield much more
realistic figures. In this case the big figures are really the
purchases of dollar oil which we make in order to supply sterling oil
for the sterling area countries and to Europe, Latin America, etc.
The saving on tobacco, films, and by retaining basic petrol rationing
would be of the order of £50 millions over the three years. This gives
a total deficit over the period in U.S. dollars of about £450 millions.
We should therefore have, say, £300 millions available - little enough
in all conscience - for helping Canada with her U.S. balance of payments, for meeting any dollar deficit of the sterling area countries
and for dealing with possible difficult countries in Latin America and
the hard currency countries of Europe. I would say that this is
certainly workable.

6.   Total Balance of Payments

Our total balance of payments on trading account would probably
be workable. I think we could work to a pattern on trading account of
this kind:-

	1946 £m	1947 £m	1948 £m
Imports, excluding oil	1,075	1,180	1,300
Exports	600	1,000	1,175
Other net receipts	150	180	200
Surplus or deficit	-325	-	+75

The level of total imports contemplated here compares with imports
in 1938 at present prices of £1,500 millions - i.e. we should start
this year, as we are doing, with imports slightly above 70% of 1938
and we should increase to, say, 87% of 1938 in 1948. The export figures
in the table are perfectly feasible; at the end of this year they will
be running at £1,000 millions a year if plans are carried out - and
the actual effect of the crisis would be to ensure that plans were
carried out. We should also have a tied market. The figure I have put
for 1948 is less than 25% above 1938.

The effect of this would be that in the three years we should have
an adverse balance on trading account of £250 millions. Taking into
account the fact that we have to pay the sterling area for £300 millions
worth of gold, this might be distributed as follows:-

	£ millions
Deficit with U.S.A.	450
Deficit with Canada	250
Surplus with sterling area and rest of world	150

We should try to borrow £250 millions of new money from Canada; we have £300 millions to spare in gold and dollars from the end of paragraph 5 and we have a convertible surplus with the rest of the world. So far so good.

7. Military and Political Expenditure

This very favourable picture in which we potentially have about £450 millions to play with brings out the real crisis in our position – the political and military expenditure. Lord Keynes has put this at £1,000 millions in the three years on existing plans. On the basis of the figures above, this is clearly not a starter because we should not possibly be able to borrow a further £5 or 600 millions from the rest of the world for these purposes. Indeed, it looks as if something like £500 millions would be the upper limit for this type of expenditure – in so far as it is expenditure which affects our balance of payments. On the other hand, as there would be no question of sterling becoming convertible, it might be possible so to arrange matters that, in fact, India and Egypt did lend money to us. But this whole problem, which is serious enough on the assumption that we get the U.S. loan, becomes really critical if we do not. The implications upon the European position are extremely serious because France and Holland and the rest could not reasonably expect to secure loans from U.S.A. except small ones on Export-Import Bank terms. Yet in order to recover they must have American goods. We could not step into the place of U.S.A.

8. As regards military expenditure in the Middle East and Far East, I think the only policy would be something of the kind which Lord Keynes suggests.

The European problem would become the central one. I think we should have to seek some general arrangement with France, Holland, Belgium, Norway and Denmark by which these countries pooled their gold and dollar securities and operated a joint buying policy in U.S.A. and in other countries which were not on a sterling basis. Each of these countries would have to submit an import programme divided between its purchases within the group and its purchases outside the group and we should have to decide how the scarce gold and dollar reserves of the group could best be used. This has the most furious political implications, but I believe it would be the only way to tackle the problem and to enable the limited resources over the transition period to be used in the way best designed to secure recovery – and incidentally to prevent us from holding all the babies. The British and French zones of Germany would have to come into the same arrangement and would have to be a joint charge upon the joint gold and dollar resources. I do not pretend to have worked this through in detail, but it seems to me the only possible starter. I believe, as a matter of fact, it could be rather an attractive proposition.

In short, I think it would be a mistake if Congress turned down the loan for us ourselves to adopt an isolationist policy. I think we should seize the opportunity of trying to build up a group based upon sterling with the object of making the best possible use for the rest of the world outside U.S.A. of the dollars which U.S.A. thought fit to make available.

9.   These notes are all rather bitty and, as I say, I have not thought
the thing through, but I think that they indicate the orders of
magnitude and the sort of problems which would be likely to arise. I
think we could pull through without having to embark upon such
austerity as would reduce the British economy to a standstill.
Indeed, I suspect that the really important issues are not in the
import programme but altogether elsewhere. I would not defend any of
these figures for my life but I think they show orders of magnitude.

R.W.B.C.

12 February 1946.

---

11. What happens if we do not get the US Loan? Comments by Lord Keynes

I agree with Mr Clarke's conclusion "that the really important
issues are not in the import programme but altogether elsewhere".

But no-one, of course, has faced the virtual impossibilities of
the reductions in military and political expenditure which will be
required in the absence of an American loan. For, even on the
assumption of an American loan, the position is all but intractable.

The estimate of gold and dollar resources in paragraph 4 seems to
me much too optimistic. The figure for gold production assumes that
South Africa lends us or accumulates in sterling balances a substantial
sum without security. We should have great difficulty in borrowing or
realising £250 million in U.S.A. if we walk out of Bretton Woods and
I.T.O. If we want to raise the wind on this scale in U.S.A., we should
have to agree, I think, to remain for the time being in Bretton Woods
and enter into I.T.O. conversations without, however, our present
commitments. That, I think, would be our right policy. Even so, I
should say £250 million is too high. Altogether it would be wiser to
substitute £600 for £750 million.

The point about Mr Clarke's statistics which leaves me somewhat
perplexed is the following. He replaces the American loan by other
American borrowing and the use of gold reserves to the amount of £450
million. He loses from the loan £937 million. He reduces military
and political expenditure from our previous estimate of £600 million
to £500 million. Thus he loses 937 and gains 550, a loss on balance
of £387 million. Out of what economies is this realised? He is
also, of course, assuming that we reach complete equilibrium in
three years, whereas I have never supposed that complete equilibrium
could be possible under five years. One also has to remember how
quickly loans of the Export-Import Bank type are eaten up in interest
and amortisation. Mr Clarke's dollar borrowing and realisation programme would cost us $50 million a year, which in four years is £50
million, for which he has made no provision.

I agree that there is nothing to be gained by action on the import programme whilst we are waiting for the U.S. loan. Film interests and others are already quite well aware of the consequences of a failure to grant the loan without our making impolite threats.

As I mentioned in another note, I agree that, military and political expenditure apart, the position would not be desperate. Our position would be in several respects a very great deal stronger than it would have been if it had been we who had broken off last autumn and rejected an American offer.

On one remote, at present academic, issue I might mention that I do not believe that a sterling system would insulate us against the effects of an American depression. Those effects would show themselves primarily in reduced imports from India, Malaya and other parts of the sterling area. I do not see how the existence of the sterling system would help that much.

(Signed) Keynes

13.2.46.

---

12. What happens if we do not get the US Loan? Minute by R. W. B. Clarke to Sir David Waley

1.   I was certainly wrong in not including interest and amortisation on the dollar borrowing plus realisation of U.S. securities. This means I am £25 to 50 millions too optimistic, both on the U.S. balance of payments and on the total balance of payments over the three year period.

2.   <u>Gold and dollar resources</u>

I agree that a great deal depends on what South Africa is willing to do. But over the period as a whole, we shall pay for most of her gold with goods.

On possible borrowing from U.S.A., I feel that Keynes is pessimistic. The Export—Import Bank loans are tied to U.S. goods; there would be very strong pressures from American exporters to provide them. It would also be wrong to under-estimate the commercial borrowing. The American tobacco interests in particular are very eager to retain the U.K. market and it would be certainly possible to pledge the Imperial Tobacco assets in U.S.A. Indeed, the present form suggests that we should be inundated with requests to sell us American goods on favourable credit terms; many cases have already come to my notice, particularly in machinery. In three years this might add up to quite a lot.

However, if Lord Keynes feels that my estimate of £750 millions for our resources is too high — and I may note in passing that our gold and dollar reserves at the beginning of January were, in fact, £470

millions and not £450 millions – I would reduce it. This would correspondingly reduce the size of my error in omitting the service of U.S.
loans. To the extent that gold receipts were written down from £300
millions, there would be corresponding increases in our surplus with
the sterling area and rest of the world in the last part of paragraph 6.

3.   Now for Lord Keynes' mystery about the £387 millions which I have
saved compared with the Washington balance sheet. The Washington estimate was a deficit of £1,250 millions, of which £650 millions was in
respect of current trading and £600 millions in respect of military
expenditure. The whole of the saving on the overall balance comes from
the current trading. I give a deficit on current trade in the three
years of £250 millions compared with the £650 millions Washington
estimate. Part of this is secured from a cut in imports; some comes
from what I believe to be a better estimate of invisibles; the rest
comes from increased exports. I am fairly confident that the import
programme can be held to the level which I suggest in paragraph 6;
but of course this would mean a slowing down of easement of civilian
standards, and the modest cut in tobacco, etc. We should be bound to
have a better chance of exporting more in 1947-8 because we should have
a tied market. Even as it is, I should not be at all surprised –
indeed, I should expect – that our current trading account will reach
balance in the first half of 1947.

4.   On the question of five years versus three, I still feel that if
we do not reach complete equilibrium – with the fingers crossed about
military expenditure – by the end of 1948, we shall never reach it.
Surely some American depression is certain by then and I cannot see why
our position should be better in 1950 than at the end of 1948.

5.   A point which I failed to make in the previous note was that we
should probably have to embark upon direction of exports to countries
which were outside the sterling and near-sterling group – in particular
to North America, but probably also to Latin America, and may be <u>away</u>
from some other countries. It is not easy to see how far this would,
in fact, be necessary – because we should expect to have a surplus on
current trading with the sterling area and the rest of the world. But
it has to be borne in mind.

6.   <u>Military and political expenditure</u>

    I have great difficulty in working out the real implications of
military and political expenditure in these circumstances. If sterling
was not convertible and if we were giving no undertaking to make it convertible, surely a straight issue would be reached with the Middle East
and India. Either they would have to lend us the money for our troops
there, or we should have to move our troops out. A straight choice
would have to be made. The position would be quite different from
what it is under the U.S. loan, for there is a third alternative of
paying them, in effect, in dollars and of frittering away the whole of
our loan on the lines set out by Lord Keynes in C.P.(46)58. The
danger is that with the loan the third alternative of frittering the
loan away will gain the day.

7.   I feel even more uncertain about the effect of the political
expenditure upon the balance of payments. Suppose we lend France the
money to buy Australian non-ferrous metals. This increases Australia's

sterling balances. It is not clear that this is a charge upon our balance of payments over the critical three years except to the extent that Australia wishes to import more and draw her sterling balances down. With inconvertible sterling, however, she would surely not be able to import more from countries outside the group - and as far as U.K. is concerned, we should be exporting to her as much as we could on supply grounds anyway. In effect, Australia would be lending the French money, and this would be Australia's own affair. With convertible sterling, however, we put up the money, and it is just the same as a subsidy by us to Australia.

Of course, if we were selling U.K. goods to France and financing them by loan, this would be a charge upon our balance of payments. But it may well be that most of this political expenditure is related to supplies from other countries and not to supplies from the U.K. In that case, if sterling is inconvertible, the sterling area country is really lending the money. In a non-convertible world, we should have to examine the military and political expenditure with great care from this point of view.

The same point applies in expenditure in Burma and Malaya. I am afraid I have not much idea of how the figures might work out on this basis, but it is possible that they might be less frightening. Another point is, of course, that if we do go for a pooling of gold and dollar securities with the Western European countries we might avoid having to lend them money. We should, at any rate, stop the idea - which I am afraid may become very prevalent after the loan goes through - that U.K. is relatively rich again and can syphon off her dollars to other countries. My point is that surely the balance of payments calculus is different in a non-convertible world. Is it not true that in the short view - which is what we are considering when we ask whether we could carry on if the loan failed - the only really important thing is the balance of payments of the sterling and near-sterling group with the rest of the world?

8.   I do not think for a moment that a sterling system would insulate us against the effects of an American depression. I was thinking much more of the I.T.O. side. The real problem when an American depression starts is for us to maintain our export employment, for this is the dynamic factor in our employment situation. I am doubtful whether we can mop up unemployment developing in the export trade by fiscal action to increase home investment or consumption. If the cotton industry, for example, is devoting 50% of its output to exports, it is very difficult to take that up in domestic consumption when export demand drops. I suspect that the only answer is bilateral arrangements of one kind or another. We might, for example, agree with New Zealand to maintain our imports of dairy produce provided that they increase their imports from U.K. of hydro-electric power plant or Post Office equipment. But this sort of thing is pretty incompatible with I.T.O.

9.   If you would like me to revise my note at this stage to take account of Keynes' comments I am, of course, ready to do so.

R.W.B.C.

15 February 1946.

13. Relevant facts on rejection: Note by R. W. B. Clarke

[This note was appended to a minute headed "If Congress rejects the Loan" addressed to Lord Keynes and Sir David Waley. The minute is incorporated in the text at para. 119. Ed.]

These figures are all highly speculative.

Our Resources

1. We start 1946 with gold and dollar reserves of £470 millions, of which say £220 millions is disposable. Allowance for gold production in 1946-8 would raise the available amount to at least £450 millions.

2. This is not all available for financing U.K. deficit with U.S.A. Canada would probably want some; we should have to use some for difficult countries; the sterling area would probably have some adverse balance; some of our political and military expenditure in 1946 costs gold and dollars (e.g. Germany). We should not reckon on much more than £300 millions for financing the U.K. deficit with U.S.A.

3. We might be able to borrow from Export-Import Bank. We could also do some commercial borrowing, e.g. to finance tobacco purchases. The value of our U.S. market securities pledged as R.F.C. loan collateral exceeds the outstanding R.F.C. loan. In addition, £75 millions direct investments are pledged; other U.K. assets in U.S.A. (largely unrealisable) are approximately estimated at £150 millions. But both Export-Import and commercial borrowing are very expensive indeed, and we should lose considerable long-term dollar income by selling securities. But if we were not conducting economic war against U.S.A., we could borrow some.

Deficit with U.S.A.

4. Our 1946 adverse balance with U.S.A. may be £250 millions, assuming no food easements. This will fall as we move away from U.S. sources of supply.

5. In 1946-8, we shall need £200 millions of food at least, allowing no dollar easements and some cuts in consumption (e.g. dried eggs). We shall need £300 millions of raw materials, machinery, and petrol (including sterling area petrol need). This makes £500 millions, against which we can put maximum of £200 millions income. The deficit on these essentials for the three years is £300 millions, which mops up the resources in paragraph 2 above.

6. Tobacco, films and petrol for private motoring would, if uncut, cost £200 millions in the three years. This could probably be cut by £50 millions without catastrophe - reduction of 20% in U.S. tobacco, cut films by one-half, retain basic petrol rationing. Bigger cuts would probably be difficult.

7. Broadly speaking, we could buy our basic food and industrial supplies from U.S.A. against reserves and new gold production; the extent of cut in tobacco, films and private motoring would depend upon

the amounts of borrowing we could still do in U.S.A. It should be possible to borrow the £150 millions, which would maintain these on a cut basis.

8.   The position would get easier through the years. Our reserves would fall low at end-1946 and in early 1947, but would tend to recover as commercial loans became arranged and as requirements of food and petrol fall.

9.   We could probably get a food cut in the second half of 1946; it would be difficult (but not impossible) to maintain austerity in 1947-8.

Balance of Payments elsewhere

10.   Our balance of payments on trading account with the rest of the world would be reasonable. We should want to borrow at least £250 millions from Canada (new money). We could have a surplus of about £200 millions with the sterling area, and the rest of the world (after buying the sterling area's gold), provided that our exports developed with real force. But this estimate is by no means impossible.

Military and political expenditure

11.   Our availabilities for military and political expenditure would thus be,

     say, £200 millions trading surplus with sterling area and rest of world (paragraph 10)

     say, £100 millions reserves (paragraph 2).

12.   Lord Keynes has put our commitments at minimum of £1000 millions on present plans. It is clear that this is quite impossible unless we can borrow the money from within the sterling area (or the rest of the world). We may in fact silently borrow £100-150 millions in the first half of this year, the inertia of war-time arrangements continuing. By being fairly dilatory, we could perhaps borrow more. In any case, we could presumably borrow from Palestine. We could perhaps lend the European countries some U.K. and Colonial exports. But we could not finance European reconstruction nor finance world security. The extent of the commitments which we could undertake would require very careful examination, as would the possibilities of an expanded dollar pooling. But it is clear that they could not be even a shadow of present plans.

Long-term policy

13.   We should clearly need some direction of exports, especially to North and South America and to difficult sterling area countries and away from non-payers.

14.   We should have to retain Government purchase of food and materials which are largely supplied from U.S.A.

15. We should have to seek to balance the sterling area's accounts with U.S.A. by end-1948. This would involve some developments like the following:-

　　(a) Pressure to increase U.K. agricultural production, especially sugar and dairy produce.

　　(b) Long-term supply arrangements with Dominions and Argentina for meat and dairy produce.

　　(c) Pressure to expand U.K. steel production.

　　(d) Continued pressure to switch from U.S. cotton (and development of U.S. types in Africa).

　　(e) Strong attempt to get timber from Russia (at present hopeless).

　　(f) Develop Middle East oil (but not easy in relation to paragraph 12).

　　(g) Increase Rhodesian tobacco production.

　　(h) Rapid expansion of U.K. film industry.

　　(i) Special attempts to restore Malayan tin and rubber.

　　(j) Renewed development of gold production within the Empire.

R.W.B.C.

20 February 1946.

---

14. If Congress rejects the Loan: Minute by Lord Keynes to Sir David Waley

　　Without wanting to share responsibility for this paper, I should be content for it to go forward in this form, subject to the following points:-

1.　I think there is something which verges on a fallacy in taking credit for £230 million gold production. We shall not receive this gold as a present, but in return for exports and foreign currencies we have supplied to gold-producing countries, with possibly a little of it lent us by them. This means that, whilst the gold in question is available for financing the sterling area deficit with U.S.A. taken in isolation, it has to be brought in as a debit item in our balance of payments elsewhere. Thus, I think that Mr Clarke is shy by this £220 millions in addition to the amount, which he does not, but should, state in the memorandum, by which he expects to cut our imports and expand our exports compared with the estimates we used in Washington. I think this ought to be brought out.

Perhaps the clearest way of bringing it out is to start from the £1,250 millions cumulative deficit which we assumed in Washington. At that time our idea as to how to meet this was £937 million from the American loan, £250 million from Canada, and £63 million through miscellaneous loans and disposal of capital assets, supplemented, if necessary, by a draft on our gold and dollar reserves. The failure of the American loan would cause a gap of £937 million. The only means of meeting this gap are by –

(i)   using our reserves more exhaustively

(ii) borrowing from the Sterling Area

(iii) cutting down our military and political expenditure overseas

(iv) cutting our imports compared with the Washington estimates

(v)   expanding our exports faster than the Washington estimates

(vi) some borrowing from U.S.A. in spite of the main loan falling through.

Mr Clarke is not very clear as to how far he is relying on each of these sources. I think his text implicitly makes fairly definite assumptions, but I have not managed to work out just what they are.

2.   I should be inclined to high-light still more than he has that the main reaction of the loss of the American loan must be on our military and political expenditure overseas. For I cannot believe that the gap can be bridged in practice unless we go all out in economies in that direction. As Mr Clarke points out, that is fraught with all sorts of political consequences. It brings this out to put the orders of magnitude of the loan and of the political and military expenditure side by side. The American loan is for £937 million. In the Washington estimates the political and military expenditure was put at £600 million. The revised estimate of the latter, prior to the recent changes of policy now under consideration, was £1,000 million. Thus, it comes out in the wash that the American loan is primarily required to meet the political and military expenditure overseas. If it were not for that, we could scrape through without excessive interruption of our domestic programme if necessary by drawing largely on our reserves. The interruption of our domestic programme which is politically and economically possible so long as the military and political expenditure goes on on its present scale is strictly limited. The main consequence of the failure of the loan must, therefore, be a large-scale withdrawal on our part from international responsibilities. (Perhaps there might be no harm, in private conversation, in letting the State Department appreciate a little more vividly than I think they do at present that this would be inevitably the most striking consequence.)

I should be grateful if I could have a copy of Mr Clarke's note to take with me to America.

(Signed) Keynes.

22.2.46.

15. What happens if?: Minute by R. W. B. Clarke to Lord Keynes

[This may not be the final version of the minute. Amendments in Clarke's writing on the typed copy have been incorporated. Ed.]

I am getting this note off too quickly, in order to catch you before you leave.

I am satisfied that I have not cheated on new gold production. The sterling area's gold production in 1946-8 will be £300 millions, of which I thought we might get "at least £230 millions". This must be offset by British exports or loans from sterling area, but the figure in paragraph 10 of my statistical note took care of this.

The note is still obscure about the relation with the Washington figures. I am in difficulty here, for there was never a detailed statement for 1946-8. You will remember there was a lengthy cabled discussion which came to an unresolved end when the negotiations reached their climax. I have been referring back to the cables, but this is really an essay in exegesis. However, I think the following figures, changed to the basis now used by the Bank and ourselves, are compatible with the figures you were using in Washington.

	1946 £m.	1947 £m.	1948 £m.	Total 1946-8 £m.
Imports f.o.b. (excluding oil)	1,150	1,250	1,350	3,750
Overseas war expenditure	300	175	125	600
	1,450	1,425	1,475	4,350
Exports	650	975	1,175	2,800
Net invisibles	50	100	150	300
	700	1,075	1,325	3,100
Deficit	750	350	150	1,250

Our latest estimates for the three-years, assuming we get the loan (and do not do overmuch about military expenditure), may be something like this:-

	1946 £m.	1947 £m.	1948 £m.	Three years 1946-48 £m.
Imports f.o.b. (excluding oil)	1,100	1,225	1,350	3,675
Overseas Government expenditure	450	350	200	1,000
	1,550	1,575	1,550	4,675
Exports	600	1,000	1,150	2,750
Net invisibles	150	175	200	525
	750	1,175	1,350	3,275
Deficit	800	400	200	1,400

The "Government expenditure" now includes political expenditure; in Washington such political expenditure as was forecast was included in "net invisibles".

The main difference between the table above and the Washington table is an additional 400 for Government expenditure (pretty statistical in character) and an additional 225 for net invisibles, which were badly under-estimated in the Washington negotiations - which did not allow for drawing imports from U.K.-owned stocks abroad (e.g. cotton and wool), nor enough for shipping.

This gives a deficit of 1,400, of which we should draw 937 from U.S.A. loan, 281 from Canadian loan ($1¼ billion new money), 50 from U.S. and Canadian pipeline extending into 1946, and the remaining 132 from sterling area and other borrowing, and use of gold and dollar reserves.

How do I cope with the 1,400 deficit if we fail to get the U.S. loan? The short answer is:-

(i) Use the disposable gold and dollar reserve - 220.

(ii) Borrow 150 (net of service) from U.S.A. by other means.

(iii) Still borrow 281 from Canada, and still keep the 50 Lend-Lease pipeline and Canadian cuff element in 1946 imports.

(iv) Cut imports and film royalties by 150.

(v) Achieve the export figure, instead of missing it (no statistical saving).

This gives me 850. I need another 550. If I buy 200 gold from sterling area out of income, this makes 750. This can only be obtained by cutting Governmental expenditure from 1,000 or by borrowing from the sterling area and the rest of the world. In fact, we have to cut the 1,000 level of Governmental expenditure to a figure of 250 plus borrowing from the rest of the world. Much of the latter is linked with Governmental expenditure, especially if sterling is inconvertible. I suppose we may borrow 100-150 from inertia of war-time arrangements, and I should have thought we might borrow to some extent from South Africa, and oddments from Switzerland, Portugal, etc. Is it reasonable to say that we might borrow 250, and so have to cut Governmental expenditure (in so far as it does in fact impinge upon the U.K. balance of payments in conditions of inconvertible sterling during the period) to something like 500 for the period? This should not, to my mind, be absolutely impossible, for the extent to which these loans do in fact affect our balance of payments (i.e. represent U.K. exports directly or indirectly) under conditions of inconvertible sterling is open to some question. This is a very crucial point, which required detailed examination. I would not care to commit myself on what are the military and political consequences without seeing this argument much more clearly to its logical conclusion than I do now.

But I hope this meets your criticism, to the extent that it is a statistically logical analysis.

R.W.B.C.

23 February 1946.

16. What happens if?: Minute by Lord Keynes to R. W. B. Clarke

Thanks for your note of February 23rd with the statistics of reconciliation. I am reconciled as well as the statistics and agree that, without my taking responsibility for the actual figures, you have met my criticism by producing a statistically logical analysis.

Nor have I any reason for questioning your estimates except that perhaps net invisibles, which I agree were put too low at Washington, may now be a bit too high. A great deal depends on shipping, and there, I admit, I am optimistic, so that, if I am right, this would go some way to justifying your figure.

(Signed) Keynes.

23.2.46.

III The Dollar Crisis of 1947

17. Exhaustion of the Dollar Credit: Memorandum by the Chancellor of the Exchequer (CAB 129/17)

1.   Last Thursday (C.M.(47) 30th Conclusions, Minute 5) I warned my colleagues that we were racing through our United States dollar credit at a reckless, and ever-accelerating, speed.

2.   This is not my first warning on this subject. Last February I circulated a warning by the late Lord Keynes on the overseas deficit (C.P.(46) 58) and, simultaneously, a paper by myself on the balance of payments for 1946 (C.P.(46) 53). Again, on 23rd October (C.P.(46) 401), I circulated a further, and slightly more strident, warning, indicating in emphatic language that we were in serious danger of using up the United States and Canadian Credits too fast. Since then, the speed at which we have been exhausting these Credits has been rapidly mounting, and the situation now shows every sign of going out of control, unless we face the facts and pull ourselves together. In three or four weeks, I shall be submitting to the Cabinet proposals for the Import Programme from July 1947 onwards, in two six-monthly periods up to June 1948. I ask, meanwhile, that no decision should be taken, involving a still more rapid exhaustion of the residue of the Credits.

3.   The United States Credit of $3,750 millions was finally granted in July 1946. By the end of 1946 we had already drawn $600 millions. If this rate of drawing had been maintained, we should have exhausted the Credit in September 1949. This, having regard to our difficulties, was a pretty poor prospect. But, since the beginning of 1947, we have drawn a further $500 millions. On 1st April, in order to meet the ever-rising demands of the various Departments, the Treasury will be compelled to draw a further $200 millions. This will only leave us $2,450 millions of the American Credit. I must underline to my colleagues the simple arithmetical truth that, if we continue from now on to draw these dollars at the same rate at which we have been drawing them since 1st January, i.e., at the rate of $700 millions a quarter, the United States Credit will now be exhausted in February 1948.

4.   Even if we make some allowance for the fact that, at the beginning of April, we shall still have some unspent balances of our drawings in hand, we cannot spin out the United States Credit, at the present rate of spending, beyond June, 1948. This is a looming shadow of catastrophe, and I will not have it said hereafter that I have left my colleagues unwarned until the eleventh hour.

5.   The chief reasons for this very rapid worsening of our prospects are, first, the rapid rise in American prices, i.e., the rapid depreciation in value of the dollars lent to us, and, second (though this is partly a consequence of the depreciation of the dollar), our

ever-rising dollar bill to feed the Germans. Since the loan was negotiated in December, 1945, the value of the dollar, as measured by American wholesale prices, has fallen by 30 per cent. In 1946, the British taxpayer, even after allowing for dollar receipts from the sale of German exports, had to find some $60 millions to feed the Germans. It is, in itself, a most unwelcome and unexpected mis-use of our American Credit. From January 1947 to 1st April, a period of three months only, we shall have provided no less than a further $60 millions for this same high purpose. And we may have to find another $30 millions on 1st April. At present, as an incident in the arrangement for the fusion of the British and American Zones, we are paying the American share, as well as our own, of food supplies, particularly wheat, for both the Zones!

6.   If, and when, the American Congress votes the necessary appropriations, we should recover part of this excessive burden now falling on the British taxpayer.

7.   The practical conclusions for immediate action are two: the export drive, sadly handicapped by the fuel shortage, must be sustained, and stimulated, to the utmost; on the other hand, the import programme must be kept within the most severe limits. This may mean the rejection of many attractive proposals, such as an early increase in the sugar ration; but it will do the nation no good, in this highly critical situation, to give temporary advantages which cannot be continued. I am, indeed, doubtful, on a preliminary study of the facts, whether we can afford to maintain, let alone increase, our present food supplies from dollar sources. It is most important to switch, as much as we can, from dollar to non-dollar sources of supply. It is, of course, an illusion to suppose, as some seem to do, that imports bought from non-dollar sources do not have to be paid for by British exports.

8.   I therefore ask my colleagues to ponder deeply, and to be prepared for the taking of hard, and difficult, but necessary, decisions in the early future.

> H.D. (Hugh Dalton)
> Treasury Chambers, S.W.1.
> 21 March 1947.

---

18. Import Programme 1947/48: Memorandum by the Chancellor of the Exchequer (CAB 129/19)

I have repeatedly warned my colleagues – most recently in C.P. (47) 100 – that we were racing through our United States dollar credit at a reckless pace, and that they should be prepared to take hard and difficult, but necessary, decisions in the early future.

The attached memorandum by the Treasury on the Import Programme for 1947-48 brings us face to face with these decisions.

2.   The Treasury originally proposed a cut of £200 millions in the Import Programmes submitted by the Departments, of which £150 millions was on food (mainly hard currency). (As explained in paragraph 12 of the Treasury Paper, the programme of the Ministry of Food was designed to improve the standard of consumption above the 1945-46 level.) This proposal was designed to carry forward to June 1948 $800 millions of unused North American credits. This with our reserves, would have enabled us to finance a similar, and no worse, Import Programme for 1948-49. A preliminary review of these proposals was made by a group of Ministers, and the proposals were remitted for further consideration at the official level. As a result, a revised proposal has been put forward for consideration by the Cabinet, namely that we should make a cut of only £80 millions in the food programme, all in hard currency. The other cuts originally proposed would stand. This would mean a hard currency deficit over the next twelve months of more than $2 billions.

3.   As a result, we shall carry forward, at June 1948, not $800 millions of the credits, but at most $500 millions. That is all that will be left of the original credits of $5 billions. And for the import year 1948-49, even assuming a favourable trend of import prices, and success in forcing our exports against a possible sag in the sellers' market, we cannot expect a hard currency deficit of less than $1,250-1,500 millions.

4.   If, therefore, we accept only the modified cut of £80 millions in the food programme, we are running a very grave risk that in 1948-49 we might have to make far more drastic cuts in our imports of food, and also of raw materials, which would immediately affect employment and our export income, unless we supplement our reserves of hard currencies either by increased exports or by further assistance from the Americans.

5.   I ask my colleagues to pay special attention to paragraph 33 of the Treasury Paper. Action on these lines must be pressed forward at once, with a full sense of urgency. Otherwise we are sunk.

6.   As regards further assistance from the Americans, I will state my views orally. But we should certainly take the earliest opportunity of making the whole position clear to them. We are entitled to point out to them that all the assumptions on which the original line of credit was negotiated have been falsified:-

(a) The credit was not as large as we originally asked for and thought necessary.

(b) Since then, costs in the United States have risen rapidly. The wholesale price index in the United States has risen 40 per cent. since December 1945.

(c) Owing to the slow recovery of the non-dollar world, we cannot get convertible currency for our exports and we remain far more dependent for supplies on the American Continent than we foresaw.

(d) We are still having to use large quantities of our scanty dollars, not for our own people but for the Germans.

The net result is that not only is this country having to buy more, and at higher prices, from the Americans than we had contemplated, but that we are not alone in this position. Already "strong countries", such as Sweden and Canada, face drastic decisions about their dollar imports. The shortage of dollars is a world shortage, and only the Americans have it in their power to put it right.

7.   To sum up, I ask my colleagues for the following decisions:-

(1) The food Import Programme for 1947-48 to be reduced by at least £80 millions from hard currency sources. The reduced food programme should be authorised for the next six months only. The subsequent six months must be reviewed in September in the light of our foreign exchange position towards the end of this year.

(2) Reduction of the other Import Programmes on the lines set out in the Treasury Paper.

(3) An export target of 140 per cent. of 1938 volume to be reached by the second quarter of 1948.

(4) The long-term proposals in the Treasury Paper to be pressed forward vigorously.

(5) An early approach to the Americans on the whole question.

> H.D. (Hugh Dalton)
> Treasury Chambers,
> 28 May 1947.

---

19. Import Programme 1947/48: Memorandum by the Treasury

[This memorandum, only parts of which are reproduced, was attached to the Chancellor's Memorandum on the same subject. Ed.]

The Balance of Payments Problem

1.   We now face a crisis in our external financial position which affects our ability to import our food and raw materials.

At the end of May nearly half the two North American Credits will have been exhausted. We have $2 billions of the United States Credit and $570 millions of the Canadian Credit (£640 millions in all) left from the original total of $5 billions.

We have also £325 millions drawing rights on the International Monetary Fund. We can draw on these at a rate not exceeding £81 millions a year and subject to limits on the amount we can draw at any time within a year. We cannot count with certainty on being able to draw upon these monies, for they are meant to meet a temporary situation and not a continuing disequilibrium. The Board of the Fund, acting on behalf of all the Members, including particularly the United States, are bound to scrutinise carefully the situation of any Member which is drawing heavily.

We have reserves, mainly of gold but including some dollars, of some £625 millions. Ordinary prudence requires us to regard £250 millions of this reserve as a "war chest" – a reserve to meet an unforeseen crisis in international affairs. Reserves are meant to be drawn upon at time of need, but they are our final defence and we must handle them with great caution. Moreover, they are the central reserve, not only for ourselves but also for the sterling area, and while we need not, perhaps, concern ourselves with the difficulties which will confront some members of the sterling area, there are others, such as Australia, New Zealand and the Colonies, who will have to look to us to tide them over temporary difficulties. In the uncertain conditions of the next three or four years, the handling of our reserves will be of crucial importance. The willingness of other countries to sell to us for sterling will be influenced by the rate at which we are drawing upon these reserves; if they take alarm about our position they will want gold for their supplies.

2. Our balance of payments is worse since last October. The following events have produced this:-

(i) 10 to 15 per cent increase in world prices, equivalent to an extra import cost of £200 millions a year. This increase falls immediately upon us, but any corresponding upward adjustment of our export prices, even if it is assured, takes longer to produce results. On this latter point see paragraph 30 below. In any case, a rise in export prices does not compensate the extra dollar cost of our imports.

(ii) The fuel crisis has cost us two months' exports and has set back the export drive by nine months: this is equivalent to a loss of export income of £200 millions in 1947. This estimate makes the favourable assumption that the end-1946 export level is regained by this autumn, and that by the second quarter of 1948, exports will have reached 140 per cent of 1938 volume.

(iii) The losses suffered by United Kingdom agriculture have delayed the recovery of a major potential dollar saver.

(iv) Political difficulties, war damage, and the coal shortage have delayed the progress of recovery in Europe and the Far East; this delays the prospect of a switch to other sources of supply.

(v) The cost of the restoration of Germany's economy, which is crucial to the restoration of Europe, has increased and may increase still further.

(vi) There is a cumulative dollar shortage showing itself in the world – even in strong countries such as Sweden and Canada. This threatens to create a world economic crisis. The International Monetary Fund has only just begun operations; only one small loan has yet been made by the Reconstruction Bank.

(vii) Quite recently the Canadians have informed us <u>very confid-
entially</u> that they are in acute difficulties about their United
States dollar position and they are unlikely to be able to allow
us to draw upon the Canadian Credit as we need it.

3.   Last October it was hoped that the total deficit for 1947 would be
about £200 millions. This was subsequently increased to £350 millions
in the Economic Survey. On the present import programme, however, the
total deficit for the year 1947 will be over £700 millions. On the
import programmes as originally submitted (Appendix B), <u>and assuming a
favourable course of exports</u> (i.e., achievement of the target of 140
per cent of 1938 volume by the second quarter of 1948), the deficit in
the second half of 1947 will be £400 millions and in the first half of
1948 will be £150 millions - a total of £550 millions for the year
mid-1947 to mid-1948.

4.   The hard currency deficit is even more serious, for half our
imports come from hard currency sources. On the same basis as above,
the hard currency deficit for mid-1947 to mid-1948 will be about £650
millions. This would mean that the United States and Canadian credits
would be exhausted by the middle of 1948 (Appendix C).

5.   We dare not take this risk. We have no hope of being able to
stand on our own feet so early as the middle of 1948. We might by then
get some relief from lower prices, but this would signal the end of
the sellers' market for our exports as well. European and Far Eastern
production will gradually recover, but this cannot relieve us of the
bulk of our hard currency expenditure by the year 1948. With the
credits gone we should be forced into catastrophic import cuts of food
and raw materials.

6.   The crisis which is coming upon us differs in kind from any other
we have experienced. Currency depreciation or adjustment or repudiation
of external indebtedness provides no way out. Our overseas income is
insufficient for our overseas needs. Our food consumption and our
industrial activity depends upon our ability to export. We are not
yet exporting nearly enough. Superimposed on this is the hard currency
problem which can be solved only by a recovery of the non-dollar world;
this is not yet in sight. No juggling can dispose of these two basic
facts which will condition our life for the next few years.

This crisis has been developing inexorably since the early years
of the war and has been concealed successively by lend-lease, borrowing for sterling and the United States and Canadian credits. We have
been living beyond our means, not only in consumption levels, but
also in overseas financial commitments. We are faced now with a
reduction in the whole of our standard of living, or a supreme effort
for five years which will enable us to restore our pre-war standards
with prospect of improvement.

The rapid worsening of our position requires immediate short-term
measures - a sharp cut in imports and an increase in the proportion of
our output which goes in exports.

Cut in the Import Programme

7.   The first Treasury proposal was for an immediate cut of £200 millions (of which £150 millions would fall on food) in the import programme for the year mid-1947 to mid-1948. The purpose of this was to enable us to carry forward to the year mid-1948 to mid-1949 some $800 millions of unused North American Credits. These, together with our reserves, would have enabled us to finance a fairly tolerable import programme for that year. It must be emphasised that the immediate position for mid-1947 to mid-1948 is not the crucial issue, for we could buy practically all the imports we could secure if we choose to use up the whole of the North American Credits for this purpose. But this would bring catastrophe in mid-1948 to mid-1949.

8.   It was proposed that the cut should fall almost exclusively on the hard currency imports, for these are a direct and immediate charge on our reserves. For this purpose the hard currencies are shown in Appendix E and a further sub-division is made between the other sources of supply. It must be emphasised, however, that certain sources of supply are hardly less difficult than the so-called hard currency sources. It is entirely wrong to think that imports from non-dollar sources cost us nothing; indeed, we cannot get imports from any source except by sending exports or by paying dollars or by borrowing from that source.

9.   A major cause of this crisis is the rise in import prices. The proposed reduction in our purchases should have a useful effect in easing the pressure in world markets. This cannot affect the price of our imports much in 1947-48, but it has an important potential effect upon 1948-49. The cut should likewise ease the demand upon our shipping and increase its foreign exchange earnings and relieve the pressure on the freight market.

10.   A cut of the scale proposed cannot be secured by pruning "non-essentials". About 50 per cent of the hard currency import programme represents food; 40 per cent represents raw materials, petroleum (other than for private motoring), machinery and other supplies for industry and agriculture; only 10 per cent represents the so-called "luxuries" - tobacco, films, private motoring, consumer goods. Even if decisions were taken literally to stop smoking, close the cinemas, prohibit private motoring, &c., this would save only about £80 millions a year.

11.   The Treasury proposal was discussed with the Departments principally concerned with particular reference to the effect of the proposed food cut of £150 millions. The view was taken that a cut of this scale would be too severe and an alternative proposal has been made that the cut should be £80 millions, all from hard currency sources. The other proposals made by the Treasury have been accepted departmentally. The following table shows the various proposals:-

	Total £m.	Hard Currency £m.	Cut proposed by the Treasury £m.	Alternative proposals £m.
Food –				
"Basic"	754	442	150	80
"Supplementary"	116			
Raw materials	609	267	25	25
Petroleum	87	49	4	4
Machinery	42	36		
Goods for industry	45	12	2	2
Seeds and animals	23	2		
Consumer goods	32	10	2	2
Tobacco	53	46	14	14
Films	15	15	3	3
	1,776	879	200	130

On the alternative proposal, the cuts must all be made on the hard currency programmes. The savings must be made, as far as possible, in the second half of 1947, and the position will, in any case, be reviewed again in September, when the firm programme requires to be fixed for the first half of 1948.

12. _Food_. On the alternative proposal of a cut of £80 millions in food from hard currency sources, the lay-out of consumption might be as follows:-

(i) An immediate cut to 1s. 2d. in the meat ration, the ration to remain at this level until the end of June 1948. The carcase meat portion to be 1s. for most of the period, but reduced to 10d. for about two to three months. The recent reduction of one-third in manufacturing meat to continue until the end of June 1948.

(ii) Maintenance of the present fats and sugar ration.

(iii) Abolition of bread rationing and unrestricted flour consumption.

(iv) Maintenance of the present tea ration (unless cut necessary on supply grounds). A 50 per cent cut in coffee compared with the present rate of distribution.

(v) Restoration of the bacon ration from 2 oz. to 3 oz. during January to June 1948.

(vi) The usual increase in the cheese ration from 2 oz. to 3 oz. during the winter months.

(vii) Consumption of dried eggs, together with shell eggs, to be equivalent to 98 eggs per person in 1948-48 compared with 87 eggs

per person in 1946-47. Stocks of dried eggs to be exhausted by
June 1948. In 1948-49 to rely entirely on shell eggs (estimated
at 86 per person).

(viii) Increased supply of liquid milk with the same quantity of
condensed milk distributed during the winter of 1947-48 as was
distributed last winter. Issue of milk powder would have to be
discontinued some time during 1947-48.

(ix) Maintain supplies of points canned meat and canned fish.

(x) 40 per cent reduction in dried fruit and 62 per cent reduction
in canned fruit, compared with 1946-47.

(xi) Citrus fruit at about the same level as 1946-47. A 66$\frac{2}{3}$ per
cent reduction in apples compared with 1946-47 (no imported apples
during the winter). 50 per cent increase in bananas, three times
as many tomatoes and 25 per cent more of other fresh fruit than
in 1946-47.

(xii) Considerable increase in fresh fish consumption and a 25 per
cent cut in poultry compared with 1946.

This programme would provide a total caloric intake approximately
at the 1946 level. The effect of the alternative proposal compared
with the cut originally proposed by the Treasury is to restore a number
of important items and in particular increases next winter in the bacon
and cheese ration and the maintenance of supplies of points canned
meat and canned fish. It must be remembered in considering this programme that some £40 millions of the £442 millions hard currency food
programme represents improvements in consumption and that there is a
substantial quantity of supplies from other sources - some £75
millions - which will contribute to improve the standard of consumption
above the 1945-46 level. On the alternative proposal, the total food
programme for 1947-48 would be some £790 millions compared with £677
millions (at lower prices) in the year mid-1946 to mid-1947.

/The remainder of the memorandum deals with other cuts in imports, the
need to persuade the American administration to take a less restrictive
view of Article 9 of the Anglo-American Financial Agreement, military
expenditure overseas, and export targets. Ed./

Summary of Immediate Plan

31. The immediate implications of the alternative proposal may be
summarised as follows:-

(i) Cut in food as described in paragraph 12.

(ii) Continuation of present clothing ration (unless production
increases).

(iii) Other cuts in manufactured goods for the home market,
including newspapers, motor cars and household requisites.

(iv) Cuts in petrol, tobacco and films.

(v) To provide enough steel for steel-consuming exports (plus machinery, &c., for United Kingdom) will interfere with housing and other building, and so will the cut in raw material imports.

32. On the original proposals of the Treasury we could reasonably hope to reduce the hard currency deficit for 1947-48 to some £450 millions and in July 1948 we should thus still have had some £200 millions of the United States and Canadian Credits together with our reserves. We could then have reasonably hoped to afford an import programme for 1948-49 of similar volume to that then proposed for 1947-48. The alternative proposal worsens this position considerably. It means that instead of carrying forward £200 millions into the second half of 1948, we may only be able to carry forward, say, £125 millions. Furthermore, since the original Treasury Memorandum which proposed the £200 millions cut was prepared, the position has continued to deteriorate and our reserve position at the middle of next year is likely to be less favourable than we then hoped.

While the arguments for the alternative proposal are recognised and the danger that a food cut of the scale proposed might have damaging effects upon industrial production is understood, the fact remains that the alternative proposal runs serious risks for the 1948-49 import programme.

33. These additional risks for the future make it all the more urgent that we should immediately press forward the measures which are necessary to enable us to right our position. The crisis in our ability to buy food and raw materials will continue until our export income is enough to meet our import needs. Nothing can change this fact. The following are the main things which must be done:-

(i) Coal. We must increase coal production so that it meets essential needs of home production and provides a reasonable volume for export. Coal is of fundamental importance to the whole matter. If we take risks on our import expenditure, we must make more certain of our export income.

(ii) Power and Transport. These other essentials to our whole economy are affected by supplies of coal and by supplies of steel which in turn depends upon coal.

(iii) Agriculture. We must expand our agriculture as fast as possible and particularly expand livestock and other production which saves expensive dollar imports. For this purpose, housing in agricultural areas should have high priority and the industry should be given sufficient priority for supplies of machinery, &c.

(iv) Building. We do not see how the production required to secure the necessary volume of exports in the next twelve months can be obtained without setting free some part of the resources of material and labour at present allocated to building.

(v) Import-Saving Production. We must develop production in this country of materials and other supplies which will save expensive hard currency imports. This should be done with the same determination as the corresponding war-time measures for saving bulky imports.

(vi) <u>Alternative Sources of Supply</u>. Departments are switching as far as they can, but the important items in the import programme should once more be re-examined and every effort made to **create** alternative sources of supply.

(vii) <u>Guidance of Exports</u>. This must continue to be pressed forward even at the cost of some disappointment to other old customers. In particular we should do what we can to guide exports to Canada and Latin America, especially Argentina. These will, for the next few years, remain a large and indispensable source of supply.

Conclusion

34. The result of the original Treasury plan, as far as this can be predicted in a rapidly changing situation, would have been –

(i) To stop the immediate decline in our position.

(ii) To create an essential margin, so that we should be able to avoid catastrophic cuts in food and raw materials in the next two years.

(iii) To allow time for the constructive proposals summarised in paragraph 33 to begin to take effect.

(iv) To help to carry us over the interval – the length of which no one can foretell – until the prices of our imports at last begin to fall.

(v) To tide over the United States Presidential Election year without catastrophe, and to allow dollar starvation to reach the point where the Americans are driven, in their own interests, to produce more dollars.

35. The alternative plan will contribute towards the same results, but the gain secured under each of these heads will be correspondingly less, and the risks of early disaster correspondingly greater.

Appendix F

Prices and Quantities

1. The following table estimates the quantities of the import programme, in comparison with 1946 and 1938:-

	Retained Imports 1938		Retained Imports 1946		Programme July 1947-June 1948	
	at 1938 prices	at current prices	at current prices	Quantum as % of 1938	at current prices	Quantum as % of 1938
	£m.	£m.	£m.	%	£m.	%
Food	380	995	631	63	850	86
Raw materials	245	596	395	66	525	88
Manufactured goods	84	225	75	33	125	56
Tobacco	21	55	70	127	51	93
Seeds and animals	9	31	23	74	20	65
Oil	31	69	76	110	88	128
	770	1,971	1,270	65	1,659	85

2. The increase in prices over the whole programme compared with 1938 is estimated at over 150 per cent. The increase in food is about 160 per cent; in raw materials about 140 per cent; and in petroleum 120 per cent. These represent the current f.o.b. prices as shown in the import programmes for the first half of 1947; they are considerably more than the increases shown in the regular Board of Trade indices, because of the time-lag between f.o.b. prices and the arrival of the imports in United Kingdom.

3. British export prices are running at about 110 per cent above 1938. The evidence suggests that the terms of trade have moved against us sharply.

4. The import prices of food and raw materials are now $12\frac{1}{2}$-15 per cent above those of 1946.

20. The World Dollar Crisis

[In June 1947 after a short visit to Ottawa with Sir Wilfrid Eady, Sir Richard 'collected together the best picture I could make of "the world dollar shortage", both for UK and international purposes' in a memorandum which he intended to use as the basis for Chapter V ('Preliminary to the Marshall Plan'). He claimed that it was the first time 'the world dollar shortage' had been analysed world-wide and its dynamics brought out. 'The rapid deterioration, obviously spreading into 1948,' he wrote, 'put the sense of energy into the creation of the Marshall Plan.'

In his draft he reduced the memorandum to less than half its original length by omitting the early and concluding sections. In what follows the early sections have been restored but the second half is left in the form to which he reduced it (paras. 25-33). Ed.]

The World Dollar Crisis

/̄The figures indicate orders of magnitude only./̄

How the Dollar Crisis affects us

1.   Our basic problem is our adverse balance with the American Continent. Assuming the import cuts, we shall import $3 billion of goods and
services from the American Continent in 1947-8. Our exports to the
American Continent will not be more than $1 billion. We must therefore
find $2 billion a year. This is a continuing charge, which (apart from
borrowing) can be met in only three ways:-

(i) Reduce imports still further.

(ii) Increase exports.

(iii) Earn dollars from our trade with the rest of the world.

2.   A fall in prices would help. A fall by 20% (restoring our terms
of trade to the 1938 level) would reduce the gap by $½ billion.

3.   Reduction in dollar imports can be achieved otherwise only by
greatly increased supplies from other sources (and of course greater
U.K. agricultural production). In order to _increase_ our consumption,
still more supplies will be needed from other sources. Increases on
this scale are obviously impossible unless the rest of the world
recovers and European and Far Eastern sources of supply are developed
again. This recovery requires vast capital investment to set the
European and Asiatic economies on their feet; we cannot finance this.

4.   We are pressing our exports to the American Continent as hard as
we can. The figure of $1 billion would be rather more than pre-war
export volume. But the market is limited.* The seller's market in

---

*   In 1937, U.S.A. imported $¾ billion of manufactured goods, Canada
     $½ billion, Latin America $1¼ billion - total $2½ billion, of which
     U.K. did one-sixth. The market may now be $5-6 billion at present
     prices.

North America is drawing to an end and there are signs of difficulty
in Latin America. We are up against very keen U.S. competition in
markets which U.S.A. has regarded as its own preserve; we are also up
against European competitors in search of dollars. We have lost six
years' contacts in these markets, and indeed we never concentrated on
these markets before the war; many of our most suitable industries
(e.g., textiles and pottery) have been seriously disrupted by the war.
Obviously it is uphill work in these markets, unless Canada and Latin
America are so short of dollars that they are forced to discriminate
stringently against U.S.A.

5.   The natural way for us to fill the gap is to earn dollars from
our sales to the rest of the world where we can readily expect a
surplus in our balance of payments. However, even taking full account
of South African gold, Malayan rubber, etc., the net contribution which
we can receive from our surpluses with the sterling area will not be
much over $\pounds\frac{1}{4}$ billion. There is no obvious sign of dollars from the rest.

6.   The size of this transfer problem, in the very best conditions, is
hardly manageable. This same problem created continuous difficulty
before the war but the balance was then $1:\frac{1}{2}$ not $3:1$, and was in effect
filled by South African gold and Malayan rubber and tin.

7.   But if the world is short of dollars and fails to recover its
production, there is obviously no solution at all within the present
framework of thought. There may be a bilateral solution, especially
as production develops, so that we get more room to manoeuvre for
imports. But there is no solution at all compatible with present ideas
and commitments.

8.   Indeed, our commitments under the Anglo-American Financial Agreement make the whole problem much worse. Unless we can rely on earning
dollars from the rest of the world to meet our deficit with the
American Continent, we must obviously cut down our imports from the
American Continent to the bone. But under non-discrimination, we have
to cut down our imports from other sources likewise. This in turn
forces them to cut down their imports from us, and so ad infinitum.
Not only is trade between U.K. and the American Continent brought to a
standstill, but also trade between U.K. and the rest of the world.

9.   The convertibility obligation can bring about the same result in
a rather different way. With sterling convertible and dollars short,
the rest of the world will manage its affairs so that it earns as much
transferable sterling as it can. It cuts down imports from us, in
order to get sterling to finance its dollar deficit. In the arithmetic
above, we clearly cannot accept this. We therefore curtail our imports
from the rest of the world to stop them from getting sterling ... and
so ad infinitum again.

10.   To sum up, the effect upon U.K. of a world dollar crisis is:-

   (i) To stop the growth of non-American production, and thus to
   maintain our huge import bill with the American Continent.

   (ii) To increase competition in American markets - the only
   source of earning dollars.

(iii) To prevent us from securing dollars from the rest of the world to finance our deficit with the American Continent.

These jointly prevent us from solving our dollar problem, and force us to run through the Credits and our reserves - a process intensified by convertibility, which gives the rest of the world a chance to push their dollar problem on to our back. This process inevitably leads (especially in conjunction with non-discrimination) to a drying-up of world trade - and may literally mean starvation and unemployment on a substantial world-wide scale. The world dollar crisis reacts upon U.K.; the consequent U.K. crisis reacts back on the rest of the world and may create a world catastrophe.

The Evidence of World Dollar Crisis

11. Obviously a world dollar crisis is developing. The U.S. trade figures show it:-

		Monthly rate ($m)		
		Exports	Imports	Surplus
1946	1st quarter	762	353	409
	2nd quarter	829	398	431
	3rd quarter	784	411	373
	4th quarter	873	472	399
1947	1st quarter	1,199	471	728
	April	1,296	512	782

The striking fact is the growing deterioration in the first quarter of this year, with the gap still growing. The pattern is very like that of the U.K. dollar drain, which has increased from $100 millions a month in the second half of 1946 to over $300 millions a month in April.

12. Besides the rapid worsening of the U.K.'s position ($2 billion in 1947-48), there are the Canadian and Swedish crises. The Europeans are all critically short of dollars; there are signs of trouble in the smaller Latin American countries; an interesting indicator from the Far East is the inability of Siam to buy any oil from Standard (while buying from Shell). A trend of this kind must have rapid results; a situation is obviously untenable in which only one-half of the world's imports from U.S.A. are being paid for by exports and gifts. The U.S. surplus in the first five months of 1947 will be equivalent to the whole British loan.

13. How does the surplus arise? Exports have risen in volume in the last year from double pre-war to nearly treble pre-war; imports are only about 25% above pre-war volume. The increase in the prices of both imports and exports has been about 25% in the last year, and both are now about double pre-war. Price is an important factor in the size of the surplus, but there has been no improvement in U.S.A.'s terms of trade.

14. How is the surplus financed? In 1946 the surplus was $8.1
billions. This was financed by $3.1 billions Government expenditure
and other gifts; $3.3 billions loans and credits (of which Export-
Import 1.0, Lend/Lease and surplus property credits 1.7, U.K. Loan
0.6), and the remaining $1.7 billions in gold and dollars.

15. The official U.S. view is that the 1947 surplus will again be
about $8 billions. But it looks likely to be much more (there is a
big - and probably growing - surplus on services as well as on goods).
It has been reported in the press that the surplus for the first quarter
was as much as $3 billions, of which $1.2 billions was financed by gold
and dollars, $0.7 billions by U.N.R.R.A., Lend-Lease and Army spending,
etc., and $0.5 billions by the U.K. Loan, leaving $0.6 billions to be
covered by Export-Import and other public and private credits, etc.
Taking the full year 1947, it is difficult to put Government expenditure above $2 billions, U.K. Loan $2½ billions, Export-Import $1
billion and other credits of $1 billion. This only gives $6½ billions.
The British Loan is the major factor preventing a general crisis in
1947. An $8 billions surplus in 1947 might be manageable. But a $12
billion surplus is likely to create a general crisis by the end of
1947.

16. Looking forward to 1948, one can see no obvious reason for the
pressure on the U.S. balance of payments to diminish. There will be
greater pressure to export, and imports may fall. One cannot possibly
put the figure below $8 billions.

The Background to Action

17. It seems likely that by the end of 1947 - or at any rate in the
first half of 1948 - the general crisis will be upon the world unless
special action to the tune of $6 billions a year is taken. It is not
only a problem of 1948; it will continue to be intense for some years.
The crisis is solely a reflection of the fact that U.S.A. vastly
expanded her industrial and agricultural capacity during the war, while
the rest of the world has, economically speaking, been devastated. We
all need the American goods - food, oil, steel, cotton, tobacco,
machinery, trucks. Discrimination is not an issue in 1948.

18. Any action will present considerable difficulty for U.S. public
opinion, which is not prepared (and has been badly misled by the
Administration into thinking it has done fine so far). At the same
time, one would hope that we shall not fall into the trap of letting
the Administration use Congress as the bogey. Any serious proposal
to fill the gap is the exercise of U.S. economic power on a terrific
scale, and will certainly be devised in the manner which best secures
U.S. political and commercial advantages. Old-fashioned isolationists
may oppose the use of economic power, but they are not even a strong
minority.

What Would Help Us

19. Our interests are so wrapped up with those of the world as a whole
that any plan would help us. But we want to be clear what is best for
us.

(i) We need some direct help to finance our deficit with U.S.A. In 1947-8 this will be £$\frac{3}{4}$ - 1 billion and though this will be the first of our hard currency deficits to decline, it will remain considerable.

(ii) Help for Canada is important to us in order to enable the Canadians to continue to let us draw on their Credit, and, indeed, in order to let them lend us more.

(iii) If, as one suspects from the figures, Latin America is beginning to run out of dollars, this creates the certainty that the Latin American countries will take all their transferable sterling in dollars.

20. We then come to the more indirect means of getting help which would enable us to earn dollars /in exchange/ for our surplus with the Eastern Hemisphere. The earlier figures show that the scale upon which we shall wish to do this is very large indeed. This really breaks down into three parts:-

(i) Western Europe.

(ii) Suez to Singapore.

(iii) The rest of the Eastern Hemisphere.

Western Europe is a central crisis and I do not think that there would be a tremendous amount of dollars for us in aid given to Western Europe. However big the dollar flow it would be a long time before the Western European countries could supply us either with goods to substitute for Western Hemisphere goods or to supply us with gold and dollars. The reconstruction of Western Europe is a longer term affair. It is necessary but not sufficient to solve our problem.

21. I agree with Mr Cobbold that the area from Suez to Singapore is of decisive importance to us. This area is not seriously short of dollars at present; it has quite significant dollar earnings. Fundamentally it is short of sterling, i.e. it faces a serious deficiency of current sterling as soon as we stop the rate of drawing down of sterling balances. By far our best way to earn a large number of dollars would be for this area to be put in funds so that it could continue to buy heavily from us.

22. For the rest, we should probably not derive much advantage from dollars going behind the iron curtain, but my belief is that a good deal of reconstruction money is needed in the S.E.A.C.* area and particularly Indonesia. It may well happen that purchases of Japanese cotton textiles - which are absolutely vital to this area - will have to be cut out because they are dollar purchases. The benefit we should derive from dollars in this area would be in the restoration of commodity production rather than in direct payment for the goods we send.

---

* South East Asia Command.

23. A fall in world prices would be of substantial value to us, not only by virtue of the fall in prices itself but also because it increases the value of our reserves in terms of commodities.

Possible U.S. Action

24. The only courses of action open to the Americans in order to close the gap are:-

(i) To cut their exports.

(ii) To increase their imports.

(iii) To lend the surplus goods abroad.

(iv) To give away the surplus goods.

25. The scale and duration of the problem is such that as soon as the Americans see it, they are bound to think in terms of large inter-governmental loans and grants: freer import measures are trivial in this sort of money. Some would think of using the IMF, but the righting of great trade disequilibria is not the Fund's business (and would not give much money anyway) and the purpose of the Bank is to develop countries, not keep them alive. Private lending could not begin to cope.

26. The experience with the British on the Loan is not encouraging for loans. How many countries could reckon to repay them? However, the same query could be put to the International Bank loans. Some countries (e.g. Canada) could certainly repay, and there could well be part of a package.

27. Next, general subsidies - i.e. subsidies of, say, 50% on food, coal, steel, shipping. Contrary to I.T.O.; and likely to be very awkward for some countries and perhaps diminish their production. But in this indignation, one has to remember that the purpose is to reduce the "dollar gap", that one of the main reasons for the "gap" is the great increase in U.S. primary prices, and export subsidies are familiar in U.S.A.

28. Of course the redistribution of the gold in Fort Knox is always there, especially joined with a doubling of the price of gold; and it could also be done through the IMF and so be fitted into the inter-national machinery. But the mystique of gold cuts both ways. The idea of $20 billion lying in Fort Knox appears a little nonsensical: but once it is given away it has gone - it is easier to replace $2 billion of wheat than $2 billion of gold. Of course if the distribution is really a loan (via IMF or otherwise), much would turn on the ultimate IMF terms and controls.

Conditions

29. It must be expected that the Americans would make conditions. One line of possibility would be to try to develop the concepts in the U.K. Loan Agreement - use of the assistance to strengthen IMF and ITO and bring others in compulsorily. An entirely different line of thought would be more on power political lines: requiring a more acceptable government, access to bases, etc. Another and more imaginative course

would be to abandon the idea, politically speaking, of helping countries, and seek to help continental blocs (e.g. Western Europe or South and South-East Asia) economically more powerful than the present units, and sympathetic to U.S.A.; and obviously this would require "plans" and inconsistencies with the international doctrines.

30. From the British point of view, the general international rather than the Continental or individual course is the best, for three reasons:-

(i) The problem is a world dollar shortage, and will so continue, and the solution should be related to this.

(ii) The continental systems leave a formidable problem of how to handle the dollar deficit of the rest of the sterling area.

(iii) A Western European bloc including ourselves should develop independently as an economic group getting temporary U.S. aid but outside the U.S. political ambit.

What Happens if the Americans give no Aid

31. The prospects of any of these schemes of large scale American assistance are extremely uncertain. The idea of a special session of Congress in the autumn is coming to the fore. But the process of getting quick congressional approval to whatever the U.S.A. Administration ultimately decides must be a tortuous process.

32. We cannot draw up any sort of timetable. The following, however, may be regarded as fairly established facts:-

(i) The U.K. will be in a serious crisis for the first half of 1948. Unless there is congressional action this autumn on an adequate scale the 1948 import programme determination in September and October will be critical.

(ii) Canada will be in a dollar crisis by the end of this year.

(iii) The Brazilian difficulties are the first real sign in Latin America. Latin America has a lot of dollars but is using them very fast.

(iv) It is expected that the U.S. coal allocations to Europe for the third quarter of this year will not be fully taken up; (the timber allocation system in Europe has virtually broken down already because of the inability to afford supplies).

(v) If we are to have no releases of sterling balances there will be an acute crisis in the Middle East and India before the end of this year.

33. If by the end of this year the dollar shortage is running at the rate of, say, $5 billion a year - that is, if there is still a gap of that size after allowing for possible use of gold and dollar balances, etc. - then a cut of about one-third in U.S. exports would be inevitable.

R.W.B.C.

16 June 1947

21. Alternative Courses of Action: Memorandum by R. W. B. Clarke

1.   In the autumn, Ministers will face one of three major situations:-

Situation A. Substantial Marshall aid certain.

Situation B. No or inadequate Marshall aid likely.

Situation C. U.S. Credit nearing exhaustion, but uncertainty
              about Marshall aid.

2.   Situation A is most unlikely by autumn and need not concern us
here.

3.   Situation B will require drastic action internally and on import
programme, and a major reversal of engines in the whole field of overseas commercial and financial policy. This is analysed in the Appendix,
and the chief points are:-

(a) Internal Policy: Drastic action, equivalent to national
mobilisation, to expand export production (e.g. coal and textiles),
stimulate import-saving production (e.g. agriculture), and stop
long-term capital projects.

(b) Import Programme: Cuts much more drastic than those proposed
by the Treasury in April.

(c) Overseas Policy: Bilateral bargaining for supplies; development of payments agreements; some direction of exports.

(d) Commitments: Abandonment of non-discrimination and convertibility obligations of Loan Agreement; postponement of I.T.O.;
no more dollars for Germany; review of military and other
commitments overseas.

This series of policies would have to be carried out with great vigour
and sacrifices in order to make it succeed, and would be seriously
damaging to us unless we went at it whole-heartedly.

4.   Situation C is most likely. There now seems little chance of
Marshall aid before the Credit is exhausted. Ministers will thus have
to choose between:-

(a) A gamble on Marshall aid, which would drain away our remaining resources very fast, and leave us in desperate straits (with
our bargaining power gone) if the Marshall aid were too little and
too late.

(b) Vigorous remedial action on the lines contemplated in
Situation B. We could not however make the major reversal of
overseas economic policy (with its Loan Agreement implications)
while Marshall aid was being negotiated. Our power to organise
alternative sources of supply or to influence the terms on which
we continue to get supplies, e.g. from Canada and Argentina, would
be weak until we could get a free hand for bilateral bargaining.

The immediate action would therefore be primarily in the field of internal policy and import cuts, with such manipulation of our financial and trading arrangements as could be achieved without overt variance with the Loan Agreement obligations. The need for drastic internal action as outlined in paragraph 3(a) above and in greater detail in the Appendix is as important in Situation C as in Situation B, both for our own balance of payments and as an essential condition for success in our approach to the Americans for Marshall aid.

R.W.B.C.

23 July 1947

Appendix

1.   The following deals with the clear situation envisaged in Situation B, in which no or inadequate Marshall aid is likely. The general background would be:-

(i)   World dollar shortage raging with great intensity, forcing sharp import restrictions in Canada, Latin America, Europe and elsewhere. The fact that sterling was still convertible would make these countries discriminate less strongly in favour of U.K. and against U.S.A. than they would otherwise do. A number of countries will be short of sterling.

(ii) Prices of dollar goods falling.

(iii) Pressure on non-dollar sources of food and raw materials (even if convertibility is still operative).

(iv) Fall in U.S. exports, tending to reduce employment in U.S.A. but not sufficiently decisively to make a U.S. slump.

(v)   European economic activity falling as a result of failure to buy the necessary minimum of food and fuel.

(vi) The U.K. would be the only major trading country with a significant reserve of gold and dollars.

The Import Problem

2.   Our central problem would be to finance our imports from the Americas in 1948 and 1949. We could reasonably expect to finance our imports from elsewhere with our exports.

3.   Import programmes for 1948 and 1949 are being worked out, which will show the extent of our inevitable dependence upon the Americas. The present programme for the year mid-1947 to mid-1948 gives the scale. Our import bill from the Americas will then be $3 - 3\frac{1}{4}$ billions (£750-800 millions), and our exports there only $\frac{3}{4}$ billions (£185 millions) - a deficit of $2\frac{1}{4} - 2\frac{1}{2}$ billions (£550-600 millions).

4.   This is a formidable import programme including:-

	Imports from the Americas mid-1947 to mid-1948 ($ millions)	% of U.K. <u>Consumption</u>
Wheat	400	75
Maize, barley, oats	120	50
Meat and bacon	475	40
Sugar	100	40
Oils and fats	160	40 (by value)
Cheese	60	33
Tobacco	100	75
Copper	60	30
Zinc	25	50
Lead	25	30
Aluminium	30	80
Softwoods	135	55
Hardwoods	15	35
Cotton	100	40
Woodpulp and paper	40	15
Hides and skins	60	80

And a great deal else besides, including practically the whole of the steel which would enable us to export steel as such, all the machinery we plan to import, and much of our oil (including most of the oil equipment for the British companies and their expenses in Venezuela; dollar expenditure on the oil and oil equipment and tanker programmes is of the order of $350-400 millions).

5.   Radical cuts in this programme will be extremely difficult to make, and if made confront us with the prospect of a decay of industrial activity - a downward spiral towards the plight of Germany to-day.

General Overseas Economic Strategy

6.   The intensifying world dollar shortage will <u>hamper</u> European and Asiatic production. Europe and Asia need substantial foreign investment put into them, and their production cannot expand fast without it. There will be a tendency towards drying-up of economic activity throughout the non-dollar world.

7.   There would be no chance of filling the gaps in our dollar programme from non-dollar sources. But if we started early enough, our bargaining position to get non-dollar supplies would be strong. We should still have some gold; we should be the main source of manufactured exports; we could begin by exploiting this position without overmuch regard to our long-term commercial interests (for the Americans would not be able to get into the markets we left at any rate until they

had begun to organise tied credits).

8.   The first question to decide is whether U.K. should go all out for supplies at the risk of intensifying other countries' difficulties (and thus damaging our own medium-term prospects) or whether we should seek to do all we could to develop trade within the non-dollar world (if necessary at some cost to ourselves in supplies).

9.   This arises with great force in terms of individual and crucial supplies. Should we take Australian wheat from India, or Mauritius sugar from the Middle East, or Rhodesian copper from France, or Anglo-Iranian oil from the sterling area and European markets? If we do not do so, we lose supplies or pay gold for their equivalent. If we do so, we push other countries further downhill and write off our chances of getting increased supplies from them.

10.   On the monetary side, there would be advantage in maintaining the free expendability of sterling over as wide an area as possible – though not of course providing U.S. dollars – in order to keep trade as multilateral as possible and enable countries to offset their surpluses in trade with each other with their deficits. The present sterling area system and our arrangements with Western Europe could be modified in this direction. This would constructively help in maintaining trade, at no cost to us in gold or dollars (for we clearly could not allow the balances arising in this system to be converted, except under special arrangements).

11.   On the supply side, we should have to start on a bilateral basis, and later widen the bilateral arrangements as we saw fit. We are examining the main elements in possible bilateral arrangements with Canada, Argentina, Brazil, France, Belgium, Sweden, Eire, Denmark, India, Australia, New Zealand. Until these are ascertained on a quantitative basis, it is difficult to be precise.

12.   These arrangements would vary very widely, and in some cases might provide very close integration of policy; they could, for example, lead to definite dollar pool arrangements and also for specific inter-change of supplies. Our advantage would <u>prima facie</u> best be served by making such intimate arrangements primarily with the stronger countries which had supplies to offer complementary to our own (e.g. Australia, New Zealand, Eire, Denmark) rather than with countries which would be likely to be a drain upon our resources and which would raise difficult questions of allocation of scarce supplies.

13.   Canada and Argentina present major difficulty. But there are strong bargaining weapons on our side. Once we reach the point at which we <u>must</u> be prepared to forego supplies (because we literally cannot afford them), they are faced with a crisis because they have no alternative market. This state of affairs would not develop immediately, but it would give us some cards. They would however require specific supplies, and we should have to manage our affairs to enable us to give them. It is at least possible that we should be able to cut the prices and to pay for the supplies partly in goods, partly in gold, and partly in credit.

14.   It seems certain that some direction of exports would be necessary in connection with some of the bilateral agreements. We should seek to avoid universal export licensing machinery (and some administrative

relief might be possible via C.D.3 procedure). Plans would have to be made in advance in order to enable direction to be put into operation at all quickly.

Import Programme

15. We might reasonably hope to conduct our trade with the non-dollar world in a way which would enable us to get that part of our imports with no net gold and dollar loss.

16. The deficit with the Americas is so large ($2 billions (£500 millions) at least in 1948) that we cannot possibly hope to deal with it by bilateral bargaining and financial manipulation. It would more-over be fatal (especially in the early stages) to plan on the basis of rapid exhaustion of our reserves and other resources in the hope that something would turn up in 1949 - or 1950 or 1951.

17. The cuts which would be needed in our 1948 import programme from the Americas would mean going considerably beyond the Treasury's original recommendations in April. There are possible but drastic expedients which have not yet been proposed, e.g. stopping the oil companies' development programmes (a very profitable foreign invest-ment). But the bulk of the strain would fall on food and raw materials (in particular meat, sugar, dairy produce, timber, non-ferrous metals). It must be recognised on the other hand that some fall in prices is to be expected, and an overall 10% on the dollar programme can save £75 millions.

18. It is thus impossible to predict the scale of physical import cuts which would be required. It largely depends upon the price situa-tion. But it seems certain that sharp cuts would be necessary in the present food consumption level, and cuts also in the imports of raw materials. And these involve loss of industrial production and a gradual downward spiral in economic activity.

Implications on Commitments

19. This whole line of policy is entirely at variance with the U.S. Loan Agreement commitments. The abandonment of non-discrimination and of convertibility in the sense of the Loan Agreement is implicit throughout. It does not seem that withdrawal from I.M.F. would be necessary, but early adoption of I.T.O. would clearly go by the board.

20. Policy on Germany would need immediate reconsideration, and also policy on military commitments overseas.

U.K. Internal Policy

21. The practical problem for U.K. would be to ride the storm with lower imports. We cannot make great adjustments quickly in our economic structure without considerable distress. We should run risks of a downward spiral of activity, with cumulative frustration. It would be of prime importance to give people something to look forward to, and to show that a plan existed for getting us through, with backs to the wall. For this reason, it would be necessary to present a plan for recovery by our own efforts by 1950.

22. The internal problem would still be the same, in its fundamental
outline, as it is now. We should require a desperate export drive,
and in particular special action for:-

(i) Agriculture. In the 1947-8-9 harvests to run no risks of
insufficient labour; this might mean radical interference with
educational arrangements. We should go forward with a "famine"
food programme, and direction of labour to agriculture, and to
building of rural houses.

(ii) Capital Projects. The building and investment programmes
generally should be drastically cut down, to save timber and
steel and manpower. We should not have resources for satisfying
our elementary consumption needs plus exports plus investment.
There will in any case be substantial investment programmes
connected with the recovery plan (e.g. copper refinery, housing
for miners and agricultural workers, etc).

(iii) Textiles. Woollen textiles would be of prime importance.

(iv) Coal. As always, fundamental.

(v) Allocation of raw materials to develop exports and cut down
investment.

23. In order to make the adjustments quickly enough, drastic action
would be needed; it is difficult to see how this could be done without
direction of labour and indeed a complete and total national mobilisation, as far-reaching as that of 1940. It would be only by these
drastic means that we could hope to get through.

R.W.B.C.

23 July 1947

---

22. Exchange of Letters between Sir Wilfrid Eady (HM Treasury) and C. F. Cobbold (Deputy Governor of the Bank of England)

My dear Cobbold,

While I was away on leave a paper on convertibility was prepared,
largely out of material supplied by the Bank.

There is one additional piece of information which we would like
and which I think you could conveniently present for us satisfactorily.

The material you provided does not deal in any detail with the
question of the Sterling Balances. The Government may be open to
criticism on the ground that the American Loan may be regarded as
"wasted" to the extent that it was used for repaying debt. There is
obviously an answer to this. The general line of the note prepared by
you is valid to the extent to which convertibility was exercised in
relation to currently accruing Sterling. But it is not equally valid

to the extent that Sterling Balances, either in the Sterling Area or non-Sterling Area, were drawn down. The Government might be attacked for allowing the debt to be redeemed. Can I ask you to have a note prepared on this aspect of the question.

I might add that it is rather urgent to have this material ready as the early Debates in Parliament are almost certain to range over this field. I should therefore be grateful if you could have this put in hand.

If you or Mynors wants to ask me more about the meaning of this letter please let me know.

Yours,

C.F. Cobbold, Esq.

13 October 1947

My dear Eady,

Thank you for your letter of 13th October about Convertibility. I do not need to tell you that the question you ask is an extremely difficult one and one that cannot be answered exactly in terms of statistics. In the first place it is obviously impossible, where a country was drawing U.S. dollars from us during a certain period, to say how much of those dollars were paid for our of current sterling accruals and how much by the reduction of existing sterling balances. Again the whole purpose of the convertibility arrangements was to enable one country to use its working sterling balances to pay any other country, so that the origins of the sterling which may appear at a particular moment on one particular country's account are imposs- ible to determine exactly.

In what follows I have tried to see what broader conclusions the figures seem to suggest in the more important instances and to give you some figures in support of these conclusions.

As a general proposition, even if it proved to be true that some of the Loan had been used to repay debt, it would seem curious to describe as "wasted", money used to discharge more or less pressing overseas obligations.

Although there is inevitably a lot of interplay between sterling area and non-sterling area, it is necessary and convenient to take the sterling area separately from the rest of the non-sterling area. (Egypt and Sudan are regarded throughout as "sterling area".)

1.   I take first the non-sterling area. For the purposes of the argument one can take two periods and sets of figures.

(a) First, one can take the difference in the net sterling banking
liabilities as at 30th June, 1946 and as at 31st August, 1947 (i.e.
as near as we can go to the date when the American Loan was first
available and the date on which convertibility was suspended).
During that period net banking liabilities to the non-sterling
area (excluding U.S.A., U.S. dependencies, Canada and Newfoundland
which it seems appropriate to disregard) increased by £92 million.
Some £50 million of this increase was due to a change in the
figures for France and the rest was spread rather widely. The
countries with which we had the most active convertibility agreements show little change, e.g., Belgium moves from £29 million to
£28 million and Argentina from £125 million to £134 million. The
only considerable decreases are for Norway (£40 million) and
Greece (£14 million): in these two cases something like £8
million and £2 million respectively found their way into dollars
through the convertible account system.

(b) Secondly, one can take each convertibility agreement and look
at the difference between the net sterling liabilities at the end
of the quarter immediately before the agreement came into force
and at the 31st August, 1947. On this basis (Schedule 1 attached)
there was not in any case a heavy decrease and in one or two cases
there were increases: adding the differences together there was
a net decrease of £7 million. In one or two cases (notably
Belgium and to a less extent Argentina) the figure ran up at
certain dates during the period of the agreement and ran down
again in the last weeks before convertibility was suspended.

(c) So far as the non-sterling area is concerned it therefore
seems reasonable to conclude that such part of the dollar drain as
was attributable to these countries did not, either over the
period 1st July, 1946 to 31st August, 1947 or in each particular
case over the period when the convertibility clause was in operation, reflect any considerable reduction of balances held by non-
sterling area countries. The figures quoted also seem to confirm
the general conclusions of paragraphs 5, 6 and 7 of the note on
Convertibility which I sent to Bridges on 8th September and paragraphs 3 and 5 of my letter to Bridges of 11th September. Thus so
far as the non-sterling area world is concerned there is no case
to answer on the allegation that a large part of the loan was
"wasted" in the repayment of sterling debt.

2.   In the case of the sterling area the question is even more
difficult to answer accurately. The Washington Loan involved no change
in the procedure by which other sterling area countries could spend
sterling outside the sterling area. As before 1st July, 1946, so
during the period until the 31st August, 1947 and so even now,
expenditure outside the sterling area by these countries is at the
discretion of each local control. Thus there were no new "convertibility" arrangements with these countries. On this point, however, I
may perhaps repeat what I said in my letter to Bridges of 11th
September:-

"The emphasis on convertibility and non-discrimination in the
Loan Agreement doubtless encouraged sterling area controls to
relax both as to the amount they bought and as to where they
bought it from, and in the last period importers and potential

imports covered their exchange at the earliest possible moment,
whilst exporters may have been slow to collect proceeds. The
agreements concluded in the summer with sterling area countries
had little effect on the rate of drawings, though they may have
encouraged rather quicker drawing <u>before</u> the agreements were concluded on the grounds that less drawings would be possible <u>after</u>
conclusion. These agreements did not, as is often suggested,
release funds which were previously blocked – they blocked the
great bulk of funds which had previously been free, leaving only
the "released" portions free."

There is no doubt that the sterling area as a whole, including the
Colonies, tended to be lavish with dollar expenditure during the
period, but that is perhaps not exactly relevant to your enquiry.

The sterling area countries which during the period 1st July,
1946 – 31st August, 1947 drew extensively on our U.S. $ resources
(see Schedule 2a) were:–

South Africa	(£81 million)
India	(£42 million)
Eire	(£22 million)
Australia	(£14 million)
New Zealand	(£10 million)
Egypt & Sudan	(£10 million)

The next step is presumably to see whether, in the case of any of
these countries, there was over the same period a reduction in sterling
balances which might be attributable to the net dollar expenditure.

The attached figures show that the countries which drew down
sterling balances heavily during the same period (see Schedule 2b)
were:–

India	(£136 million)
Egypt & Sudan	(£39 million)
Ceylon	(£27 million)
Australia	(£23 million)

The total reduction during the period of £232 million for the sterling
area as a whole is little more than the total decrease for these four
countries: increases and decreases for the rest of the area were comparatively minor and approximately offset each other.

Of the countries in these lists:–

South Africa is not in question because gold sales to us
exceeded dollar drawings.

Australia is out because the £23 million decrease in balances was
almost wholly accounted for by the £20 million gift.

Eire and New Zealand are out because their sterling balances did
not change over the period.

Ceylon, although taking some dollars from us over the last few
months, showed a net surplus of dollars over the period.

The question really comes down therefore to India where it can be argued that £40 million of dollars out of the Loan went in repayment of sterling debt and Egypt where £10 million may be said to have gone the same way. On top of this, of the minor increases and decreases in sterling balances over the rest of the field (which as stated above cancel each other out) some of the decreases may have reflected net drawings of dollars for a few million pounds. But by doing the sums a little differently it can equally well be maintained that in all these cases, including India and Egypt, they financed their total dollar expenditure out of gross current sterling receipts, using their accumulated balances for expenditure in the sterling area: this would indeed have to be our defence (and a perfectly legitimate one) if the U.S. Administration were to raise Article 6 (i) of the Loan Agreement.

The wider question as to whether we should have imposed a complete unilateral block on Indian and Egyptian balances at an earlier stage so as to prevent them spending any accumulated balances either inside or outside the sterling area, has been discussed in various other contexts and I cannot usefully add to that discussion here: even if we had done so there is no guarantee that they would not have used gross current sterling receipts for expenditure outside rather than inside the sterling area. As to dollar expenditure one or two further comments may be useful. Egyptian expenditure was governed over the period by "target" agreements concluded with H.M.G. As to India it is true that, in common with many other parts of the sterling area, they had relaxed their control over dollar expenditure in the later part of 1946 (though they tightened up again later). But India would certainly argue that we were not providing them with any "new" dollars during this period but were merely selling them back for current transactions some of the dollars earned by current transactions which they had sold to us against sterling during the war.

The general conclusion seems to be that at one extreme it could be argued that some £50/60 million of dollars spent by the sterling area reflected repayment of sterling debt: at the other extreme that the whole of the dollar expenditure was against gross current sterling receipts. It is an argument incapable of proof one way or the other, as it depends on which way you look at the figures. It can however be said with some confidence that even the most extreme measures to block sterling balances would only at best have prevented a part of this dollar expenditure, and that at the cost of a major dispute with the countries concerned.

If you would like to discuss this further or there is any more information we can give you, please let me know.

Yours sincerely,

(Signed) C.F. Cobbold.

16 October 1947

Sir Wilfrid Eady, K.C.B., K.B.E., C.M.G.

Schedule 1

Convertibility Agreements

£ millions

Date Agreement became effective	Country	Net sterling banking, etc. liabilities[*]	
		At end of quarter preceding Agreement	At 31st Aug. 1947
3.10.46	Argentina	(30. 9.46) 135	134
27. 2.47	Portugal	(31.12.46) 25	23
"	Belgium & Luxembourg	(") 31	28
"	Netherlands	(") 19	24
21. 4.47	Italy	(31. 3.47) 35	34
2. 6.47	Brazil	(") 68	62
1. 7.47	Norway	(30. 6.47) 36	37
"	Spain	(") 11	9
8. 7.47	Czechoslovakia	(") 9	9
"	Finland	(") 6	4
15. 7.47	Iran	(") 22	22
"	Uruguay	(") 18	18
"	Sweden	(") 28	33
"	Ethiopia	(") 2	$1\frac{1}{2}$

[*] Excluding Loans to H.M.G. Only country affected is Portugal: 61 at both dates.

Schedule 2(a)

U.S. Dollars provided for Sterling Area Countries
1st July, 1946 - 23rd August, 1947

£ millions

	1946	1947			Total
	2nd half	Jan./ Mar.	Apr./ June	1 July/ 23 Aug.*	
For transactions with U.S.A.					
Malaya	− 25.0	− 11.5	− 13.8	− 8.2	− 58.5
South Africa	18.7	12.8	16.8	13.8	62.1
India	2.5	7.0	16.8	17.7	44.0
Australia	− 5.0	−	8.7	10.5	14.2
Eire	5.0	3.8	6.7	6.5	22.0
Egypt	−	2.2	4.0	1.0	7.2
New Zealand	1.5	2.5	3.0	2.8	9.8
Ceylon	− 2.0	−	−	.5	− 1.5
Colonies (excluding Malaya & Ceylon)	− 3.2*	2.0	7.5	6.2	12.5
Other countries	2.5	2.8	3.8	6.2	15.3
	− 5.0	21.6	53.5	57.0	127.1 (say $508 mn.)
For other transactions					
Malaya	− .5	− 1.2	− .5	.2	− 2.0
South Africa	4.2	4.2	5.2	5.0	18.6
India	− .2	− 3.0	.5	.7	− 2.0
Eire	−	−	−	.5	.5
Egypt	−	−	.5	2.2	2.7
Ceylon	−	−	.2	.2	.4
Colonies (excluding Malaya & Ceylon)	−	.5	.5	3.2⁰	4.2
Other Sterling Area and undefined	.7	.5	2.0	3.6	6.8
	4.2	1.0	8.4	15.6	29.2 (say $116 mn.)
Total	− .8	22.6	61.9	72.6	156.3 (say $624 mn.)

*   Provisional

⁰   Hong Kong 1.5, British East & West Africa 1.0

Schedule 2(b)

Net Sterling Banking etc. Liabilities to
Rest of Sterling Area

£ millions

	Total	Of which			
		India	Australia	Egypt & Sudan	Ceylon
At 30th June 1946	2,923*	1,310	143	401	63
At 31st August 1947	2,691⁄	1,174	120	362	36
Decrease	232	136	23	39	27

Excluding Loans to H.M.G. of 61; of which India 20 and Egypt & Sudan 8.

⁄ Excluding Loans to H.M.G. of 48; of which India 17 and Egypt & Sudan 7.

23. How the US Loan was Spent

[I have not found the original of this document: it may have come from the Bank of England. What stands out is the large increase in dollar disbursements in 1947 in the Western Hemisphere. Ed.]

Top Secret

How the U.S. Loan was Spent

(All figures in U.S. $ millions)

Note: These figures are reasonably accurate for the second half of 1946 and the first two quarters of 1947. Figures for the third quarter of 1947 are the best estimates that can be made at this·stage, and subject to considerable revision in detail as further information becomes available.

| | 1946 | 1947 | | |
	2nd half	January-March	April-June	July-September
1. We have purchased the following goods and services in U.S.A.:-				
Food and drink	110	147	98	93
Tobacco	160	9	3	34
Raw materials	50	81	78	80
Oil and tanker freight	100	66	53	48
Machinery and other manufactures	100	50	73	82
Ships	15	9	88	44
Films	35	15	16	14
Food, etc. for Germans	55	66	57	85
	625	443	466	480
2. We earned from U.K. exports and re-exports to U.S.A.:-	85	48	52	60
3. We had other net earnings from U.S.A. on U.K. account:-				
Invisibles	70	–	3	–20
Other items/	90	18	2	20
	245	66	57	–
4. The U.K. deficit with U.S.A. was therefore:-	380	377	409	420
5. We also provided U.S. dollars for U.K. purchases in the Western Hemisphere as follows:-				
Canada	–	48	168	190
Central America	90	72	110	145
Argentina and other Latin America	50	30	45	120
	140	150	323	455
6. In our dealings with European and other countries, we acquired (–) and spent (+) the following U.S. dollars:-	–40	–	35	165

Residual item comprising net receipts on capital account and "Errors and Omissions".

	1946	1947		
	2nd half	January–March	April–June	July–September
7. We provided U.S. dollars <u>net</u> for sterling area countries as follows:-				
<u>For transactions with</u> <u>U.S.A.</u>				
Malaya	-100	-46	-55	...
South Africa	75	51	67	...
India	10	28	67	...
Australia	-20	-	35	...
Eire	20	15	27	...
Other	- 5	38	73	...
	-20	86	214	335
For other transactions	15	4	34	60
	- 5	90	248	395
8. We paid the U.S. dollar part of our and the sterling area's subscriptions to the International Bank:-	35	-	-	-
9. Our net dollar outgoings were therefore:-				
4. U.K. Deficit with U.S.A.	380	377	409	420
5. Other U.K. Purchases in Western Hemisphere	140	150	323	455
6. European and Other Countries	- 40	-	35	165
7. Sterling Area Countries	- 5	90	248	395
8. International Bank8	35	-	-	-
	510	617	1,015	1,435 +
Our drawings on the U.S. Credit were:-	600	500	950	1,300 +

+ Approximate reconciliation:

Drawings on U.S. Credit	1,300	
+ Sale of gold for $	80	
+ Purchase of $ from I.M.F.	60	1,440
- Increase in $ balances	- 45	1,395
Unexplained (net payments probably over-estimated)		+ 40
		1,435

4 November 1947

IV   Policy Towards Europe, 1948-1949

[After General Marshall's speech at Harvard on 5 June 1947, a conference of ministers met in Paris later in the month and set up a committee on European economic co-operation under the chairmanship of Sir Oliver Franks. This reported in September 1947 in a document drafted by Sir Richard Clarke, and after further discussion the Organisation for European Economic Co-operation (OEEC) came into existence in March 1948. In these and subsequent developments Sir Richard was deeply involved as chairman of the London Committee, co-ordinating official action in Britain in relation to the European Recovery Programme (ERP).

All four of the documents that follow were drafted by him. Two preceded the creation of OEEC: a note on Western European economic policy covering the submission to ministers of three reports from the London Committee; and one of the reports concerned which deals with the form and functions of the proposed organisation. Two were written after OEEC had been at work for some time: a memorandum to Sir Edward Bridges, Permanent Secretary of the Treasury, on the idea of a Western European Federation; and a minute of a meeting of senior Treasury and other officials to discuss European co-operation in January 1949. Ed.]

24. Western European Economic Policy: Minute by R. W. B. Clarke to Sir Wilfrid Eady

1.   The Chancellor will wish to consider where we are going on Western European union, especially in the economic field.

2.   A short OEEC meeting is to be held in Paris on 13th March which will set up a Working Party to hammer out the function and structure of the continuing organisation for the participating countries. Mr Bevin intends to attend this meeting which will be of major importance both vis-a-vis U.S.A. and as providing an opportunity for H.M.G. to state its attitude to European economic co-operation and to give a lead to the whole enterprise. Mr Bevin is also meeting some of the Western European Foreign Ministers on the 7th March on the general question of Western European union, of which the economic foundations are naturally of prime importance.

3.   In the last few weeks the London Committee has been hard at work developing its ideas on the purpose and nature of the continuing organisation and a submission will shortly be made to Ministers. This concentrates, however, on the more formal side of the problem and the Chancellor will wish to consider the wider implications.

4.   The Chancellor may care to read three papers which have been discussed in the London Committee and which carry the general agreement
of all officials in Whitehall who are considering E.R.P.* These are:-

   (i) GEN.209/23 - an analysis of the long-term European dollar
                   problem as reflected in the U.S. Administration's
                   Country Reports and statistical documentation
                   for E.R.P.

   (ii) GEN.188/133- a paper setting out the London Committee's views
                   on the major problem which the European countries
                   have to tackle and of the means by which they
                   should set about it.

   (iii) GEN.188/138, which is a submission by the London Committee
                   to Ministers seeking instructions on the purpose
                   and form of the continuing organisation (an
                   amended draft with no changes of substance will
                   be submitted to the London Committee on Monday
                   and will proceed to Ministers).

5.   The central problem of all the participating countries is their
deficit with the Western Hemisphere. Even in the last year of E.R.P.
(1951/2) they will have a deficit of $3¼-3½ billions and will be
covering less than two-thirds of their imports from the Western Hemisphere by their (and their Colonies') dollar earnings (the latter
estimated on an extremely optimistic basis). Apart from Switzerland
(and possibly Sweden) all the participating countries are in the same
boat; all have this chronic deficit with the dollar area. This is not
a short-term and transitory thing; it is a permanent element in their
economic structures. It arises partly from the loss of shipping and
invisible earnings; partly from the relative increase in the price of
food and raw materials, and partly from the disruption of trade with
Eastern Europe and Asia. Another important factor is the substantial
increase in Western European population since before the war which
increases dependence upon imported food.

6.   The effect of this is that Europe will never become independent
of American aid (with all the Congressional uncertainties and political
implications of this) unless there is substantial modification of its
industrial and agricultural structure. It is not even certain that a
balance could be achieved by reduction in the standard of living, for
the effect of lower food supplies on production and the lack of
imported raw materials might involve a permanently diminishing spiral
of economic activity.

7.   What this really means is that all the European countries are
confronted with the same basic problem as we are. Incidentally,
Belgium's dollar deficit is worse than ours in the long run.

8.   This points to the conclusion that the whole of Western Europe's
economic activity and planning must be directed to secure a balance
with the Western Hemisphere and to make the European economic structure
viable.

---

* European Recovery Programme.

9.   Seen in this context, the projects for customs union, etc., fall
into their right perspective. The hard fact is that a customs union
would do nothing whatever by itself to contribute to the major European
problem. Indeed, its effects would be more likely to be damaging to
the main objective than helpful. It would encourage manufacturers in
all these countries to produce for the European market instead of
seeking to earn dollars and would actually impede the reconversion of
the European economy to dollar saving and dollar earning. For
example, it would permit the Belgian azalea growers to grow more
azaleas for the U.K. market and it would permit our chocolate biscuit
manufacturers to produce more chocolate biscuits for the Belgian
market. Actually, of course, this productive capacity in both countries
should be employed to build up exports to the dollar area. By this
token it is arguable that we should not seek to increase general intra-
European trade at all for it is more likely to hinder than to help the
process of readjustment.

10.   What we want the continuing organisation to do is to see what
means are possible of securing dollar saving and dollar earning by co-
operation between the European countries. This would be the touchstone
and we and the other countries would feed in suggestions for this
purpose. It is perhaps simplest to illustrate by an example. Take
steel. The European countries as a whole will, for many years to come
(on present form), be dependent upon the supply of U.S. steel. We
should raise this on the continuing organisation and there would be
discussions between the steel industries with a directive stating
that they had to plan what was the most economical way to produce the
amount of steel which Europe needed for its own purposes and for export
to the outside world. The development programmes would then be adjusted
accordingly. Similarly, in the case of food, the problem would be
posed of how Europe was going to feed itself in the long run and an
attempt would be made to square the agricultural programmes accordingly
so that more staple foods were produced in Europe (and the Colonies)
so that we could at any rate be sure of a basic standard of living.
Another project might be to examine the full development of fish
producing resources of the European waters and an active stimulation of
the consumption of fish in order to substitute for meat from the
Western Hemisphere. A rather different type of problem would be the
discussion of suitable means to develop trade with Eastern Europe and
Russia. Yet another might be co-operative action in the stimulation
of tourism in order to facilitate dollar earning American tourists
(there is probably very big scope for this). In fact we should want
to get a system of European planning (or rather part planning and part
private enterprise, for the social institutions differ very widely
even among the countries with governments of the same colour) with
this specific aim of dollar saving and dollar earning in view.

11.   At the same time we must develop proper means for permitting
intra-European trade. It now appears certain that there will be great
pressure upon all European countries' gold and dollar reserves during
the E.R.P. period and that at the end of that time Europe will be
critically short of gold and dollars. It is therefore necessary that
we should develop a European payments system in which settlements are
made without gold and dollars passing between European countries. A
plan for this purpose is being considered with France, Benelux and
Italy which will turn upon credits being made in the E.R.P. period by
the European countries with intra-European surplus to the European
countries with intra-European deficit - this to be linked up with the

use of local currency proceeds from the sale of E.R.P. goods. Europe
has to find a means in fact of conducting its affairs without the use
of gold and dollars. The only use to which the latter can be put is
for the purchase of essentials from the Western Hemisphere – there are
not enough dollars for that and there are certainly not enough dollars
to permit the European countries to pay them to each other.

12. This is the sort of concept which we have in mind for the development of European economic co-operation. This visualises very practical
action, commodity by commodity, on a rather empirical basis, treating
every problem on its merits in the light of the major objective and
dealing with it by whatever administrative means are practicable. This
is vastly more promising than the attempts at a grandiose "general"
plan like a customs union which might even make the problem worse
rather than better.

13. The U.K. could fit into this rather well. The securing of dollar
viability for ourselves is the crucial issue which faces us in the next
four years and we shall in any case have to modify our economy – the
whole pattern of consumption, production and trade – in order to secure
this objective. It seems reasonable to suppose, on the face of it,
that if other countries are working for the same objective we can derive
benefit by co-operating with them. At the same time this will limit our
freedom. If it appears that a piece of European co-operation is
desirable for this general objective, we should have to play our full
part in it. This might lead to a point at which we should have to amend
our steel development programme or adjust our agricultural production
very radically (e.g. stop producing beef). If we go into this business
at all we should go into it with our eyes open to this extent. It is
very difficult to believe that the adjustments which we should have to
make in our own economy would be as serious as those which we should
have to make if we were trying to pull through on our own efforts
alone; there must be <u>some</u> advantage in doing this on a wider scale.
But we do not know what this will involve and we shall never, in fact,
be able to compare it with the painful adjustments which we should
have to make if we were seeking dollar viability on our own resources.
In a matter like this, however, one is bound to take a leap in the
dark sooner or later. It is quite impossible in fact to provide a
number of plans of action, worked out in detail covering the next
four or five years, between which a choice can be made.

14. All one can really say on this is that we are committed
irrevocably to European economic co-operation. If we wished to do so,
we could not get out of it without sacrificing E.R.P. There is no
doubt that the central problem of Europe is the restoration of dollar
viability. It therefore seems sensible to go ahead rather actively
with European co-operation specifically designed to produce dollar
viability.

15. But this having been said, the conclusion does follow that we
should be bound to surrender a certain amount of freedom of action and
that as this action develops it will have the automatic effect of
drawing the economies of the European countries much closer together.
As it develops, indeed, (and especially if it develops successfully)
it may be found that a major obstacle will be the decision in a particular case about which country shall have a dollar deficit – for example,
is it desirable for the U.K. to supply steel to Denmark to prevent
Denmark having to buy steel from the United States or should U.K. export

the steel to Argentina (reducing its own dollar deficit) and leave Denmark's dollar deficit untouched? This may lead to suggesting a very far reaching pooling of financial resources. Such a pooling would, of course, be equivalent to complete economic union. It would obviously be quite impossible to embark upon this without far reaching measures of political and military union as well. But this is the sort of problem which may emerge as a practical issue as time goes on.

16. A great advantage of the empirical means of approach is that it avoids all the difficulties about the Commonwealth, for it would be perfectly easy for the sterling Dominions to co-operate with U.K. and Europe on this basis without raising any problems of imperial preference. Moreover, it would be possible to resist the examination of certain specific commodities which might create difficulty for the Dominions.

17. A very crucial question in this context is Germany. The Western zones of Germany, taken as one sector, are less viable in terms of dollars than almost anywhere else in Europe. This raises the whole question of level of industry and Germany production, consumption and trade pattern. It is fairly clear that if Western Europe is engaged on a life and death struggle for economic survival, it will not be able to afford to buy large quantities of consumer manufactured goods from Germany and we should be confronted with the real decision whether Germany is to become viable or whether Germany is to be kept unquestionably "safe" from a security point of view.

R.W.B. Clarke

27 February 1948

---

25. The Continuing Organisation: Report of the London Committee on European Economic Co-operation

[This report was submitted by the London Committee of British officials (of which R. W. B. Clarke was Chairman) set up under the Marshall Plan to handle problems of European economic co-operation. In the spring of 1948 the OEEC had not yet come into existence and this report discusses what form of continuing organisation is required. Ed.]

The Continuing Organisation

1.   There will be a meeting of the Committee of European Economic Co-operation in the middle of March, at which a working party of the 16 participating countries will be set up to consider the functions and constitution of the continuing organisation provided in the Paris Report. From these discussions will emerge the shape of the continuing organisation, and thus the nature of the European economic co-operation which will take place in the period of the European[*] recovery programme.

---

[*]   For the purposes of this paper Europe means the 16 participating countries and their dependencies.

Purpose of Continuing Organisation
<u>_____</u>

2.   In our view, it is desirable that the purpose of the continuing
organisation should be formulated precisely. If it is given vague
terms of reference (e.g. "to foster European economic co-operation")
it will never set to work at all, and it will spend its time discussing
the various countries' hobby-horses (French proposals for customs
unions, Belgian proposals for transferability, Italian proposals for
increased trade in fresh fruit, etc.). It must have a clear objective.

3.   The central problem of the participating countries, singly and
collectively, is the trade deficit with the Western Hemisphere.
According to the United States' calculations, only one-third of the
participating countries' imports from the Western Hemisphere in 1948-
49 will be paid for by exports; in 1951-52, even on very favourable
assumptions, these countries' exports to the Western Hemisphere will
cover less than two-thirds of the imports they require. This means
that on present plans, at the end of the four years of the European
recovery programme, the participating countries (singly and collectively and taking their dependent territories' dollar earnings into
account) will not nearly be in balance with the Western Hemisphere.
This would mean that either a further Marshall Aid programme would be
required or the countries would face an acute standard-of-living
and employment crisis.

4.   Clearly we cannot contemplate being in such a position ourselves;
nor can we tolerate that Western Europe generally should be in such a
plight. This would be failure of the attempt to rebuild Europe.
Moreover, the signs of this impending failure would appear long before
the four years were out, and Congress might well decide to write the
whole Plan off, and would stop throwing good money after bad.

5.   In our view, therefore, it is necessary that the main activity of
the continuing organisation must be to right the participating
countries' deficit with the Western Hemisphere, that the various
countries' national action should concentrate on this, and that
European co-operation should be specifically directed to this purpose.
This could be expressed:-

> "The purpose of the continuing organisation shall be
> to ensure the success of the European recovery programme,
> and in particular to ensure that by the end of the European
> recovery programme period, the participating countries will
> become independent of extraordinary outside economic
> assistance".

The last phrase is a quotation from the draft European Co-operation
Bill. It provides the most acceptable definition of the purpose of
the continuing organisation from the American point of view.

Functions of Continuing Organisation
<u>_____</u>

6.   The functions of the continuing organisation could best be
defined in relation to the purpose, giving wide authority to initiate
and carry out co-operative action for this purpose. Our general idea
is that the problem should be attacked in two ways:-

(i) by building up production in Europe (and Colonies) to replace imports from the Western Hemisphere, and by building up exports to the Western Hemisphere: this would be examined commodity by commodity, by Governments in association with the industries concerned.

(ii) by taking general measures, e.g. to reduce trade barriers in Europe and to develop improved payments arrangements within Europe, consistent with the main objective.

7. The continuing organisation should thus be empowered to examine and foster all forms of co-operative action designed to reduce the participating countries' deficit with the dollar area. It would proceed step by step and commodity by commodity, concentrating first upon the measures which could provide the greatest economic benefit, and upon which agreement could be readily secured. The organisation would of course have to work by securing agreement between the countries concerned on specific problems; there could be no question of instructions being given by the organisation to the individual members.

8. The method of operation would vary widely from case to case. The governmental, industrial and social structures of the Western European countries are diverse and cannot be fitted into one pattern of co-operation. It would therefore be necessary to develop a wide range of techniques of co-operation, each suited to the particular problem to be solved. Under the auspices of the continuing organisation, a network of inter-governmental agreements (often associated with inter-industrial agreements) would take shape, all directed to the main purpose.

9. Participation in European co-operation on these lines would require the United Kingdom (and other European countries) to make adjustments in economic structure which will create difficulty. But we cannot avoid the need to make such adjustments. If we seek to right our position by our own efforts alone, changes in our industrial and agricultural structure will be inevitable – either deliberate or imposed by the force of events; our present pattern of production, consumption and trade will require considerable modification to eliminate the dollar deficit. If on the other hand we embarked upon a far-reaching <u>automatic</u> policy of European co-operation (such as a customs union, developing towards complete economic union), great changes would likewise be required; free imports from Europe would have radical effects upon all our industry and agriculture. There is no reason to suppose that the changes which would flow from the type of co-operation outlined in the paper would be greater and more difficult than in either of these alternatives, and there is some reason to think they would be less.

10. The fact does remain, however, that this line of approach deliberately limits our freedom of action in the economic field; it will involve making commitments to other participating countries; it is likely to involve some changes in our economy which will create serious problems. But it is submitted that we really have no choice; by accepting Marshall Aid, we commit ourselves to European economic co-operation, and the scheme proposed at least seeks to secure that this co-operation will be constructive in character and will be carried out in a controlled manner. Moreover, this concentration upon <u>specific</u> dollar-saving and dollar-earning co-operation presents the least

possible difficulties with the sterling Dominions, who are now co-
operating with us towards the same objective.

11. There are certain specific functions of the continuing organisation to which we attach importance, and on which it is submitted that
our Delegation should be given precise instructions:-

(i) <u>Allocation</u>. It is certain that the effect of the European
recovery programme will be to widen the scope of allocation of
scarce commodities. This is a tendency which we cannot resist.
We should, however, seek to develop the existing international
machinery for allocation rather than set up new allocation
machinery under the continuing organisation. In particular, we
should retain the present system of world-wide allocation of
certain foods, nitrogen and seeds by Food and Agriculture Organisation Committees, and if necessary accept this machinery to
cover other foods and feedingstuffs; timber, coal and pitprops
should continue to be allocated through the Economic Commission
for Europe; in other cases, it may be necessary to establish
world-wide machinery for some, and work through the continuing
organisation for others. New subjects for allocation should be
treated on the merits of the commodity, and we should resist all
proposals for a major change in existing allocation machinery.

(ii) <u>Colonial Development</u>. There would be advantage in setting
up, within the framework of the continuing organisation, machinery
for co-operation on questions of Colonial development between
those of the participating countries who are Colonial powers.
Such machinery would not be in any sense exclusive - i.e. direct
contacts and consultations between one or more of the Colonial
powers, such as have been taking place since the end of the war,
would not be precluded and would, in fact, certainly need to
continue and to be extended. But the establishment of formal
machinery under the auspices of the continuing organisation should
serve to ensure that the major aim of that organisation - namely
dollar-saving and dollar-earning is kept fully in mind in plans
for Colonial development; and it would not give the appearance,
as might the establishment of <u>formal</u> machinery outside the framework of the continuing organisation, of exclusive arrangements
between the Colonial powers.

It is specially important that we should avoid any impression
that we are ignoring the Dominions. We should therefore make it
clear that we shall continue our normal practice of close consultation with them on matters affecting Colonial areas adjacent
to them, and that we shall have careful regard to their views on
any specific projects.

(iii) <u>Customs Union Study Group</u>. The continuing organisation
should exercise such supervision over the Customs Union Study
Group as may be consistent with differences of membership.

(iv) The Continuing Organisation should be empowered to consider
the measures which should be taken (consistent both with the main
principle indicated in paragraph 5 above and with the International
Trade Organisation and the International Monetary Fund) to free the

channels of intra-European trade, to expand its volume, and to facilitate intra-European payments.

Form of Continuing Organisation

12. In order that the work should be effective, it is necessary that the continuing organisation should be controlled by strong national delegations representing governments. The matters with which it will be dealing will be of primary importance, and will certainly involve difficult decisions for the participating countries. The only way to make this at all possible is for the delegations to be strong, carrying the confidence of the governments.

13. It is very important that the effective control should be in the hands of the national delegations, and that these should be strong enough to exercise this control and to prevent the secretariat (or an "independent" chairman) from taking action on its own. These intimate problems of economic co-operation involve to a greater or less extent a limitation upon the nations' freedom of action in matters of decisive political and economic importance. This can be done only by representatives of governments, and serious damage can be done by tactless intervention by "international" officials. For the same reason, we propose that the continuing organisation should elect its own chairman from time to time.

14. Membership should be open to all countries which are willing to participate in a joint European recovery programme (subject of course to certain obvious exceptions). Germany should be fully associated with the continuing organisation, and should have the responsibilities and rights of a full member. Preliminary arrangements for this are being worked out by the United States, France and ourselves at the Tripartite talks now in progress.

15. It will be necessary for the United States Administration to be closely associated with the work of the continuing organisation, but we feel that the United States of America should not be a member. The continuing organisation should be a European undertaking, and it should be in a position if necessary to present a collective view to the United States Administration. We should not seek "friendly aid" from the Americans for the working party meetings.

16. The continuing organisation will have to work with other inter-governmental bodies, and in particular with the Economic Commission for Europe, and the Food and Agricultural, International Trade and International Labour Organisations, etc. This may present considerable difficulties in practice, for in some cases the wider United Nations organisations are more appropriate (on grounds of membership) while in others the wider United Nations organisations are already dealing badly with (and without the essential purpose of the continuing organisation) subjects in which the continuing organisation would have to act with vigour. The continuing organisation will not wish to supersede these other inter-governmental bodies, and reasonable working arrangements will no doubt be possible in practice. But there is bound to be some difference of objective until the United Nations organisations accept (and work on) the basic importance of restoring the economic balance between United States of America and the rest of the world.

17. The problem of the Economic Commission for Europe will be particularly troublesome. We propose, however, that in view of the importance
of maintaining United Nations organisations and of maintaining economic
collaboration in certain fields with the Eastern European countries, we
should continue to suppose the Commission even though this may involve
great difficulties of demarcation. In particular, the Commission should
continue with its present functions on coal, timber and inland transport.
A time may come at which the Commission becomes an arena for conflict
between participants in the European recovery programme and opponents
of it, but in the meantime we should suppose it, while watching to
ensure that it does not obstruct or duplicate the working of the continuing organisation of the programme.

18. An important question at the Paris Conference was the limitation
of the existence of the continuing organisation to the period of the
programme. This was necessary to obtain the support of the Scandinavians and Swiss. While formally and for tactical reasons it may be
necessary for us to leave this question open, we should proceed on the
assumption that, in fact, the continuing organisation will develop
permanent functions.

19. We propose that the seat of the continuing organisation should be
in one of the smaller capitals, e.g. Brussels. The French would not
agree to its being in London, and we should not agree to its being in
Paris.

20. The fifteen points in the Annex have been suggested as agenda for
the working party by Benelux. These seem acceptable, subject to the
various additions and qualifications set out in this paper.

21. It will be necessary for the working party to frame a draft
multilateral agreement between the participating countries, as
envisaged in the United States Administration's Bill, for embodiment
in the bilateral agreements with the United States Administration. A
further submission will be made to Ministers on this.

Conclusions

22. The London Committee asks authority for Ministers to instruct our
delegation to the working party to proceed on these lines, and in
particular on the following points:-

  (i) Purpose of the continuing organisation (paragraph 5) and
  general function to carry out this purpose (paragraph 6).

  (ii) Working of continuing organisation by agreement of members
  concerned (paragraph 7).

  (iii) Functions in allocation, colonial development, customs union
  study group, intra-European trade (paragraph 11).

  (iv) Control by strong national delegations and not by "executive"
  secretariat (paragraphs 12, 13).

  (v) Membership open to all European countries; effective participation of Germany (paragraph 14).

(vi) United States of America not to be a member (paragraph 15).

(vii) Need for close co-operation with other inter-governmental bodies (paragraph 16).

(viii) Continued support for the Economic Commission for Europe (paragraph 17).

Cabinet Office, S.W.1.

2 March 1948

<u>Annex</u>

<u>Points of Guidance for the Working Party</u>
<u>Benelux Proposals</u>

1.   The continuing European organisation will be created by multi-lateral agreement.

2.   Member can be each country which adheres to a joint programme for European recovery based on self-help and mutual co-operation.

3.   The working party shall make proposals as to how Germany shall be represented in the continuing organisation.

4.   The organisation should be set up as an instrument of constructive and firm European economic co-operation and it will assume the various functions necessary to ensure the success of the European recovery programme.

5.   The delegates of the member-countries will decide in all matters in mutual agreement.

     In case matters are under discussion which do not affect all members, only the delegates of the members concerned will decide.

6.   The organisation will ensure, to the fullest extent possible by joint action, the realisation of the economic conditions necessary to enable the general objectives to which each country has pledged itself to be effectively achieved.

7.   It is assumed that the organisation will be simply and flexibly organised.

8.   The secretariat will work in conformity with the rules agreed to by the delegates of the member-countries.

9.   The charter of the organisation should be elaborated in such a way that assistance can be given in the administration of a foreign aid programme as far as it needs joint action.

10.   The organisation can make recommendations to the participating countries, to foreign countries which make means available for carrying out a programme of recovery and to international organisation.

11. The organisation will make periodical reports to the participating countries on the extent to which the programme is being realised.

12. The organisation will make periodical reports to the countries which make means available for carrying out a programme of European recovery.

13. The organisation will operate in close contact with existing international organisations generally under or affiliated with the United Nations. It is understood that the exact division of functions between the existing organisations and the new organisation cannot be arbitrarily laid down in advance.

14. The organisation must be adopted as the programme progresses in the light both of the opportunities for multilateral action and the adequacy of the existing organisations to provide the types of assistance required.

15. A draft multilateral agreement should be elaborated according to the undertakings and pledges contained in the report of the Committee for European Economic Co-operation.

---

26. Western and other Unions: Memorandum by R. W. B. Clarke to Sir E. Bridges (Head of the Treasury and Secretary to the Cabinet)

1. The touchstone of Western Union is the setting-up of a Western European Government, no matter how limited its powers. Once there is an independent Western European Executive, separate from the constituent governments, a new political unit is born. The powers of the Executive automatically grow, as in the history of all Federations, and the nations are merged into a new entity.

2. Does the U.K. envisage entering a Western European Federation of this kind at any time in the visible future? Our policy surely depends upon the answer to this question. We can either move towards this objective or seek other forms of co-operation with Western Europe. But we cannot do both of these at once, and we shall be very ill-advised to take steps towards Federation unless we are ultimately willing to go the whole way.

3. There are useful forms of co-operation with Western Europe which do not lead towards Federation, just as there is ample scope for co-operation with U.S.A. without Atlantic Union. We are in no way committed to move towards Federation, certainly not in E.R.P., though perhaps some of the Foreign Secretary's speeches could be interpreted that way. We have a reasonably free hand, which makes it all the more important that we should not in fact go down the Federation road unless we want to.

4. The decision has to be total, embracing military, political, economic, diplomatic and cultural considerations. Nor can it be said that on certain assumptions Federation would be advantageous, but on others disadvantageous. A judgment has to be given, in the light of

all the expected circumstances, <u>including</u> the estimated effect of our own decision.

5.   Before very long, Ministers will have to take a decision which, if favourable to Federation, will be substantially committing. We cannot continue for long without a European policy; unless we know where we stand on this point, we shall have great difficulty in O.E.E.C., in Customs Union Study Group, and (one would think) in 5-Power Treaty discussions.

6. At one time, I thought this decision could be postponed for a long period, and that we could proceed pragmatically; an Open Conspiracy of bureaucrats and business men would link the affairs of the Western European countries closer and closer together, and we should advance by almost imperceptible stages to a point at which so many questions were in fact being settled internationally that one had the substance of Western European Government without its form. But little progress has been made so far, and it is not obvious (at any rate on the economic side) that any further advance will happen (the O.E.E.C. exercises in October/November will be significant). I am now inclined to think that the political steps have to be taken first.

7.   The idea of a Western European Federation derives from the search for a "Third Force" to stand between U.S.A. and Russia – a military, political and economic unit strong enough with its overseas territories to stand on its own, established with U.S. assistance, but maintained by its own power. A Federation of U.K., France, Benelux, Western Germany would dispose of great resources, particularly of industrial manpower and capital equipment, though weak in indigenous supplies of food and raw materials. If such a unit existed fully organised, it would surely be extremely powerful, with its population of over 150 million (plus overseas territories) and its steel production capacity of nearly 50 million tons. If it could be created, a Federation would be a new factor in the world balance of power; it could be decisive in stopping war, by establishing with U.S.A. a decisive preponderance of power.

8.   Indeed, this Federation has such impressive potential strength and such power to change the world situation, that if the U.K. could call it into being fully fledged at the drop of a hat, it should surely do so, even if this risked a sacrifice of U.K. interests.

9.   The strength of a Federation is unquestionably stronger than that of its constituents (the arguments were stated at length by Madison and Hamilton,* and are as true now as they were then). The decisive advantages are:-

(a) the ability to mobilise all resources according to a common plan.

(b) the access of morale and self-confidence arising from political and ideological unity.

As the real weakness of post-war Europe is <u>moral</u>, rather than material, these arguments for Federation are of first-class weight. Indeed, it

---

* James Madison and Alexander Hamilton, authors of <u>The Federalist</u>.

is readily arguable that the introduction of a new seminal idea into
Europe is the only possible way to restore morale.

10. If this Federation could be established in full working order –
militarily, politically and economically viable – by the end of five
years from now, and if no war intervened, our prospects of maintaining
peace after that period would surely be much greater than they would be
in the absence of Federation. This consideration is of such crucial
weight that it amounts to a prima facie case for Federation in U.K.'s
wider interests.

11. Unless results can be secured as quickly as this, and unless we
can be reasonably sure that war will not intervene, there does not seem
much point in the idea. Until a substantial degree of cohesion has
been reached, and until the group is viable, its existence and participating in it might be definitely dangerous for U.K. (If U.K. had been
part of a federation with France and Benelux in 1940, we should have
been forced to commit more forces to the European battle – and the
group not being militarily viable in Europe, Britain might thus have
been lost too). We should inevitably be expanding resources for
developing the Federation which we could otherwise use to provide
alternative means of defence. By committing ourselves to Europe, we
should be closing the door to alternative policies (e.g. union between
U.S.A. and the Commonwealth). The risks are very grave indeed unless
we can be sure of getting pretty quick results.

12. By the end of five years, it would be necessary to achieve the
following minimum positions:-

   (i) a Western European Government established, responsible at
   least for defence and foreign affairs (and possibly civil rights).

   (ii) a combined Commander-in-Chief.

   (iii) a combined Foreign Secretary.

   (iv) agreed financial arrangements for defence.

   (v) each constituent in reasonable balance of payments equilibrium.

   (vi) some sort of Parliament, from which authority derives to the
   Government and some sort of common citizenship.

   (vii) establishment of enough prosperity in each constituent to
   prevent social unrest and to counteract attractions of communism.

13. When this stage had been established, rapid progress could be made
towards common monetary reserve and dollar pool, customs union, common
planning agencies, etc. But this comes second, not first.

14. If we could get to the position in paragraph 12 by the end of
1953 without a catastrophe in the meantime, it would be well worth
while; it could make peace reasonably certain.

15. But the difficulties are formidable:-

   (i) The Commonwealth. The relationship with Western Europe would
   be formally closer than that which now exists with the Commonwealth.

It is hardly conceivable that the Dominions would join. Some
sort of loose relationship would no doubt be possible, but inevitably the Commonwealth ties would be weakened.

(ii) Germany. The idea of Federation is useless unless Germany
is in. If Germany were out, not only would be power of the
Federation be greatly reduced (and its central raison d'etre
thus eliminated), but also there would be the gravest danger of
Germany joining the other side - from many points of view, Germany
and Russia are natural partners. But would France have Germany
in? And indeed would we? And what would be the U.S. implications?

(iii) France. Is there any reason to suppose that France's basic
difficulties would be solved more easily within a Federation?
Would Federation make the French pay taxes, or the peasants send
food to the towns?

(iv) Viability. The group is not readily viable; it is ill-
balanced economically; it has great export potential, but it does
depend upon imported food. It is conceivable that U.K. will regain
viability pretty fast, with oil and rubber and gold; but France
and Germany?? Federation greatly strengthens political and
military viability but it does not create economic viability -
five bankrupts don't add up to one solvent. The economics tend
to be competitive rather than complementary, and therefore the
units do not solve each other's problems by solving their own.

(v) Dependence upon U.S.A. In the period before viability was
reached, the embryo Federation would be wholly dependent upon
U.S.A., both economically and militarily. The Federation would
therefore not have full responsibility for its own progress;
this would greatly weaken it and it would prevent the moral
force from being exerted.

(vi) The Social Problem. There is as yet no economic ideology
to counter communism. Laisser faire capitalism has few supporters
in Europe (it has never had any in Germany), and social democracy
has no future except in the British Commonwealth and Scandinavia.
There is no positive economic doctrine. The idea of Federation
may be a substitute to rally the people, but it is not a way of
life. In other words, do the seeds exist for social stability,
even in a Federation?

(vii) In addition are all the well-known practical difficulties.

16. There are no attractions whatever for the U.K., except for the
central attraction of preventing war - which is of course decisive for
us. Our ties with the Commonwealth are bound to be weakened. We
should have only a one-third share in the Federation, and would be in
a continuous wrangle to get our way, no doubt playing off the French
against the Germans in order to do so. Economically, it is difficult
to see any benefit for us; we are much the richest and have much the
highest standard of living; the other parts of the Federation would
be a continuing drain upon us. No increased opportunity would be
opened up for British citizens.

17.   One is forced to the view, indeed, that to sponsor or join a
Federation would be an act of great self-sacrifice in the common,
interest (overwhelmingly ours too) of avoiding war. In the period of
creating the Federation, moreover, we should be running great risks.
The difficulties are tremendous; the risk of failure to form it at all
would be very great; attempts to form it might well exacerbate the
Russians and lead us to war in the worst possible circumstances; we
should face an alarming and critical period before the conditions in
paragraph 12 were satisfied. We might find, indeed, that far from
becoming a viable and powerful independent unit, the Federation would
be a group of countries held uneasily together by a fear of Russia and
by American doles and armaments. To have sacrificed the Commonwealth
and our independence for this – to be Mussolini to America's Hitler –
would be an intolerable end for the United Kingdom.

18.   If one takes such a serious view of the military-diplomatic
situation as to be ready to consider such expedients in order to prevent
war, one should also consider other possibilities. If we regard the
possibility of war in the next ten or fifteen years as sufficiently
real to be taken into account, we must face this in all its implications. The fact of the matter is that we are not militarily viable,
and never shall be again. If war comes, we cannot hope to maintain
our independence.

19.   We have not yet realised how weak we are – not in numbers of
aircraft and tanks and sailors, but in real war potential. In the
last war, our efforts were unparalleled. We mobilised into the Forces
22% of the labour force; we produced in the U.K. about 70% of the
total equipment used by the British Empire forces. But we sold assets,
borrowed or were given supplies to a value of well over £10,000
millions. In retrospect, we played too big a part in the fighting
effort. But this was inescapable at the time, and would be again.
In a future war, we should utterly and absolutely depend upon United
States aid – to an extent that would mean that we were no longer a
partner in the war, but a satellite or mercenary.

20.   In the last war, this position was concealed by the fact that we
were first in; at the formative stage we were in the lead; the course
of the war made it a genuine Anglo-American partnership. But by the
end of the Germany war, and throughout the Japanese war, the economic
realities were making themselves felt; 1945 was no longer the partnership of 1942–43. Next time, it will not even nominally be a partnership; it is doubtful whether there will be Combined Chiefs of Staff
and Combined Boards in any precise sense, if at all; the relationship
will be that which now rules in the Bizone. In other words, we shall
not be fighting the war as an independent nation; the Americans will
be paying the piper and calling the tune.

21.   In any case, we should lose our independence afterwards. War can
end only with the victory of U.S.A. or the victory of Russia; in
either case, the victor would <u>have</u> to establish world government over
North America, Europe and Russia; this would probably be necessary as
a practical matter to cope with the physical problems of the post-war.
In this process, we should retain at best a formal independence – a
nominal front of independence.

22.   If this is so, it is surely worth sacrificing independence before-
hand to prevent war. But we must do it in the most effective way. We

have seen the difficulties of European Federation. My own belief is
that more certain and favourable results to this country would be
secured by Union between U.S.A. and the British Commonwealth. To me,
this is a much less fantastic notion than the Western European
Federation.

23. This seems wholly possible; indeed, one can visualise the sort
of negotiations which would lead to it. We have already worked together in conditions of extreme intimacy. The organs of combined
military organisation are already in being, and could be rapidly
extended into complete unity. The language and basic institutions are
not fundamentally dissimilar.

24. This would not break the Commonwealth up, like the Western
European Federation; it would submerge the Commonwealth in a wider
unity. In fact we should stick together, for it so happens that on a
white population basis, the Commonwealth would have a one-third interest,
and the idea of a two-thirds majority – giving the Commonwealth
countries a vote if they all stood together – is familiar in American
political institution.

25. Economically, the union would be highly favourable to us, for it
would solve the dollar problem for ever; it would open up tremendous
new opportunities for the British people, who do now seem condemned to
penury.

26. The Americans would get great advantage out of it, for we should
be a profound stabilising influence, and would give them just what they
need to carry out their responsibilities as world leader.

27. If this Union was formed, it would operate in Europe with powerful
effect, taking such steps as necessary to build up an alliance with
viable Western European states. It might sponsor a Federation of
France, Benelux and Germany. But as a matter of fact, the resources
of the Union would be so formidable that it is doubtful how far it
would be necessary to adopt panic measures; it would have virtually
all the world's naval and maritime power, nearly all the oil, at least
two-thirds of the world's industrial capacity, all the food it needed.
This, with unity of control, would surely be decisive. It can be
argued that this decisive preponderance already exists, because U.S.A.
and the British Commonwealth would indubitably fight together if war
broke out. <u>But the vital thing is the mobilisation of this power as
one unit serving a common plan, military and political.</u> At present,
this does not begin to exist, nor is it likely to do so.

28. If radical measures are being considered, as they must be unless
we are ready to gamble on peace, this is immensely the most favourable
for us (and also, as a matter of fact, for the Americans). One has
only to think of what one's reaction would be if one woke up in the
morning and saw in the newspaper that an Atlantic Union had been
created, compared with one's reaction if a Western European Federation
had been created.

29. The project of Atlantic Union involves a clean break in our
present relationships with the United States. We have to appear as a
worth while partner to be treated as an equal entrant into a new
enterprise embodying the entire Anglo-Saxon tradition. The immediate
need is to become independent of U.S. aid; this is the essential

preliminary. We should never get into a real union with the United States as a beggar.

30. We should tell them straight, and as soon as possible, that we do not intend to enter a Western European Federation, and have no intention to concentrate our activities upon Europe as a primarily European power. At the same time we should state the extent to which we are prepared to help in European economic recovery - a very long way. Such a statement would in no way contravene either the O.E.E.C. Convention or the Bilateral Agreement. But it would put an end to American hopes of a united Europe.

31. My own view is that many Americans would probably welcome this. In any case, I cannot believe they would refuse to give us a second E.R.P. appropriation. If they did refuse, the result would not be catastrophic. We put our U.S. dollar needs in 1949-50 at $940 millions. We shall not get more than $750 millions anyway, of which we shall have to pass on probably $350 millions in the payments scheme - leaving a net of $400 millions. If we had no E.R.P. at all, we should earn E.R.P. dollars from Europe in a very big way, and we might well make a very reasonable plan which would yield dollar viability in say three years with no more than a loss of $1,000 millions in our reserves. We should still have $1,000 millions of reserves left.

32. It is surely well worth risking the loss of part of our reserves in order to get the right relationship with U.S.A., and one which could develop into Atlantic Union if events moved propitiously. I think it most unlikely that the Americans would take umbrage; there would no doubt be an anti-British burst from the long-haired, but if it appeared that we were prepared, if necessary, to abandon E.R.P. aid and stand on our own feet, the results might be surprising.

33. Of course if we (and U.S.A.) are really thinking in terms of rearmament and serious war-preparation, E.R.P. as such is dead anyway, for viability in 1952-53 for Europe is obviously out of the question. A new political-economic-military idea will have to emerge from Washington. By the time the second E.R.P. appropriation comes along, something new may well be in the field - and I cannot think of anything better than Atlantic Union.

34. The practical conclusion which I would draw from this, in terms of immediate policy, is:-

(i) Do nothing in Europe to lead towards Federation; i.e. keep all military and other discussions on a strictly country-country basis, not creating European institutions with a life of their own.

(ii) Concentrate in O.E.E.C. upon practical measures to bring about recovery (i.e. fields of activity) and to promote unity between Continental countries (e.g. transport and electric power); vigorously eschew customs unions and structural integration.

(iii) Seek to divert U.S. policy away from concept of U.K. as part of Europe (i.e. chief mendicant) to concept of combined operations between U.S. and British Commonwealth.

(iv) Make a categorical statement to U.S. that we shall not enter

Western European Federation or anything like it, but will help European recovery up to the hilt.

(v) Be prepared to risk losing the second E.R.P. appropriation.

(vi) Sound out the Commonwealth, particularly Canada.

R.W.B.C.

27 September 1948

27. Policy towards Europe

[This minute records a discussion on 5 January 1949 between senior officials, some from the Treasury (Sir Edward Bridges, Permanent Secretary; Sir Henry Wilson-Smith, Head of the Overseas Finance Division; Mr F. G. Lee, who later became Sir Frank Lee, Permanent Secretary of the Treasury; Mr D. H. F. Rickett, who later became Sir Denis Rickett, Second Permanent Secretary to the Treasury; and R. W. B. Clarke). Others were from the Foreign Office (Mr Roger Makins, Deputy Under-Secretary of State, who later became Lord Sherfield), the Dominions Office (Sir Percivale Liesching, Under-Secretary of State), the Board of Trade (Sir John Henry Woods, Permanent Secretary); also present was the Government's Chief Planning Officer (Sir Edwin, later Lord, Plowden). Ed.]

The following were present at an informal discussion on 5 January, 1949, to discuss European co-operation: Sir Edward Bridges, Sir John Woods, Sir Henry Wilson-Smith, Sir Edwin Plowden, Sir Percivale Liesching, Mr Lee, Mr Makins, Mr Rickett, Mr Clarke. There was general agreement with the following appreciation, although there were differences of emphasis.

1.   Since post-war planning began, our policy has been to secure close political, military and economic co-operation with U.S.A. This has been necessary to get economic aid. It will always be decisive for our security.

2.   The means to this is now the Atlantic Pact. We hope to secure a special relationship with U.S.A. and Canada within this, for in the last resort we cannot rely upon the European countries. Although we may maintain a special relationship in fact, this will not be overtly recognised (at any rate while we are still a claimant for U.S. economic aid). However, we must in practice establish the position that U.S. will defend us, whatever happens to the Europeans.

3.   In order to get U.S. aid, we have had to accept certain U.S. concepts (e.g. I.T.O. and convertibility). Our policy has been to work these out in good faith, and to abandon them only when it is clear to the Americans that we are forced to do so by hard facts and not duplicity. This policy is sound.

4.   Under U.S. pressure, and as a condition of E.R.P., we are pledged to European economic co-operation in O.E.E.C. We must seek to make

O.E.E.C. a success; if it fails, we must show clearly to the Americans that this is not our fault.

5.   On merits, there is no attraction for us in long-term economic co-operation with Europe. At best, it will be a drain on our resources. At worst, it can seriously damage our economy.

6.   Economic co-operation in a structural sense (e.g. Customs unions, integration in extreme forms) is impossible without political feder-ation. This must be ruled out of practical consideration.

7.   But economic co-operation in this sense is irrelevant to European economic recovery. Its results could not appear for many years.

8.   We have a major interest in European <u>recovery</u>. Failure of Europe to recovery spells communism. The Atlantic Pact is hopeless unless France, Benelux, etc., secure economic stability.

9.   At the same time, it is doubtful whether the European countries <u>can</u> recover - i.e. can be independent of U.S. aid by 1952 at the standard of living which is necessary to maintain social stability. This means that we must secure a de facto special position with U.S.A. And that we must not burn our boats in Europe.

10. Our policy should be to assist Europe to recover as far as we can. We should be prepared to assist the Europeans to earn sterling; we should be prepared to let them have supplies. But the concept must be one of limited liability. In no circumstances must we assist them beyond the point at which the assistance leaves us too weak to be a worth-while ally for U.S.A. if Europe collapses - i.e. beyond the point at which our own viability was impaired. For example, we should not be prepared to provide them with dollars (except where this suited us in our own interests). Nor can we embark upon measures of "co-operation" which surrender our sovereignty and which lead us down paths along which there is no return.

11. O.E.E.C. will break down (and with it the whole E.R.P. programme) unless we continue to take the lead. Discussion in O.E.E.C. is now becoming sterile and effective activity will break down unless a new idea is injected. If O.E.E.C. is to break down, the breakdown should be made to come because the other countries have rejected a clear, definite and reasonable lead from us. This is necessary for our relations with U.S.A. - in particular to prevent us from being written off as a failure alongside the other countries.

12. We should therefore accept the idea of M. Spaak that we should put forward a European plan. We should advance this as a plan for European recovery, and not as a plan for long-term co-operation.

13. The general principles of the plan should be:-

   (i) It should be frank and realistic.

   (ii) It should say what we think each major country should do.

   (iii) It should say what we ourselves intend, and it should be reasonably forthcoming on U.K. assistance in the next four years, particularly in the solution of sterling problems.

(iv) It should not compromise our own viability.

(v) It should be defensible in European interests as a whole.

14. It must be admitted that it is doubtful whether the other countries would welcome such a plan. It would be bound to propose highly unpalatable courses of action. We cannot go far with "co-operation" – integration, specialisation, co-ordination of investment, customs union, and all the other attempted escapes from unpalatable action.

15. Work is now proceeding accordingly. It will not be possible to table a plan at O.E.E.C. before the end of February. It is not yet certain that it will be possible to produce a tolerable plan at all.

16. Mr Spaak should be told that we are working on a plan, and we should seek to restrain him from calling Ministerial meetings to discuss this until we are ready. We should also discuss the E.C.A.[*] before we submit a plan.

---

[*] European Corporation Administration.

List of Persons Referred to in the Text

Allen, R. G. D. (later Sir Roy). 1906– . Statistician. HM Treasury, 1939–41; Director of Statistics, British Supply Council, Washington, 1941–2; British Director of Research and Statistics, Combined Production and Resources Board, 1942–5; Statistical Adviser, HM Treasury, 1947–8; Professor of Statistics, University of London, 1944–73.

Anderson, Sir John (later Lord Waverley). 1882–1958. Governor of Bengal, 1932–7; Lord Privy Seal, 1938–9; Home Secretary, 1939–40; Lord President of the Council, 1940–3; Chancellor of the Exchequer, 1943–5.

Arnold, General Henry H. 1886–1950. US Deputy Chief of Air Staff, 1940; Commanding General, US Army Air Forces, 1942–6.

Beaverbrook, Lord. 1879–1964. Canadian newspaper proprietor. Minister for Aircraft Production, 1940–1; Minister of State, 1941; Minister of Supply, 1941–2; Lord Privy Seal, 1943–5.

Bevin, Rt. Hon. Ernest. 1881–1951. British trade union leader. General Secretary of Transport and General Workers Union, 1921–40; Chairman of TUC, 1937; Minister of Labour and National Service and member of War Cabinet, 1940–5; Secretary of State for Foreign Affairs, 1945–51.

Brand, Lord Robert Henry. 1878–1963. Banker. Head of British Food Mission, Washington, 1941–4; representative of HM Treasury in Washington, 1944–6; Chairman, British Supply Council in North America, 1942 and 1945–6.

Brand, Hon. T. H. Banker. Director of Lazard's.

Bridges, Sir Edward (later Lord). 1892–1969. Civil Servant. Secretary to the Cabinet, 1938–46; Permanent Secretary, UK Treasury, 1945–56.

Byrnes, James F. 1879–1972. American lawyer. Associate Justice, US Supreme Court, 1941–2; Director of Economic Stabilisation, 1942–3; Director, Office of War Mobilisation, 1943–5; US Secretary of State, 1945–7.

Clayton, William Lockhart. 1880–1966. Founder and Chairman of Anderson, Clayton & Co., Cotton brokers. Assistant Secretary of State for Economic Affairs.

Cobbold, Cameron F. (later Lord). 1904– . Executive Director, Bank of England, 1938; Deputy Governor, 1945; Governor, 1949–61.

Cripps, Sir Stafford. 1889-1952. British laywer. Ambassador to USSR, 1940-2; Minister of Aircraft Production, 1942-5; President of the Board of Trade, 1945-7; Minister of Economic Affairs, 1947; Chancellor of the Exchequer, 1947-50.

Crowther, Geoffrey (later Lord). 1907-72. Economist, editor, and business man. Editor of *The Economist* 1938-56. Staff of the Ministry of Supply, 1940-1; Ministry of Information, 1941-2; Deputy Head of Joint War Production Staff, Ministry of Production 1942-3.

Dalton, Hugh (later Lord). 1887-1962. Economist and politician. Minister of Economic Warfare, 1940-2; President of the Board of Trade, 1942-5; Chancellor of the Exchequer, 1945-7; Chancellor of the Duchy of Lancaster, 1947-50; Minister of Town and Country Planning, 1950-1.

Eady, Sir Wilfrid. 1890-1962. Civil servant. Secretary, Unemployment Assistance Board, 1934-8; Chairman, Board of Customs and Excise, 1941-2; Joint Second Secretary, UK Treasury, 1945-52.

Gordon, Lincoln. 1913- . American economist. US government service with National Resources Planning Board, 1939-40; National Defence Advisory Committee, 1940-1; War Production Board, 1942-5. Subsequently US Ambassador to Brazil, President of Johns Hopkins University, etc.

Halifax, Lord. 1881-1959. Viceroy of India, 1926-31; Cabinet Minister, 1932-40; Ambassador to the USA, 1941-6.

Harriman, W. Averill. 1891- . Special Representative of President Roosevelt in Great Britain, 1941; US representative in London of Combined Shipping Adjustment Board, 1942; Member of London Combined Production and Resources Board, 1942; US Ambassador to USSR, 1943-6; to Britain, 1946; US Secretary of Commerce, 1946-8; US Special Representative in Europe under Economic Co-operation Act of 1948.

Hopkins, Harry L. 1890-1946. US administrator. Works Progress Administrator, 1935-8; Secretary of Commerce, 1938-40; Special Adviser and Assistant to President Roosevelt, 1940-5.

Howe, Rt. Hon. Clarence Decatur. 1886-1960. Canadian engineer and politician. Held various ministerial posts between 1935 and 1957. Minister of Munitions and Supply, 1940; Minister of Reconstruction and Supply, 1946.

Katz, Milton. 1907- . American lawyer. Professor of Law at Harvard University, 1940-50 and 1954-78; staff of War Production Board and US Executive Officer CPRB, 1941-3; Deputy US Special Representative in Europe (under Harriman), 1949-50; President, American Academy of Arts and Sciences, 1980.

Keynes, John Maynard (later Lord). 1883-1946. British economist. Fellow and Bursar of King's College, Cambridge; editor, *Economic*

Journal, 1911–44; India Office, 1906–8; Treasury, 1915–19 and 1940–6; leader of British Delegation to Washington, Sept.–Dec. 1945.

King, Admiral Ernest Joseph. 1878–1956. Commander-in-Chief US Atlantic Fleet, 1941; Commander-in-Chief US Fleet and Chief of Naval Operations, 1942–5.

Layton, Sir Walter (later Lord). 1884–1966. Economist and editor. Editor of *The Economist*, 1922–38; Chairman, News-Chronicle Ltd., 1930–50; Deputy Leader of Liberal Party in the House of Lords, 1952–5; Director-General of Programmes, Ministry of Supply, 1941–2; Head of Joint War Production Staff, 1942–3.

Lee, F. G. (later Sir Frank). 1903–71. Civil servant, 1926–62. Treasury Delegate to Washington, 1944–6; Joint Permanent Secretary, HM Treasury, 1959–62; Master of Corpus Christi College, Cambridge, 1962–7.

Lyttelton, Oliver (later Lord Chandos). 1893–1972. President of the Board of Trade, 1940–1; member of the War Cabinet as Minister of State, 1941–2; as Minister of Production, 1942–5; President of the Board of Trade and Minister of Production, May–July, 1945.

Marshall, General George Catlett. 1880–1959. Chief of Staff of the US Army, 1939–45; Secretary of State, 1947–9; Secretary of Defense, 1950–1.

May, Stacy. American statistician. Director of the Bureau of Research and Statistics of the National Advisory Council and the Office of Production Management.

Meade, James. 1907– . British economist and Nobel Laureate. Economic Assistant, 1940–5, and Director, 1946–7, of the Economic Section of the Cabinet Offices; Professor of Economics at LSE, 1947–57; at University of Cambridge, 1957–68.

Monnet, Jean. 1888–1979. European political figure. Deputy Secretary General League of Nations, 1918; Chairman Franco-British Economic Co-ordinating Committee, 1939; member of British Supply Council, Washington, 1940–3; author of the French Monnet Plan, 1946; Chairman, Action Committee for the United States of Europe, 1956–75.

Morgenthau, Henry, Jr. 1891–1967. Secretary of the US Treasury, 1934–45.

Morrison, Herbert (later Lord). 1888–1965. Labour politician. Home Secretary, 1940–5; member of the War Cabinet, 1942–5; Deputy Prime Minister and Lord President of the Council, 1945–51; Foreign Secretary, Mar.–Oct. 1951.

Nelson, Donald M. 1888–1959. American business man. With Sears Roebuck & Co., 1912–39; Director of Purchases, Office of Production Management, 1941; Chairman, War Production Board, 1942–4.

Pierce, Sidney. 1901–   . Canadian diplomatist. Lecturer, Dalhousie University from 1926; Canadian Department of Munitions and Supply, Washington, 1940–4; subsequently Ambassador to Mexico, Brazil, etc.

Plant, Sir Arnold. 1898–1978. British economist. Professor of Commerce at LSE, 1930–65; Adviser to Ministerial Chairman of Materials Committee and Central Priority Committee from 1940; Ministry of Production, 1942–5.

Plowden, Sir Edwin (later Lord). 1907–   . Business man. Ministry of Aircraft Production, 1940–6 (Chief Executive, 1945–6); Chief Planning Officer and Chairman, Economic Planning Board, 1947–53; Chairman, Tube Investments, 1963–76.

Purvis, Rt. Hon. Arthur. 1890–1941. Business man. With Nobel Explosives Co. Ltd., Glasgow, 1910–24; director of many Canadian companies; Director-General, British Purchasing Commission, 1939–40; Chairman, British Supply Council in North America, 1941; killed in an air crash in 1941.

Robinson, E. A. G. (later Professor Sir Austin). 1897–   . Economist. Joint editor of the *Economic Journal*, 1944–70; member of the Economic Section, War Cabinet Office, 1939–42; Economic Adviser and Head of Programmes Division, Ministry of Production, 1942–5; Economic Adviser to Board of Trade, 1946; member of Economic Planning Staff, 1947–8.

Rowan, Sir Leslie. 1908–72. Civil servant, 1934–58. Assistant Private Secretary to Chancellor of the Exchequer, 1934–7; Assistant, later Principal Private Secretary to Prime Minister, 1941–7; Permanent Secretary, Office of Minister of Economic Affairs, 1947; Second Secretary HM Treasury, 1947–9, 1951–8; Economic Minister to Washington, 1949–51; Managing Director, Vickers Ltd., 1962–7; Chairman, Vickers Ltd., 1967–71.

Rowe-Dutton, E. (later Sir Ernest). 1891–1965. Civil servant. Financial Adviser to HM Embassy, Berlin, 1929–32; to HM Embassy, Paris, 1934–9; staff of HM Treasury from 1939 (Third Secretary, 1947–51).

Rowlands, Sir Archibald. 1892–1953. Civil servant. Permanent Secretary, Ministry of Aircraft Production, 1940–3; member of Beaverbrook-Harriman Mission to Moscow, September, 1941; Finance Member in Indian Government, 1943–6; Permanent Secretary, Ministry of Supply, 1946–53.

Self, Sir (Albert) Henry. 1890–1975. Civil servant, 1907–47; Director-General, British Air Commission, Washington, 1940–1; Permanent Secretary, Ministry of Production, 1942–3; Deputy for Minister of Production on Combined Production and Resources Board, Washington, 1943–5; Deputy Chairman, British Supply Council, Washington, 1945; Deputy Chairman, 1947–57, and Chairman, 1957–9, Electricity Council.

Sinclair, Sir Robert (later Lord). 1893–1979. Industrialist. Director, Imperial Tobacco Co. Ltd., 1933–67; Director-General of Army Requirements, War Office, 1939–42; Deputy for Minister of Production on Combined Production and Resources Board, Washington, 1942–3; Chief Executive, Ministry of Production, 1943.

Snyder, John Wesley. 1895–   . American banker. Director of Office of War Mobilisation and Reconversion, 1945–6; Secretary of US Treasury, 1946–53.

Stamp, Lord (Josiah). 1880–1941. Statistician and business man. Chairman of the London Midland and Scottish Railway; Director of the Bank of England; Member of the Economic Advisory Council; Adviser to HMG on Economic Co-ordination, 1939–41. Declined offer of Chancellorship of the Exchequer, 1940.

Stark, Admiral Harold. 1880–1972. Chief of US Naval Operations, 1939–42; Commander, US Naval Forces in Europe, 1942–5.

Stimson, Henry Lewis. 1867–1950. American lawyer and politician. Secretary for War, 1911–13, 1940–5; Secretary of State, 1929–33.

Strachey, Rt. Hon. John. 1901–63. Author and politician. Minister of Food, 1946–50; Secretary of State for War, 1950–1.

Truman, Harry S. 1884–1972. Democratic President of the USA, Apr. 1945–Jan. 1953.

Vinson, Frederick Moore. 1890–1953. American laywer. Director, Office of Economic Stabilisation, 1943–5; Vice-Chairman, US Delegation to Bretton Woods Conference 1944; Director, Office of War Mobilisation and Reconversion, 1945; Secretary of US Treasury, 1945–6.

Waley, Sir David. 1887–1962. Treasury Official, 1910–47. Principal Assistant Secretary in Overseas Finance (OF) Division, 1931–46; Third Secretary, 1946–7.

Weeks, H. (later Sir Hugh). 1904–   . Statistician and business man. Director of Statistics, Ministry of Supply, 1939–42; Director-General of Statistics and Programmes, 1942–3; Head of Programmes and Planning Division, Ministry of Production, 1943–5; Director, Finance Corporation for Industry, 1956–74.

Wood, Sir Kingsley. 1881–1943. British politician. Held various Ministerial posts from 1931. Chancellor of the Exchequer, 1940–3.

Woods, Sir John Henry. 1895–1962. Treasury official 1920–43; Principal Assistant Secretary, Ministry of Production 1943–5; Permanent Secretary, Board of Trade, 1945–51.